BUILD AN EMPIRE

THE STORY OF QUEENSRŸCHE

AN UNAUTHORIZED BIOGRAPHY

BY JAMES R. BEACH
WITH BRIAN L. NARON AND BRIAN J. HEATON

FOREWORD BY PAUL SUTER

NW METALWORX BOOKS

TABLE OF CONTENTS

ACKNOWLEDGEMENTS

Many people helped contribute to the writing of this book, without whom we would not have been able to complete it. Special thanks go out to: Paul Suter for his wonderful foreword; Robert John for the great cover photo; our good friend Brett Miller for letting us quote some of the interviews you did, for letting us reference the great articles you have written on Queensrÿche and their early years and pre-history, as well as doing the interview with us yourself. To: Jason Arnopp, Dan Birchall, Charrie Foglio, Dimitris Kazantzis, Bob Nalbandian, H.P. Newquist, Martin Popoff, Dave Reynolds, Beth Rivers, Corey Rivers, Steve Slaton, Gene Stout, and Jeff Wagner, for letting us use quotes from your interviews with Queensrÿche band members and/or associated people in past years. To: Sullivan Bigg, Adam "Bomb" Brenner, James Byrd, Craig Cooke, Randy Gane, Mark DeGarmo, Jeff Gilbert, Terry Gorle, Howard Dee Gray, Kelly Gray, Tom Hall, Kim Harris, Brook Hovland, Sharon Harkins-Lundstrom, Neil Kernon, Rick Knotts, Craig Locicero, Pamela Moore, David Morris, Paul Passarelli, Scott Rockenfield, Charles Russell, Jason Slater, Tom Wilcox and Michael Wilton for taking the time do interviews with us, and/or answering questions. To: Richard Galbraith, Jill Adams Stebbins, and Brian Woodwick and for letting us print your great photographs. To our friends and super fans that also shared their memories, experiences, info and images/materials with us: Thomas Brogli, Rick Moore, Kory Pohlman, Cyrene Probart, Mike "The Rycher", and Doug Wirachowsky. And especially to our wives, Joyce, Wendy and Staci – Thanks and love always for your support and patience with us on our musical journey.

James R. Beach additional thanks: My patient and supportive wife, Joyce, and our awesome kids - Kayli, Chris and Jocelynn. My parents David and Linda Beach, my brother Jonathan Beach and his family

– thanks for always supporting me and my various projects over the years. Jim Sutton and James Tolin for help in conducting some of the interviews and for the friendship, super thanks to all of our friends and fans for your constant support of our NW Metalworx album and book projects (and concert festivals!), to my *Building An Empire* co-writers "The Brians", and of course, Queensrÿche, for all the great years of music and concerts.

Brian L. Naron also thanks the following persons and entities for my musical journey: Mom, Ace, Peter, Paul & Gene, Marc Bolan, Dennis Russo, The Doors, Jimi Hendrix, Cheap Trick, Johnny Cash, Gladys Knight, Blood Sweat & Tears, Chicago, Bon Scott, Rush, The Who, Sex Pistols, The Damned, Judas Priest, Iron Maiden, Mike Beckstead, Shoes, Girl Trouble, The Heats, Rob Whitworth, Eric 'EO' Olson, Tom G. Warrior, Le HooDoo Gurus, George Johnson, Bill Nelson, Kim Harris, L'Andrew, Kurdt, Patrick Naron, T. Dallas Reed, NW Metalworx Music, and lastly, to my wife Wendy for her love and understanding. Music = Life. Also special Rychean shout outs to: Doug Wirachowsky, Kory Pohlman, Tim Shelton, Mike the Rycher, Thomas Brogli, Dimitris Kazantzis, James R. Beach and Brian J. Heaton.

Brian J. Heaton thanks: My wife Staci, and our daughter Samantha, for their patience, love, and encouragement. My late parents, Debbie & Richard Heaton. My brother Todd Heaton and his family. Jeffrey and Wayne Douglass, for getting me started on this Queensrÿche adventure in the `80s. The late Robert Kotynski, Marshal Schoener, Larry Fulkerson, Kristi Garrison, Jorge Martinez, Marcus Magnusson, Johan Wall, Thomas Morningstar, and the whole crew for all the great Queensrÿche concerts and experiences in the '90s and '00s. My unreasonable gang from The Breakdown Room—Gregory Twachtman, John Schneiderwind, Steve Duvall, and Raf Ahráyeph—you were all the gold standard (as moderators go) 81 percent of the time. Jim Matheos and Eddie Jackson (two of the nicest guys in the music business). Adam Swanson, Alex Ward, Jonathan Rustvold, Jeff Brown, Chad Davis, Brian Kenna, Brett Miller, Matt Cocuzzo, Jason Tomasulo, Eric Weidenfeld, Jerry Deschler, Erik Onstott, for your friendship. Richie Waddell and Scott Thompson from *Focus on Metal* for your support. James "Taaaaate!" Chatary for the barrel of laughs (I told you I'd get "it" in). The late David Ascoli, who always believed in me and knew

I'd do this one day. Finally, to my co-writers, James R Beach and Brian L Naron, whose kind words and trust made it easier for me to find joy in writing about my favorite band again. Here's to our friendship and future adventures.

My work on this book is dedicated to my good friend and brother, the late Jason Slater.

FOREWORD

By Paul Suter

It was quite a long time ago now, backstage at the House of Blues in Los Angeles. I was chatting with Michael Wilton after the show when one of their closer fans came over to join us, and Michael introduced me as the man who discovered Queensrÿche.

Really? I'd always taken a degree of satisfaction from having written that fateful *Kerrang!* demo review which started the ball rolling, but the reality was that I was second in line to Diana and Kim Harris. They were already managing the band, and so enthused that they hand delivered a demo tape to the *Kerrang!* offices in London. Of course, their relationship with the band would turn out to be fraught, but if anybody discovered Queensrÿche, they deserve the credit.

As for that demo, therein lies a story too. I was a freelancer at *Kerrang!* and had a day job (as a Customs officer, believe it or not) which meant that I only visited the office once a week, and was consequently pretty low in the pecking order for new goodies just received. So how long had the cassette been sitting there before I got it? It was halfway through "Queen of the Reich" when it was given to me, so somebody had listened to at least some of it – had they thought "ewww, no thank you". And it's hard to believe that it was put aside specially for me since they were neither female nor Canadian; of course they would go on to cover Lisa Dalbello's "Gonna Get Close To You", but there were no crystal balls in the *Kerrang!* office. That Queensrÿche turned out to be one of the most exciting things I'd ever heard is all part of the story now, with the *Kerrang!* demo review generating more enthusiasm for a band nobody could actually listen to (remember, no internet then!) than any other before or since, and I'll proudly take credit for that. But discovering them, that's a bit of stretch....

Of course, we all know the story of how so many *Kerrang!* readers mailed the band wanting to hear the demo – the whole point of *Kerrang's* "Armed & Ready" demo reviews was to link up worthy bands with potential fans. The reaction was massive, and as we all know Diana Harris now had a story to tell her old friend Mavis Brodey at EMI Records…and the rest is history.

The first time I actually met the band was when I was flown out to Seattle to see them open for Dio and write a cover story for *Kerrang!*, my very first. At that point Queensrÿche were "mine." Great memories of interviewing the band the next morning on a deck overlooking Puget Sound—where the cool breeze fooled me into not realizing that I was getting horribly sunburned. Oops. And then another ooops: when I got back to the hotel I discovered that the tape had jammed and I actually had virtually nothing on tape. Thanks to the blessing that I still had my list of questions and a good memory of what the responses had been, the entire story was written by the time my plane landed in London. But if any of them ever read it and thought"I didn't say that, it was Chris," now you know why.

There were some fun times when they came to London to record *The Warning*, with fond memories of my kitchen full of Queensrÿche, beer and marijuana; Geoff threw up. But bear in mind that this was the early `80s, email and affordable international calls weren't even on the horizon yet, so my relationship with the band was entirely through the management. And when I fell victim to a nasty bout of internal politics at *Kerrang!* I really wasn't much use to them anymore, so that was that.

A year later, I moved to Los Angeles as West Coast correspondent for a number of European publications, and soon discovered that Queensrÿche were still "mine". We'd do the usual album release interviews, but I was never one to ask for phone numbers (or later, email addresses), so my relationship with the band continued to be through the record label press office and new management Leber-Krebs, big time guys who neither knew nor cared that I'd been there at the beginning. There was one nice surprise when I got invited to Eddie's wedding – or was it Michael's? – but at the time airfare and hotel in Seattle were beyond my budget so I had to take a pass on that. And Scott gave me his email address once, but it had changed by the time I tried to use it. My one contact was Geoff, who at one point recruited me to try and help out his old bandmates in Myth (this was when they changed their name to Fade To Grey) and would always call me when the band was in town, but quite reasonably his number would frequently change as too many annoying people got hold of it, and eventually they just weren't in town any more.

So when the magazine work itself started to fade away that was the end of my Queensrÿche story, and since then I've just been an observer like the rest of you, running the gamut of emotions from enthusiasm to meh to depression to sheer misery and sorrow. Over the early years, as I had watched the band rise to their multi-platinum heights from that humble cassette beginning, I'd been sure that Queensrÿche were going to become an institution akin to Rush, and it's a tragedy that it never happened. Sure, there's still a Queensrÿche, and they're pretty damn good, but for good or bad they're not the band I got so excited about all those years ago.

Yes, I'm proud of my involvement with Queensrÿche but no, I didn't discover them.

INTRODUCTION

I used to make the 48-mile drive from Tacoma, Washington, to Easy Street Records, in Bellevue, just about every other weekend. I worshiped at the "Wall of Death" and purchased records that I could not find anywhere else. Kim and Diana Harris had the best heavy metal selection around. They brought in titles nobody else would special order, especially 7" inch singles with picture sleeves. On one particular Saturday late in 1982, I was in the store shopping. Kim mentioned that he was going to manage a local band and he had their demo tape. He asked if I would like to listen to it and I of course said, "Yes." There were four or five other people in the store at this time, including Scott Rockenfield, who I would soon be introduced to. Kim slipped the cassette tape into the house stereo and the first chords of "Queen of the Reich" erupted out of the speaker system. By the time the final strains of "The Lady Wore Black" had faded, I was awestruck! I was a bit skeptical about this "local band." The music sounded far too mature and polished for what was coming out of the Pacific Northwest hard rock scene at the time. Besides, they sounded so British, like Judas Priest and Iron Maiden. But indeed, the band was from Bellevue, Washington, and not from England. They called themselves Queensreich at the time, but the band would soon change the spelling to Queensrÿche. Kim continued by saying that he knew enough people in the industry that he could get the tape heard. Of course, as many of you already know from Rÿchean lore, the Harris' went to Merry-ole-England for a "vacation" and dropped off a copy of the EP tape to Paul Suter and the mighty *Kerrang!* magazine. The rest is history.

By August 13, 1983, the 206 EP had only been out a short time. The fans and press alike were buzzing about the band. Queensrÿche had played their first two professional live shows with Zebra in late June and were getting ready for their first major tour with Dio in the fall. On this day, the band was doing their first in-store autograph session at Penny

Lane Records in Tacoma. About 70 young "Heavy Metal" kids were waiting and excited for the band's arrival in this small, but very popular record store. Kim Harris came through the door first, followed by the members of the band. Queensrÿche seemed in awe of the electricity in the room, especially Scott and Chris. Geoff wore a confident grin on his face, looking seemingly unaffected by the attention. That's a lead singer for you. The store owner kept flipping the EP over on the turntable, and it played through many times during this event. The store must have sold 150 copies of the record that day. I purchased my ASCAP copies at this event. When it was my turn to have my copy autographed, I pulled out a new style of gold metallic marking pen and asked the guys to sign on the vinyl. Michael exclaimed, "You won't be able to play this dude!" I said, "I know, it's going on my wall!" So, with wide eyed amazement, I, the band and half of the room saw the first 206 EP signed on the wax. Back then the guys would personalize their signatures with a couple of lines like, "Stay Intense" or "Keep Rocking." Their autographs were full names that you could actually read. The band looked great, the girls all loved Geoff's hair and penetrating green eyes. Queensrÿche got a big taste of being bonafide rock stars that day.

On October 1, 1983, in the Paramount Theatre in Seattle, I saw Queensrÿche perform live for the first time. I had seats in the seventh row, but by the time the show began, I was in the third row in the orchestra pit. If my memory serves me, the first song they played was "Waiting for the Kill." They played all the songs from the EP and a few songs from what would become *The Warning* - which would not be recorded or released until the next year. The band played like they were seasoned, the crowd was very enthusiastic and Dio was great, but not much of a match for the hometown heroes. Queensrÿche was dressed in leather and spandex. Scott had his gold chain drum kit and the stage back drop had the QR coat of arms and two crowns (I believe this staging was created and designed by Matt Bazemore). It was an amazing show. On my way out of the Paramount Theatre, I saw one of the gold mylar EP posters in the one-sheet display case. Well, I had to

have it. So, I jimmied open the door on the case. I still proudly display that poster, autographed and framed, on my wall.

One night during the winter of 1984, I went out to a nightclub called Astor Park. A friend of mine, Eric Olson, had just joined a popular local band, The Eagertones. The Eagertones played a few original dance tunes, but were more known for performing cover songs by The Ramones and The Romantics. As their set began, I saw a couple of familiar faces sitting at a table left of the stage. I took my rum and coke over to the table and asked if I could join the pair. Graciously, Scott Rockenfield and Chris DeGarmo welcomed me to sit with them. It was as if I was the only person to recognize them. We exchanged greetings and I bought the next round. I asked them about the latest Queensrÿche goings-on. I knew that they had been recording in England their first album. In fact, the two of them had just arrived home a few days prior and decided to go out and unwind. They told me that the album was going to be called *The Warning* and the concept of the songs revolved around technology running amok. They mentioned titles of songs, "Take Hold of the Flame" and "Roads to Madness." The real beauty of it was when Chris sang to me a few lines from the latter. "Times measure rusts as it crawls, I see its face in the looking glass. This screaming laughter hides the pain of its reality. Black, the door was locked I opened." I thought, "Wow! This sounds like it's going to be a great record." It was a fun evening. My buddy was playing in a fun dance band and I was having cocktails with a couple of great guys from my favorite band.

The band made their next big hometown concert appearance during the KISS *Animalize* tour on February 13, 1985, in the Seattle Coliseum. Many of the band's family and friends were in attendance and got their first taste of arena rock courtesy of Queensrÿche that night. The band was tight and had matured from being on the road and honing their craft. The local press was everywhere asking concert goers their thoughts on the biggest band out of Seattle since Jimi Hendrix and Heart. The band's set drew from songs from the EP and the new album, included an unreleased song, "Prophecy," and closed with "Take Hold of the Flame." Queensrÿche had everyone singing along during their set. They left the stage with a thunderous ovation. I headed to the backstage area with my fan club-issued laminate, #004, to find the room full of admirers and news cameras. It was like a scene from the winning Super Bowl locker room. Champagne and ale were flowing. Tables were full of food and excitement was in the air. The band was on a high and feeling very accomplished. They had toured the world and arrived home as stars. Cameras flashed, reporters asked all the usual dumb and obvious questions, girls hugged the band, moms and dads dried tears and accepted handshakes for jobs well done. It was great being in that room during that time. I missed half of the KISS show by the time security kicked us out of the locker room, but it was worth it. I made it home in time to record the midnight KOMO news coverage of the show and backstage events. There I was on the TV talking with Geoff, forever immortalized on video. I realized after this show that our local heavy metal band now belonged to the rest of the world.

Not all my Queensrÿche memories are pleasant ones. During the *Rage for Order* tour I went to an in-store appearance that the band made at Tower Records in Tacoma. The band was in the full "big hair" and full of themselves mode. I must say that Scott was still fairly humble and very cool as always. But I found the band as a whole to be smug and I found myself fairly irritated with them. I got my *Rage for Order* LP autographed and was heading out the door to go to the Tacoma Dome and get in line for the concert that Queensrÿche was playing. I got stopped at the door by a friend of mine, Steve. He was the assistant manager at Tower Records at that time. He said that he had free tickets to the show that night. Not only that, he had backstage passes that would get us to the side stage for the show and we might even get to meet the headliners, AC/DC! He asked if I wanted to go with him and of course I said yes. So, I sold my ticket to the first guy I saw near the venue and waited for Steve to get off work and arrive to the Dome. I waited and I waited. Cell phones were few and far between in 1986. I hear the Queensrÿche set beginning when Steve finally shows up. I thought we will quickly get our passes from will call and be inside only missing the first song or two. NOT! Will call was late setting up and could not find our passes right away. Once we were in, we tried to get to our spots on the side of the stage, but we were denied due to a "security communication" breakdown. We were finally issued seats by the ushers and only caught the last three songs from Queensrÿche's set. I was disappointed, but we still had backstage passes to meet the band. Wrong again! After waiting 45 minutes with 130 people in a room built for 75, Randy "Random Damage" Gane (QR tour keyboardist, ex-Myth), came into the room with a roadie and announced that the band was "too tired" to show up. I was the first person to leave the room. At that point I was pissed and dejected. I couldn't even get into AC/DC's set, so I just left the Tacoma Dome all together. I heard later that Eddie eventually showed up and greeted the fans who stuck it out. The moral of the story is: Rock stars are not always cool and don't be cheap. Just buy your ticket and get in line early!

In contrast, seeing Queensrÿche perform the *Operation: Mindcrime* album mostly in its entirety ("Suite Sister Mary" was not performed), on New Year's Eve 1988/1989, at the Seattle Center Arena was momentous. The band had been riding the *OMC* wave for a year and a half due to heavy rotations of the songs on the radio, on MTV, and on the VHS tape, *Video: Mindcrime*. As the 1980s waned and gave way to the 1990s, the band took a short break and played an encore featuring a medley of songs from the EP and "Take Hold of the Flame." It was a great way to spend New Year's Eve. It would also mark the last time Queensrÿche would play in Seattle for a few years.

The anticipation for the release of *Empire* was very evident at midnight on August 19, 1990, when myself and my brothers were waiting in a line at the Seattle Tower Records. There was a line from the front door that went alongside the building, up the steps and around a full city block. It was like waiting in line for a concert at the Coliseum. Hundreds of fans waited for the doors to open that Monday night to be the first to purchase and listen to *Empire* in Seattle. As we moved along in the line you could catch strains of the new music coming from inside the store. We got in and bought our LPs and CDs and then mingled outside in the parking lot while fans who bought cassettes played the new album and we all got to hear the music blaring from their car speakers. A good time was had by all, even those of us that had to be back in Tacoma for work at 5:30 a.m.

I think that most of my best memories I have about Queensrÿche have to do with the fans I have met because of the band and who have become good friends of mine. We have had great times at the events we communed to and at with each other. A few of my friends I met through the band's music. We hung out backstage during the *Promised Land* shows and partied at the *Hear in the Now Frontier* listening party at the Seattle Center Laserium. Seattle in '96, '98, '99, the Rÿchean Archÿves and Queensrÿche self-titled LP listening party, which introduced us to Todd La Torre. So, I thank Doug Wirachowsky, Kory Pohlman, Tim Shelton and James R. Beach for their friendships, and I hope Queensrÿche will bring us together for more good times.

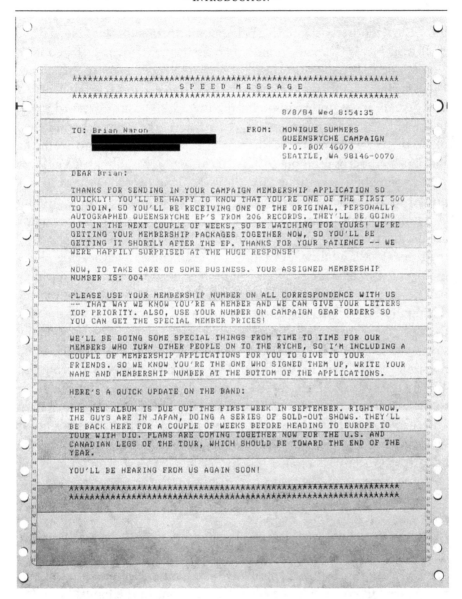

```
**********************************************************
                    S P E E D   M E S S A G E
**********************************************************

                                        8/8/84 Wed 8:54:35

TO: Brian Naron                FROM:  MONIQUE SUMMERS
    ████████████████                  QUEENSRYCHE CAMPAIGN
                                       P.O. BOX 46070
                                       SEATTLE, WA 98146-0070

DEAR Brian:

THANKS FOR SENDING IN YOUR CAMPAIGN MEMBERSHIP APPLICATION SO
QUICKLY! YOU'LL BE HAPPY TO KNOW THAT YOU'RE ONE OF THE FIRST 500
TO JOIN, SO YOU'LL BE RECEIVING ONE OF THE ORIGINAL, PERSONALLY
AUTOGRAPHED QUEENSRYCHE EP'S FROM 206 RECORDS. THEY'LL BE GOING
OUT IN THE NEXT COUPLE OF WEEKS, SO BE WATCHING FOR YOURS! WE'RE
GETTING YOUR MEMBERSHIP PACKAGES TOGETHER NOW, SO YOU'LL BE
GETTING IT SHORTLY AFTER THE EP. THANKS FOR YOUR PATIENCE -- WE
WERE HAPPILY SURPRISED AT THE HUGE RESPONSE!

NOW, TO TAKE CARE OF SOME BUSINESS. YOUR ASSIGNED MEMBERSHIP
NUMBER IS: 004

PLEASE USE YOUR MEMBERSHIP NUMBER ON ALL CORRESPONDENCE WITH US
-- THAT WAY WE KNOW YOU'RE A MEMBER AND WE CAN GIVE YOUR LETTERS
TOP PRIORITY. ALSO, USE YOUR NUMBER ON CAMPAIGN GEAR ORDERS SO
YOU CAN GET THE SPECIAL MEMBER PRICES!

WE'LL BE DOING SOME SPECIAL THINGS FROM TIME TO TIME FOR OUR
MEMBERS WHO TURN OTHER PEOPLE ON TO THE RYCHE, SO I'M INCLUDING A
COUPLE OF MEMBERSHIP APPLICATIONS FOR YOU TO GIVE TO YOUR
FRIENDS. SO WE KNOW YOU'RE THE ONE WHO SIGNED THEM UP, WRITE YOUR
NAME AND MEMBERSHIP NUMBER AT THE BOTTOM OF THE APPLICATIONS.

HERE'S A QUICK UPDATE ON THE BAND:

THE NEW ALBUM IS DUE OUT THE FIRST WEEK IN SEPTEMBER. RIGHT NOW,
THE GUYS ARE IN JAPAN, DOING A SERIES OF SOLD-OUT SHOWS. THEY'LL
BE BACK HERE FOR A COUPLE OF WEEKS BEFORE HEADING TO EUROPE TO
TOUR WITH DIO. PLANS ARE COMING TOGETHER NOW FOR THE U.S. AND
CANADIAN LEGS OF THE TOUR, WHICH SHOULD BE TOWARD THE END OF THE
YEAR.

YOU'LL BE HEARING FROM US AGAIN SOON!

**********************************************************
**********************************************************
```

- Brian L. Naron
N.W. Metal Historian

Queensrÿche and I go back almost 40 years as well. I first discovered them courtesy of the Portland, Oregon, rock radio stations, (the still in operation) KGON (92.3 FM), and (the sadly long gone) KRCK (101.1 FM). By the summer of 1983, they were playing songs from the "206" EP pretty regularly. Being a fan of some of the "New Wave of British Heavy Metal" (bands such as: Iron Maiden, Def Leppard, Saxon, Judas Priest, Motorhead, Tygers Of Pan Tang, Ronnie James Dio-era Black Sabbath, etc. etc.), I vibed on Queensrÿche right away and quickly went out and bought the indie EP at a local record store. In the fall of 1983, my freshman year at Cleveland High School, I even made my own Queensrÿche shirt in art class with the logo from the EP blazoned across the black T (with orange ink sadly as no gold or yellow available). I continued to follow the band over the years and was poised to finally see them open for Metallica in 1989 at the Coliseum (I dumbly skipped the KISS and AC/DC shows with QR opening, I admit, due to not being a big fan of those bands by then, and especially their mid-1980s albums. But I also don't remember ever hearing about the opening band for either – a common issue in the N.W. – so it may be I never even knew about Queensrÿche opening until after the fact.) during the *Operation: Mindcrime* tour. Sadly, they jumped off the trek to headline on their own shows. It was a few years later before I finally saw them live for the *Promised Land* tour in 1995. I've seen the band five times now - twice with Geoff Tate and three times with Todd La Torre fronting the band. My live exposure to the band pales of course to my co-writers, both Brian Naron and Brian Heaton have each seen Queensrÿche over 30 times. Those super fans! LOL. Bad luck and/or work deprived me of a few other times I would have loved to see the band (the Queensrÿche, Dream Theater and Fates Warning triple bill is one that definitely comes to mind), but that's the way it goes in life. Five times is actually a lot for me, as I like so many other bands and most I've only seen once or twice.

Regardless, Queensrÿche is still one of my favorite bands. They are hugely influential and pioneering progressive hard rock/heavy metal band and are still going strong. I have every album they've put out and many rare QR collectibles besides. They are one of the bands I bonded with my co-writer Brian Naron over when we first met in 1990, and our mutual love of the band we have shared since. We worked together on a huge guide to Pacific Northwest heavy metal and hard rock bands, *Rusted Metal*, and for our next book project we tackled this much needed bio on Seattle's most well-known metal band. When we started that aforementioned gargantuan book, we kept wondering when somebody else was going to do a book on "N.W. Metal" and nobody did. So, we said, "Why not us then?" Same thing with this book on

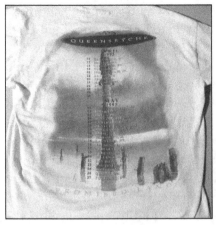

one of Seattle's most well-known groups. And what better time than to help celebrate Queensrÿche's 40th anniversary, right? What a momentous occasion. Very few bands last ten years, let alone four decades.

With this book, we dug deep into the history of Queensrÿche to tell the complete story. From their formative years of jamming with friends and forming bands, playing covers and learning to play in front of crowds, starting to write original music and pushing boundaries, to touring the world playing arenas and stadiums, selling millions of albums, and becoming a household name. Interviews with the various members of the band themselves over the years, friends, family, managers, producers and engineers, and many others involved with Queensrÿche help tell the story. We even asked various "super fans" to recount some standout moments of them seeing the band live, meeting them in person, etc.

- James R. Beach
N.W. Metal Historian

My history with Queensrÿche doesn't go back nearly as far as my co-writers. But the band's music was critically important to me growing up. As a kid on Long Island, N.Y., my first exposure to the band was a dubbed cassette copy of *Rage for Order*, back in late 1987. My friends, brothers Jeff and Wayne Douglass, had gotten the cassette from their older brother. I popped the tape into my Walkman, and walked down the hill to my apartment building, and heard the guitar lines of "Walk in the Shadows" and Geoff's opening of "What? You say..." and I was immediately hooked.

Queensrÿche quickly became an obsession in those awkward pre-teen years. It was a rough period for my family. We were poor and moved around all over Long Island. It was a very nomadic existence for me from ages five to fifteen. Thankfully, the band's music was there for me to latch onto during the `80s and `90s and help provide a sense of stability. As corny as it sounds, the music became a part of me, and a familiar "friend" as we relocated from place to place.

Summer 1990 found my family in Exeter Township, Pennsylvania (our only move off Long Island). I remember sitting with a tape recorder up against the TV speaker in the living room, recording the audio of the "Empire" video as it aired on MTV. We lost cable TV shortly thereafter, and ultimately moved back to Long Island in November/December 1990. My parents were able to scratch up enough money to buy me an Aiwa top-loading CD/cassette boombox, and *Empire* on CD for Christmas, and my Aunt got me *Operation: Mindcrime*. We had started to finally settle down as a family, moving into the school district I'd graduate from four years later. Like many kids, I bonded with others who were into heavy metal bands, particularly Queensrÿche—and a few of those friendships still exist today, 30 years later.

As of this writing, I've been fortunate to have seen Queensrÿche (in all its various incarnations) 37 times. But the road to my first Queensrÿche show was a long one. The first time I had an opportunity was the band's Building Empires tour, at Nassau Coliseum on Long Island. It was summer 1991. My parents wouldn't let me go. I pleaded with them to no avail, trying to explain what it meant to me. I was crushed and watched so many of my friends the next school year rock their *Empire*-era t-shirts they got at the show. I was known as the Queensrÿche "super fan" and amazingly, I missed out seeing them live on their biggest tour. My mom saw how dejected I was, and Christmas 1991, she went out to our local music store (Mother's Music in Patchogue, N.Y., which sadly does not exist now) and bought every single Queensrÿche import CD and cassette single they had. (I still have them all today.) She promised that the next time the band came to town, I could go.

That came later than expected, on July 18, 1995. On that date, Queensrÿche, with Type O Negative in tow, rolled into the Jones Beach Amphitheater in Wantagh, N.Y., for the Road to the Promised Land Tour. By then I was an adult and a college student, but my mother didn't forget her promise. She was working as a receptionist for a local radio station at the time and was able to get me a pair of tickets to the show. I took my best friend, Rob Kotynski. It was an incredible night I'll never forget—Queensrÿche was everything I thought they would be. Between the import singles, and my first live experience, I became a massive Queensrÿche collector and historian for the next 20 years. I met my wife, some of my closest friends and so many interesting people because of the band. A lifetime indelibly shaped by the music of five guys from the Pacific Northwest.

A lot of things have changed since then. Like Paul Suter wrote in his foreword, while the current Queensrÿche is pretty good, they aren't the same, and neither am I. But without Queensrÿche, I'd never be the person that I am today, and I'm eternally grateful for this opportunity to help tell their story.

- Brian J. Heaton
Queensrÿche Archivist
AnybodyListening.net

BRIAN HEATON AND CHRIS DEGARMO, JONES BEACH, LONG ISLAND, NEW YORK, 1997

CHAPTER 1:
BEGINNINGS

T he humble beginnings of Queensrÿche are rooted in the suburbs of Bellevue, and Redmond, Washington during the 1970s. Nestled in on the east side of Seattle, across Lake Washington, were houses surrounded by schools, small businesses and in some outlying areas, farmland. The four founding members of the band—Michael Wilton, Chris DeGarmo, Eddie Jackson and Scott Rockenfield—all developed their playing skills in those neighborhoods (Geoff Tate would show up a bit later as a Tacoma transplant). Two of the future musicians were born elsewhere, but they spent their formative years in Seattle and that is where they would remain and develop as players. All four guys had fairly regular childhoods in typical suburbs.

Michael Wilton was born in San Francisco on February 23, 1962, to Woody and Martha Wilton. He has a brother, Mark, and sister, Wendy. Michael's dad was a fan of rock music and introduced his son to groups like Led Zeppelin, The Allman Brothers, and Cream, and took him to see concerts of the Jefferson Airplane, Grateful Dead, and others at a fairly young age. His father was also a fan of jazz and turned Michael onto fusion guitarists such as John McLaughlin, Al Di Meola and Larry Coryell. Eventually, the family relocated to Bellevue in 1968 when he was six. By age eight, young Michael was learning to play acoustic guitar and trying to figure out songs from The Beatles, Jimi Hendrix, Bob Dylan, and others, from his dad's record collection. At age thirteen, in 1975, he was gifted his late uncle's bass guitar and amplifier. By the time he was in junior

high school, Michael was already forming garage bands and learning various cover tunes. During that time, he switched to electric guitar and became more serious about playing. It was also around that time that Wilton became interested in heavier music and gravitated toward Deep Purple and Rainbow (featuring guitarist Ritchie Blackmore), Black Sabbath, KISS, UFO, Montrose, Judas Priest, Van Halen and others (seeing the 1978 Black Sabbath and Van Halen concert in Seattle made a big impression on him).

"I met Mike Wilton through George Jenc," John Razor explains. "This was back when Wilton lived across the street from Interlake [High School], so he and I hadn't gone to the same junior high school. At any rate, George Jenc, Mike Wilton, and I started jamming together. Back then Mike was a bass player, George played the guitar, and I was the drummer. We played in my basement. We had a huge room that had no windows, it was perfect. It was big enough to fit an entire band, and audience, along with a huge P.A. system. Wilton secretly started learning to play the guitar and one day he just showed up and basically blew George away on the guitar. He ended up bringing Dave Radcliff over to play bass. Before too long, George just completely bowed out because he couldn't keep up with Mike, who practiced a lot. He took his music very seriously, even in the very beginning. I remember his father was really into music too. His dad had a huge record collection, mostly opera and classical, I think. That might be one reason Mike was so influenced by Queen. I remember he really dug their stuff. In fact, that was one of the tensions, because I really wanted to do more Jeff Beck, jazz-rock fusion, and he was more into the Queen-type genre."

Michael attended Highland Junior High and was friends with Brett Miller (who would later go on to play in Lipstick), Dave Goldberg and Mark Welling (future Babylon, Perennial and Bloodgood drummer). Younger student Chris DeGarmo would also become part of the group of friends interested in music once he started there.
"Chris DeGarmo was my locker partner and best friend along with our mutual friend, Dave 'Da Gold' Goldberg. We were like the three musketeers through junior high and high school. I've also known Mike Wilton since 7th grade," Brett Miller says.

Chris DeGarmo's brother, Mark, also remembers meeting Wilton early on and being impressed by his talent on the guitar. "All of us were band nerds. Wilton went to Interlake [High School] eventually, but he was younger—three or four years younger than me. I used to jam with

Michael up in the band rehearsal room at Interlake. He was known as this prodigy. He was, like, twelve years old, and already an amazing guitar player. His dad, Woody, had the most amazing record collection. Everybody back then was measured by that, and Mr. Wilton had "The Vault." Mark states:

"Of course, that all trickled down to Michael. He used to carry his guitar around—I'll never forget it—and he would come up to the band room. Many of us were hanging out and playing. We'd see who could play Rush, or whatever was the latest thing we were all 'oohing and aahing' over. I remember jamming with 'Whip' when he was really young, and all of us were older guys and were like, 'Wow! This kid can play.'"

Wilton's first live performance was a barn party in Redmond (where a Microsoft parking lot now sits in its place) in the summer of 1977. Short a player, he asked Jester drummer Matt Bazemore to sit in with the band and they jammed on tunes by Jimi Hendrix and others. Matt was impressed by Mike's "talent and graciousness." Wilton later told Bazemore that it was his first time performing in front of people. The seeds were planted....

Christopher DeGarmo was born in Wenatchee, Washington, on June 14, 1963, to Gerald and Caroline DeGarmo. His older brother, Mark, is three years older, and his other brother, Kevin, is a year younger. When Chris was around age five, his father left and his mother raised the boys on her own, usually working a couple of jobs to support them. They moved to the Bellevue area in the early 1970s, and Chris entered Highland Junior High in the sixth grade in the fall of 1974. It was tough on his family with his mom raising the kids as a single parent and money was tight. "My mom moved around a lot. I was born in Seattle. Chris and Kevin were both born in Wenatchee. But we moved around a lot. That was the other thing: we were sort of itinerant for a time," Mark DeGarmo says. "My parents' marriage broke up when we moved to Wenatchee. We moved from Seattle to Wenatchee, then back to Seattle, and then over to Bellevue. All the B's (laughs). Belleuve, Burien, Bellingham, Bainbridge Island. We moved all over the place."

Chris DeGarmo would end up getting his first guitar from his brother Mark, who wasn't interested in the gift his grandparents gave him. Chris loved music and gravitated toward others with the same interests. "My grandparents bought me a Vox guitar," Mark shares. "I was bigtime into the Beatles, as obviously a whole lot of people were then. That was the big thing on my block. I was very into music and ended up being a drummer in the long run. So I had this Vox six-string acoustic guitar stuffed under the bed. One of the earliest memories I have of Christopher is him playing the ukelele, the other thing we had we used to mess around with. We we got that Vox, it was bigger than he was. So I used to prop him up in a chair, and put it on his leg, and he would try and hold it. It had a slick varnish and I remember it slipping on him. But we would strum and play along to all of the Beatles records. I had all of them."

"That was pretty much all I listened to until about 1966 or so," Mark added. "Then I discovered the [Rolling] Stones and [Jimi] Hendrix and other stuff. We always had music going at our house, or at our grandparents. We always played music, all different kinds. But my record collection was what we ended up listening to most. A lot of Beatles, some Stones, Hendrix." As time went on, Chris was introduced to newer hard rock bands such as Led Zeppelin. Mark continues:

"One of the bigger memories I have is of one summer. Chris would constantly be nicking my Led Zeppelin tapes and making off with them. I had this little cassette player and *Houses Of The Holy* had just come out. Of course, like everyone else, I played that over and over. One summer, Chris just took my cassette player and that tape and locked himself in his room. I didn't see him for a month. One night he came out and said, 'check this out.' He played 'Over the Hills and Far Away,' note for note. I swear that he was only like 13 or 14 and played it with ease. I was always a tough critic and would tell him what I thought, but I was left with my jaw hanging open."

Brett Miller recounts a similar memory of Chris quickly learning the popular British band's songs. "I remember going to parties with Dave Goldberg and Chris back in junior high school," Miller says on DeGarmo's influences and early musical skill. "If there were girls there, Chris would find an acoustic and impress them by playing [Led] Zeppelin covers like 'Over the Hills and Far Away' and 'Stairway to Heaven'). He always did well with girls. If there was an electric [guitar] handy he would play 'Barracuda' by Heart. He was a huge Jimmy Page and Paul McCartney freak, and still does a funny McCartney impression."

While he was at Highland Junior High, Chris also became friends with another aspiring guitarist who would gift him with his first real quality electric guitar. Adam Brenner's parents had recently divorced, and he was shuffled between them and around to different schools. The budding teenagers identified with each other in that regard. "I moved back in with my dad and I got him to buy me a Fender Champ and a Fender Mustang from Bandwagon Music," Brenner says. "After I got the Fender Champ, I went to Israel for my Bar Mitzvah with my dad. I gave Chris DeGarmo that guitar because I didn't really know how to play. I just sat there with a wah-wah pedal all day for eight hours and made noise in my bedroom. I gave my guitar to Chris and when I got back from my Bar Mitzvah, I called him up. He played me, 'Over the Hills and Far Away' on the phone and I thought it was a record. I thought he was full of shit. He said, 'Yeah, I learned it!' We were kind of best friends at age twelve when we went to Highland Junior High School. So, Chris DeGarmo got good and I got jealous of him and I wanted to get good." In turn, DeGarmo encouraged Brenner to check out a popular band back then that would later feature into Brenner's setlist in his solo group, Adam Bomb. "Chris DeGarmo said, 'What about KISS?' He told me he really thought the guitarists were cool, so I thought I would check it out," Brenner states.

Adam Brenner would go on to learn to play guitar very well and became a prodigy. Before he even started at Interlake High School, he had already formed his first band with friends Gary Thompson and Scott Earl, who would go on to play in TKO and Q5, and Culprit and TKO respectively. Their garage band, Rage, was short-lived as Earl left and was replaced on bass by another Redmond friend, Eddie Jackson. Re-christened Spectrum, it would  be one of Jackson's first band experiences. "Eddie Jackson was the bass player in Spectrum for a while," Brenner adds. "He was already in high school, and we used to play 'Bad Motor Scooter' [by Montrose]. I think we did a few gigs."

Edward Jackson was born on January 29, 1961, in Robstown, Texas, to Eusebio and Alida Jackson. He has a younger brother, David, and three sisters, Erika, Dahlia (Dolly), and Olga. His family moved to Seattle in the late 1960s. Ed is the second oldest child and he grew up listening to music and singing along to songs on the radio. Eddie started playing acoustic guitar by age 14, and switched to the electric guitar and bass a short while later (after he started at Redmond High School). Jackson also experimented with drums a bit and later purchased a drum set. It likely helped him grasp a sense of timing and rhythm and was helpful with playing bass. He knew at that age, when he was in high school, that he wanted to pursue a career in music.

Jackson started jamming with friends and played in a couple of cover bands around that time, including the aforementioned Spectrum. David Morris, a mutual friend and schoolmate, also recounts the short band experience with Brenner and Thompson: "Eddie, Adam and Gary played together [in Spectrum]. Mike McCrae was responsible for introducing Adam and Gary. Scott Earl was the first bassist they played with [in a band called Rage], and then there was a short stint with Eddie Jackson after that. Sometime around 1978 was when that was. That seems about right."

"I think Eddie messed around with other people too," Morris continues. "Ron Donald was a guy that people used to come over to his house and jam there. I remember Eddie there, as well as others." Eddie eventually met a drummer named Scott Rockenfield at Redmond High. Despite Jackson being a little older, they became friends and would later get together and start jamming in the fall of 1979. Early influences on the bass guitar for Jackson were Geezer Butler of Black Sabbath, Dennis Dunaway from Alice Cooper, Mel Schacher from Grand Funk, and Geddy Lee of Rush. As time went on, Iron Maiden bassist Steve Harris was also a big influence on Eddie. His vocal ability also added to his appeal, as a bassist who could sing background parts—something that factored quite a bit into his career in music as time went on.

Scott Rockenfield was born in Seattle, on June 15, 1963, to Doug and Sandy Rockenfield. He has a younger brother, Todd, who figures into the Queensrÿche story a bit later. Scott had an interest in music early on and started playing drums at age 11. He had seen a drum set in elementary school that fall, and wanted to play them, and his parents bought him his first set that Christmas. He pounded around on it trying to learn from listening to records and picking out parts. "I first began [to be serious about it] when I was 14," Scott says. "Self-taught, I found myself listening and then trying to figure out what drummers in bands like Rush, Yes, Pink Floyd, etc., were doing. I was never much for taking lessons." He first met Chris DeGarmo in grade school during sixth grade. Chris attended other schools, but they saw each other at extracurricular events, and so on, and stayed friends over the time.

Scott attended Redmond High School and was in the same grade as Kelly Gray, whom he was friends with. Both he and Kelly shared a love of music and were learning to play. Scott was also interested in film, something he would later apply his musical talents to. As mentioned, Jackson was a little bit older than Scott and Kelly when they started as sophomores in 1970s, but he would quickly become friends with them as well.

Scott's parents were supportive of his musical interests and let him set up a practice area in their basement. He could play his drums there and invite friends to come and jam too. As time went on, it would become an important place in Queensrÿche history known as "The Dungeon." It was created in early 1979 and would be used throughout the years up until 1995. The door to enter the rehearsal room, would be adorned with stickers of local radio stations, musical instrument companies, etc., as time went on. Scott formed his first band around that time, at age 16, with a good friend who would go on to be the host of the TV show *Survivor*. "A guy named Jeff Probst knew Scott and hooked us up to play together on maybe two occasions in my basement," longtime friend

of the band, Charles Russell, shares. "Scott was three years younger than me, I believe. Years later, Scott and his father were sitting at a bar where I was a bartender. It turns out it was Scott's 21st birthday. We talked for a bit and then started hanging out on a regular basis. I slowly met the rest of the band and we all became friends."

As Michael Wilton, Chris DeGarmo, Scott Rockenfield, and Eddie Jackson all continued to learn and develop as musicians, they all played (with the various bands they assembled) parties, dances, and other small events and functions. They formed the bonds, both individually and jointly, that would eventually bring the four of them together as a band a while later....

CHAPTER 2:
JOKER ON DECK

A chance meeting of Michael Wilton and Paul Passarelli on a baseball field blossomed into a friendship and eventually a band called Joker. The boys discovered they both were aspiring musicians and quickly bonded. "I met Mike Wilton in junior high," Paul Passarelli states. "I was going to Odle and he was going to Highland and we met on the baseball field. Our teams played each other. We were the only two guys on the teams with long hair. After the game, we did the traditional handshake and he said, 'do you play guitar?' I said, 'yeah,' and he said he played guitar too. So, we exchanged phone numbers and he asked if I was a singer as well. Out of nowhere. Literally, I had never met him before. We formed Joker with John Razor (on the drums), and Dave Radcliff on bass."

Wilton, Razor and Radcliff had been together as a band for a short while and had went through a couple of name changes. They needed a strong lead singer to front the band at that point. John Razor adds: "A bit later we brought in Paul Passarelli as vocalist. Paul was a crazy man. We used to party heavily, all four of us. We would put on basement concerts at my parents' house out toward Bridal Trial/Compton Green. We had many keggers with a crap load of people there, and we played at most, if not all of them. I don't think we did any shows anywhere else while I was in the band, however. I had a huge Rogers drum set, black, double bass, with six-to-eight toms, and cymbals. The point being it was a pain to move. Plus, we had a bunch of sound equipment. We weren't really ready for any big shows anyways. We were working on building up our set of songs." Razor continues: "I actually came up with the band name, 'Joker,' back when Mike, Dave R., Paul P., and I were playing together. My (previous) bands had been 'Web' (in junior high), which evolved into 'Spaced.' Back then, I introduced Wilton to my buddy [who was a] guitarist. This dude was amazing, but he was kind of a hippy and was way too into Hendrix for Mike's taste. The name 'Spaced' worked when I was playing with that group, but Mike and the guys wanted no part of that name, so I suggested 'Joker.'"

Joker officially became a band in the fall of 1978 and they commenced on learning various cover songs and practicing. Before long, they had some lineup changes. "What happened was that Wilton was frustrated with me and Dave Radcliff, because we weren't putting as much time into practicing as he was," Razor says. "I was opting for chasing women (girls back then), working on my '57 Chevy, and partying. I showed up for our band practices (they were at my house), but I hadn't spent much time practicing in between. One day they showed up and said it was over. I didn't lose any sleep over it as I never had any realistic expectations of being a star or doing it professionally. Whereas, I think Mike always planned on making it big, and he put in the hard hours to get there." Razor was replaced on drums after a short while by Doug McGrew. Chris DeGarmo, who went to Interlake High School with Wilton and the others, joined on second guitar in early 1979. Joker was now a five-piece.

During their years at Interlake High School, friends Wilton and DeGarmo took guitar lessons from Rick Knotts, guitarist of the Eastside hard rock band Rail. They looked up to Rick and his band, who were older and had regular bookings around the Seattle area, etc., and local management. Formed in 1970, Rail continued to develop a following and had already headlined the Paramount Theatre by late 1976, playing mostly cover songs. "I gave both Chris DeGarmo and Michael Wilton guitar lessons," Rick Knotts says. "I gave Chris like two or three lessons, I didn't really give him many, but I taught Mike for several months. Taught him basic music theory and modal playing and stuff and of course they went on to Queensrÿche and a bunch of stuff. They had a band called Joker with the two of them and Paul Passarelli, who was another student of mine, and Doug McGrew who's played with everybody. And at the same time, Geoff Tate was in a band called Tyrant and their guitarist, Adam Brenner, was another student of mine." Mark DeGarmo also remembers his brother taking lessons from the older Bellevue guitar player: "Rail was the popular local band at that time, and Rick Knotts was their guitarist. I remember Chris took a couple of lessons from him. But everybody was kind of looking over their shoulder at these youngsters. We'd hear whispers of these young kids that could just play. But kismet. Chris and Michael crossed paths and the rest is history."

JOKER   Original list of songs and lead assignments   April 1979
1. Whole lotta Rosie - Ac/DC   Mike 3'50
2. Communication BreakDown - LeD ZePPeLiN chris 2:10
3. DOA - Van Halen Mike 2:10
4. Ripper - Judas Priest mike 1:54
5. Train Kept A Rollin - Yardbirds chris 7:30
6. Rock N Roll - LeD ZePPeLiN Mike 4:00
7. Bring it on home - LeD ZePPeLiN no solo 2:50
8. Can't Kuckin/Brown sugar mike Rolling stones 6:00
9. Freebird - Lynard Skynard chris 9:00
10. Come together - Beatles chris 3:25
11. Good times bad times - LeD ZePPeLiN chris 2:30
12. Stranglehold - Ted Nugent chris 6:25
13. TUSH - ZZ TOP chris 2:00
14. Ain't Talkin bout love - Van Halen Mike 3'50
15. Doctor Doctor - UFO no solo 3:00
16. Victim of changes - Judas Priest mike 7:00
17. Lights out - U.Fo Mike 4:00
18. Life in london - Pat travers chris 4:00
19. Workin Man - Rush Mike 2:00
20. Life for the Taking - Eddie Money chris 4:00
21. Jumpin Jack Flash - Rolling Stones Mike 4:00
22. Cowboy song - thin Lizzy mike 4:00
23. who Do you love - George Thourogood chris 4:00
24. Jail House Rock - Elvis Mike 1:54
25. Sin city - Ac/DC Mike 5:00
26. Symptom of the Universe - Black Sabbath Mike 5:00
27. Somebody get me a Doctor - Van Halen chris 3:00
28. out of control - Ted Nugent chris 3:25
29. I got The Fire - Montrose Mike 3:30
30. Rock Bottom - U.Fo. Mike 7:00

Wilton and the other teenagers used their lessons to help learn cover songs they incorporated into their set lists. "I'd never heard of AC/DC until Mike Wilton whipped out the first AC/DC record. I didn't know who it was, and I was like, 'Oh my God!'" Paul Passarelli elaborates. "Then we started picking songs we wanted to learn. We were both taking lessons from Rick Knotts on and off at the time. I would go after Mike went to his lesson. [It was] 'you teach me this one and then I'll go learn another and teach you that one.' Two songs for the price of one." Somewhere around this time, was supposedly when Wilton got his nickname "The Whip." His guitar teacher said he "whipped on the guitar," and the shortened version of "The Whip" stuck.

The Joker bandmates continued to learn songs from groups they liked, and the group's setlist developed into around 30 songs they pulled from. By April 1979, it included tracks by: AC/DC, Led Zeppelin, Van Halen, UFO, Montrose, ZZ Top, Pat Travers, The Rolling Stones, Rush, Black Sabbath, Lynyrd Skynyrd and even Elvis Presley. They landed their first professional gig at Lake Hills Roller Rink on May 5, 1979. "The guys in Rail were hugely kind in guiding us," Passarelli adds. "We asked them how did they get the gigs at dances and stuff. They said, 'you have to go to a booking agency,' and they

LIVE IN CONCERT!

JOKER

Lake Hills Arena

-presents-

J O K E R

SATURDAY NIGHT MAY 5
9:00 - 12:00
ADMISSION: $3.00 at the door

JOKER is

Lake Hills Arena
16732 NE 8th
Bellevue, WA
746-0102

Paul Passarelli   lead vocals
Mike Wilton   Lead Guitar
Chris Satchitano   Lead Guitar
Dave Satchitano   Bass
Russ McGros   Drums

JOKER's first show - May 5, 1979

suggested Unicam." Joker made a big impression with their first big live performance, especially their lead singer. "Paul Passarelli was the David Lee Roth of Bellevue and sported custom made DLR-style stage clothes and a big personality," remembered Brett Miller, who aside from his own bands did lights for Joker's gigs. "Paul differentiated himself from the other local singers with his rich baritone voice and was always the life of any party. We all prayed at the altar of Van Halen at time. We lived our lives according to the doctrine of David Lee Roth. We also were heavy into Bon Scott-era AC/DC, Scorpions, and Judas Priest."

Following their debut gig at Lake Hills, they were slated to be part of the lineup of 16 bands competing in a "Battle of the Bands" at the roller rink, which was a multi-weekend event that started in early July 1979. Joker competed on the third weekend, on the twenty-fourth. "I think that the Battle of the Bands [in '79] was how I officially met Craig [Cooke]," Paul Passarelli states. "Joker didn't win any level of the competition, but we outdrew everybody. I think we had 150 paid and the next highest had like 50 people. When we lost in the first round, they asked us to open up for the championship round. Like six weeks later or whatever it was. We thought that was kind of weird. But Craig said we outdrew everybody else—even the band that won the Battle of the Bands, 'Ridge.' We were literally from that area. I lived like two blocks away and worked at the Lake Hills Roller Rink."

Also competing in the "Battle of the Bands" that summer was Jester, which featured Corey Rivers on guitar and vocals, Joe Lowery on bass, and aspiring artist Matt Bazemore on drums. Amongst the other groups were Orpheus (featuring future Culprit members Scott Earl and John DeVol), Snowblind (featuring Rick Van Zandt and Izzy Rehaume who would be part of Rottweiller, and Jim Kovach who would co-found Heir Apparent), Amethyst (with members of Culprit, TKO and Mistrust), Oz (with Dan Christopherson of D.C. Lacroix), Wraith (with producer Monty Smith), Smack (featuring Jeff Olson), Mildstone, and others. The aforementioned Ridge, which included future members of Fifth Angel, would prevail eventually as the winners over Tyrant—a popular cover band that included the aforementioned Adam Brenner and Gary Thompson, and an engmatic, intense, charismatic singer with a big range and presence named Jeffrey Wayne Tate (who would later change his first name to "Geoff"). Tate made a huge impression on everyone during those battles that summer as one of the more talented singers around.

Following their performance opening for the two finalists of the Battle of the Bands on August 28, 1979, Joker decided to make some changes and replace DeGarmo with another guitarist. Brett Miller explains: "What happened was they fired Chris because he didn't have any equipment. He had to get equipment.  And they had a chance to get Jeff Olson in the band who had a PA system and all these guitars and amps. As soon as they got him, they were able to go out and do a lot more shows. Chris was a fan favorite and the girls loved him, but he didn't have the equipment." It was the age-old story of the person with the equipment, or place to rehearse, gets the gig (ala Van Halen with David Lee Roth having the PA they rented out and eventually asking him to join the band).

Joker rehearsed during the fall with their revamped lineup featuring former Smack and ROX guitarist Jeff Olson. On January 19, 1980, the new version of Joker opened for the new version of Tyrant (who split up following their loss to Ridge in the Battle of the Bands, then revamped by adding brothers Rod and Brad Young from Shifter on bass and lead vocals, respectively). They continued on playing various dances and other gigs throughout the spring that year. "Craig Cooke was booking Joker at junior highs and high schools all around Washington State," Brett Miller says. "And these were kids [who] wanted to dance. They wanted to have slow dances and the cheerleaders wanted danceable music, and we're showing up there ... it would be at a prom and they would open up with 'Hell Bent For Leather.' And there were the flashpots and smoke filling up the  entire auditorium. They were visibly upset. They let Craig Cooke know that he better not send a band like that out again."

Eventually things ran their course and Joker fizzled out. Brett Miller explains: "Jeff Olson was in the band for like a year almost—until the summer of 1980—and then he quit. Joker had a gig, I believe, opening for Rail at Bellevue Community College and they did it as a four piece. But they couldn't do as many songs and the band just kind of went on hiatus/fell apart after that." There was some intention to keep the band going, with Brett Miller learning bass guitar to fill that spot, but it never happened due to a disagreement between the two leaders, Passarelli and Wilton. "Mike and I had a little falling out after the Joker thing," Passarelli says. "Mainly because we had the PA loan together and equipment went missing towards the end of our band. If I'm paying for this monitor where is it, you know? I'm not saying anybody stole it, but it's been so long that I don't remember exactly what happened."

Wilton went off to attend the Cornish Institute of Allied Arts in Seattle, where both Ann and Nancy Wilson of Heart had attended (in the late `60s and early `70s respectively), to continue to improve his playing and knowledge on the guitar. In the fall, he met Scott Rockenfield at Easy Street Records and his path would be aligned with the drummer's after that.

After Chris DeGarmo was let go from Joker in the late summer of 1979, he landed in a group called Tempest a short while later, which included bassist/lead vocalist Mark Hovland and drummer Kevin Hodges. "Chris joined a band called Tempest, who got very popular fast by playing cool tunes like 'Black Diamond' by KISS and other good metal," Brett Miller says. "Their bass player/singer Mark Hovland had a very good voice and Chris was vindicated as a great guitarist after being kicked out of Joker. Eventually, Tempest added former ROX drummer Mark Welling (known today as the main drummer for Christian-themed rock band Bloodgood) and they became DeGarmo-Hovland-Welling. D-H-W had a real good local buzz and circulated a recording [featuring] Christian-

themed lyrics by Hovland. D-H-W broke up shortly after that when Welling left to join Geoff Tate's new progressive band, Babylon."

Scott Rockenfield continued to develop as a drummer, and in the fall of 1980, as mentioned above, he met Mike Wilton at Easy Street Records in Bellevue. They hit it off and decided to jam together. Scott was already playing with guitarist James Nelson (who would go on to play in Syre), and Wilton was added on second guitar and Eddie Jackson on bass. They named the band Cross + Fire. Nelson left after a while, and they asked DeGarmo and Hovland to join the band. "Chris Degarmo and I had known each other since the sixth grade," Rockenfield explains. "We reconnected and decided that we should start to play together." At that point, they would change the name of the band....

CHAPTER 3:
THE TYRANT OF BABYLON

 effrey "Geoff" Wayne Tate was born on January 14, 1959, in Stuttgart, Germany, to Perry and Ella Tate. His father was a member of the United States Government Diplomatic Corps, and his mother an author of children's books and an artist. While Geoff was a toddler, the Tates moved to New Mexico. Geoff's family (which by now included two sisters, Amy and Perri Ann) eventually relocated to Tacoma, Washington, when Geoff was fourteen. Geoff showed an interest in music early on, enjoying symphonies, and his mother often sang around the house. "We always sang around the house. My mother has a very nice voice," Geoff recalls. His aunt was also a professional opera singer and had tremendous vocal ability and range. He dabbled around on a variety of instruments, including playing trumpet in his school band, but eventually decided to concentrate on singing. He also developed some skill on keyboards, which he would use down the road. Geoff loved the mountains in the Pacific Northwest and started hiking at age sixteen, when he was a student at Wilson High School. He excelled in his classes and was an "A" student during his years there. He played football and considered a career in that sport until he was sidelined with a knee injury. Geoff also swam on the school team.

Geoff Tate graduated from high school in 1977 and attended Tacoma Community College for about a year before dropping out. His academic interests were political science and business. After he left college, he decided to focus on music and started auditioning for lead singer slots. In the fall of 1978, he auditioned for a garage band up in Kirkland called Tyrant. "I grew up in Tacoma and moved to Seattle in 1978 when I was 19," Tate elaborated. "I played in my first rock band when I was 17 and was a lead singer by 18. I loved writing songs and playing music and knew this was what I wanted to do with my life."

Tyrant evolved earlier that year out of a band called Spectrum that featured hot shot young guitarist Adam Brenner of Lake Washington High School, his friend Gary Thompson from Redmond High School, Eddie Jackson on bass and an older singer named Jake (who sang Aerosmith songs really well according to Brenner). Randy Nelson replaced Jackson on bass before long and they rechristened the band Tyrant, after the 1976 Judas Priest song. Jake left a while later and they started auditioning new lead singers. "We were auditioning singers and in walks this guy with a real bad afro and he could sing high Rush songs," says Adam Brenner. "We weren't sure about him, but we said, 'okay.' He told us his name was Jeff Tate with a J. He was from Tacoma and he had a cheap, brown V.W. van. So, we went for it." Tate was more into progressive rock and thought about changing his name way back then to reflect that. "Jeff was a little unsure [about the type of music we played]," Brenner added. "He wanted to change his name to Waterfall. So, me and my friends still call him 'Waterfall.'"

Tyrant practiced hard and learned a couple dozen cover songs, as well as wrote their own original composition ("Out Of Faze"). They played cuts by Rush, Rainbow, Led Zeppelin, UFO, Montrose, Pat Travers, Aerosmith, Queen, Journey and a few by Van Halen, who had turned the heads around of every aspiring guitarist with their incredible debut album in early 1978, and their opening set for Black Sabbath during that tour (they especially affected Brenner, who later followed the band around on tour, and met and hung out with Eddie Van Halen). Tyrant's debut gig was the Lake Washington High School senior party "The Main Event" on June 9, 1979. Brenner had approached the senior party organizers offering his

band to play for no charge, as they needed a gig to showcase their new band. The band was hugely popular at the 20-keg event, and the organizers did well enough they ended up paying the band "a gratuity" of $100 cash. Tyrant now had their first paying show.

Tyrant's next gig would be as one of the competing bands in the "Battle of the Bands" contest at Lake Hills Roller Rink, along with Joker, Jester, Smack and others (as mentioned in the previous chapter). Their first night was on July 17, 1979, and they faced off against Snowblind, Easy Street and Oz in the first round. Tyrant made a huge impression on the crowd and judges that night and advanced forward. "The real story from that [1979 Battle of the Bands] contest was the hot new lead singer with the band Tyrant who no one had ever heard of," Miller recalls. "His name was Geoff Tate." "Tyrant was a sensation with all of the local metalhead crowd with their sophisticated polished look and sound. Tate's Halford-esque wail was incredible. It made people stop whatever they were doing for miles around. Tyrant was probably more famous locally for their short Eddie Van Halen-clone guitarist named Adam Brenner. Adam's rich family owned the successful Brenner Brothers Bakery. They bought him the best equipment and made it possible for him to practice all day. Adam was good and he knew it. He was the first guy locally to have a Floyd Rose tremolo bar which he showed off at the soundcheck at Battle of the Bands. [He later on got signed to Geffen and changed his name to Adam Bomb.] Tyrant used to do an awesome version of Rainbow's "Man on the Silver Mountain" with Tate singing the Ronnie James Dio part flawlessly. They also played a ton of Van Halen."

Tyrant advanced all the way to the final round before being defeated by Ridge, another up and coming band with a great singer, Ted Pilot, and an amazing drummer in Ken Mary. "Tyrant went all the way to the finals," Miller adds. "The band who beat them in the finals was called Ridge. They played more poppy covers like 'My Sharona' which the judges liked better. [Members of] Ridge went on to become Fifth Angel. Tyrant broke up immediately after losing the finals, leaving Tate without a band." Despite having set list changes throughout their performances

and being very popular with the local crowd, Tyrant didn't quite make it all the way. This caused some dissention in the band, unfortunately forcing them to part ways at that point.

"We did gigs, we did the senior keg party, we did Battle of the Bands and stuff like that," Brenner says. "When the Battle of the Bands was put on by Unicam, we made it to the finals. We were kick-ass and we went up against Ridge. For one thing, we sounded just like Judas Priest and all these other great bands. When we lost the Battle of the Bands, we broke up." Brenner and Thompson eventually reformed Tyrant later that fall with Rail singer/bassist Terry James Young's brothers, Rod and Brad Young, on bass and vocals, respectively. Randy Nelson would join the winner of the contest, Ridge, in 1980 (and Perennial following that in 1982).

Despite the implosion of his band after the battles, many people had noticed Tate's vocal ability and stage presence. "The first time I saw Geoff [Tate], he was so incredible with his eye contact," says promoter Craig Cooke. "He would look at you and burn a hole in you. Every person in that hall felt he connected with them. And I'd never seen that before." Geoff was first invited to come to a Jester practice following Tyrant's split up. He liked the trio's playing and they really needed a lead singer out front. He sang Led Zeppelin's "Immigrant Song" and Judas Priest's "Dissident Aggressor" and proceeded to blow out the speaker on a Sears Silvertone amplifier. Tate declined to join the band permanently, citing their lack of practice/lack of a regular practice space at that time.

Geoff was starting to become a wanted man by the fall of 1979. Other bands were interested in getting him to join their bands and/or try out. "We needed a singer [for Orpheus] and we were trying to get Geoff Tate, because Geoff and I were good friends," John DeVol of Culprit says. "He was in a cover band at the time, and I was like, 'No, no, no. You need to be in my band.' We'd talk all the time and I'd go over to his place, but it never happened. And then [Jeff] L'Heureux came up. He wasn't really quite what I was looking for, because he was more of a Cheap Trick kind of guy, but he actually adapted to what the music was."

During this time, Tate also continued to develop his vocals and range by taking lessons from a well-regarded local teacher. "We [Geoff Tate and I] both took lessons from the Maestro David Kyle," explains Paul Passarelli. "That was due to the guys in Rail—Terry Young and Rick [Knotts]. We asked them how did Terry get to be such a great singer and screamer. And they're like, 'well, he takes lessons from Maestro

David Kyle.' So had Ann and Nancy Wilson and everybody after that. So, I took lessons from David Kyle and so did Geoff and a couple other people. We used to carpool—before it was called 'carpooling.' Geoff would be like, 'When's your lesson?' 'Saturday.' 'Mine is too.' I was like, 'Can't get my mom's car, can I go with you?' His lesson would be like an hour and I would hang out on Alki until it was my turn. He was always cool to us."

Geoff Tate soon joined the progressive group Paradox, in late-1979/ early-1980. The band would go through some turnover with guitarists and bassists throughout the next couple of months. "Paradox was Geoff Tate on vocals, Greg Mohler on guitar, Jeff Olson on guitar, and Dave Radcliff on bass," says Brett Miller. "I think the drummer's name was Greg. It was after Joker (split up). Jeff Olson played with Radcliff in Joker,

and bassists were hard to come by. Nobody liked Dave Radcliff and treated him distantly. Not invited to parties, etc. When I was auditioning for [Dave's spot in] Paradox, post-Tate, I wanted to take the band in a more 'commercial' direction with my marketing. Mohler was a bit of a purist and was writing very proggy stuff with weird time signatures. I was not very far [along] in learning the bass by that point, so I deserved to be fired." Regardless, Tate's tenure in the band was short-lived and he was on to another progressive group before long.

During the time Tate was in Paradox, he was also courted by Myth and rehearsed with them a bit. Myth was still developing original material and honing their skills as players. "Around that time, we didn't have any vocals and two of my buddies and I used to go down to Geoff's house all the time and bug him to join our band," recalls Kelly Gray. "I believe Geoff was in a band called Paradox at the time." Tate performed a gig or two with Myth that summer, but he still bounced around a bit between bands before he eventually found one that fit what he wanted to do musically.

Babylon was formed in the fall in 1980. Mark Welling had left D-H-W to join up with Geoff Tate, and former Jester guitarist and bassist Corey Rivers and Joe Lowery. "My band Jester, consisting of Corey Rivers, Joe Lowery and myself, broke up in 1980," explains Matt Bazemore. "I knew that it wasn't likely that I would find another group that could take its place in the local scene, and that I couldn't recreate the camaraderie and positive energy that I had known for a number of years. Corey Rivers and I had been playing together since seventh grade. It was over, and that was it for me for a while. I changed gears and pursued an art degree in college because I didn't want my livelihood to depend on the perpetual consensus that needs to exist if a group is to succeed."

"In the summer before I left for college [Western Washington University], I saw Geoff perform with his latest group Myth," Bazemore adds. "I'll never forget the opening solo vocal on 'Scarborough Fair.' It put a chill down my spine. Just amazing. Geoff also found time to sing with my old bandmates in a new group called "Babylon". That was a bit tough for me because I felt left out and because there was a great deal of me still in their group. The name came not from the Blackmore's Rainbow song Gates Of Babylon, but from the Blue Cheer tune of the same name, that we used to cover from Outsideinside. They still performed a song I wrote lyrics for, called The Penalty, even though they had changed them a bit, the title was still mine. I named all of our songs after Lon Chaney Sr. movies. [Babylon's] drummer [Mark Welling] had also bought his first drum set from me for six dollars."

"I met Geoff when he responded to an ad we had placed seeking a lead vocalist," Corey Rivers explains. Matt [Bazemore] and I were decent singers and were carrying the load, but singing was becoming a distraction, as we played pretty complicated stuff we needed to pay attention to. Geoff came to our rehearsal, and we did some covers we all knew. I had a recording of this audition for years on cassette tape but, after a series of household moves, I can no longer find it. I was immediately impressed with his personality, demeanor, and good looks. Geoff was a polite, unassuming, modest young man, and was very pleasant to be around. He was always kind, considerate, deferential, and unobtrusive. He obviously would attain glory [later on], but he was not a grandstander or a glory seeker in his relationships with others.

Babylon quickly gelled and started writing original, progressive material, as well as reworking some older Jester songs that Bazemore had written lyrics for. (Some of the ones with titles that were taken from the Lon Chaney Sr. silent films referenced earlier.) This was very much the direction Tate wanted to pursue with writing their own prog rock songs, versus playing cover versions of popular bands at the time. "Babylon practiced in a lavish greenhouse at Joe Lowery's folks' house," Brett Miller says. "All windows. Mark Welling was my very best friend, and I was at their practices a number of times." "Babylon rehearsed in Joe Lowery's family out-building, if you will, on their property on the shore of Lake Sammamish," Corey Rivers adds. "It was perfect, isolated from other homes and sufficiently roomy for us, friends and associates. Geoff's voice was otherworldly, and probably my favorite memory of my time with Babylon was singing harmony vocals with him. Just to hear my voice at the same time as hearing his was enrapturing. Babylon worked extremely diligently in rehearsal, as we knew we had something special with that lineup. But we were on the clock with Joe as he would soon graduate from high school, and take wing into his academic future. Babylon was exclusive originals—we did no covers. I have no recordings remaining, although I know they exist, as we frequently taped out rehearsals. Another thing about Babylon, if I dare include myself in this comment: we all had exceptional wit and senses of humor. We were constantly amused and cutting-up when we [put] our instruments down. A truly fun bunch of guys to be around. Babylon song titles I remember include: 'Sea of Darkness', 'Eire', 'Bitter End' and others."

A recording of their rehearsal demos from November 20, 1980, exists and includes the aforementioned songs, "The Penalty", "Blind Bargain," "Sabre's Edge", and "Right To Kill." Geoff Tate played keyboards (including a mini-Moog), as well as sang lead vocals (something he would continue down the road in the studio). The other members of Babylon were very talented. Corey Rivers was able to sing and play guitar really well, they had a bass player in Joe Lowery who emulated Chris Squire of Yes (including playing a Rickenbacker), and a killer drummer in Welling with a huge kit. They practiced extensively and eventually landed their first gig....

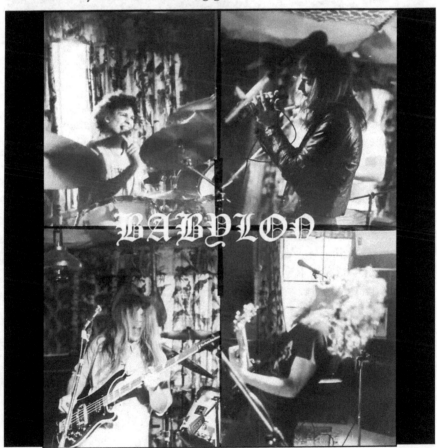

CHAPTER 4:
THE MYTH OF THE MOB

T he Mob evolved out of Cross + Fire after the lineup changes and additions of Chris DeGarmo and Mark Hovland. Hovland played bass and sang, but they decided to just have him front the band solely. That way they could have the five piece lineup in the vein of Judas Priest and Iron Maiden with twin lead guitars. "Needing a bass player, I was actually offered an audition at the time, but refused because I was trying to form a Seattle version of Motley Crue with Paul Passarelli," Brett Miller recalls. "I wasn't a very good bassist at the time anyway and didn't want to embarrass myself. Playing Nikki Sixx-type basslines I could do, but forget about playing like Iron Maiden's Steve Harris. They soon added Scott's old high school friend from Redmond High School, Eddie Jackson, who could play the intricate bass lines they wanted to. The year was now 1981. They named their new band The Mob after the Ronnie James Dio-fronted Black Sabbath song ['The Mob Rules']."

Mark Hovland's tenure with The Mob was short-lived due to him living much further away and his lack of interest in the newer heavy metal bands, especially Iron Maiden. Before Mark's departure, they did land their first gig playing at the Ellensberg Juvenile Detention Center in the spring of 1981. "One of our moms put it together," Chris DeGarmo states. "Kids broke up the chairs. It was crazy. This was the only gig our first singer, Mark Hovland, played with us."

Hovland quit after the initial concert and The Mob was now without a lead vocalist. They auditioned different candidates, but nobody worked out. They played a couple of parties without a front person, but were limited and really wanted a singer to be able to do the kind of music they were playing. Despite the limitations, people were still impressed by their skills at that point. "I saw Michael Wilton and Chris DeGarmo back when I first moved up here [to Seattle]," says Assault & Battery singer/guitarist and Floyd Rose employee Tom Wilcox. "Geoff Tate wasn't with them yet. They were so good even then at like 17 or 18 years old. It was at a party and they were playing note for note Maiden and Priest solos and I was like, 'man, I have to get a guitar!'"

Sometime during the late spring/early summer of 1981, the Mob's friend and former Joker light man Brett Miller decided to take his experience working behind the scenes running lights, building stages for Lake Hills, and working as an intern for Concerts West, to the next level as a promoter. He launched M-80 Productions in the summer of 1981 and looked to book his first concert.

Metalfest '81 was intended to be a showcase of newer local hard rock and heavy metal bands, with major label veterans TKO headlining the concert. TKO had recently added ex-Tyrant members Adam Brenner and Gary Thompson to the lineup that spring and were looking for places to debut new material before heading into the Sea-West studio in Hawaii to record a new album. "We played Lake Hills to test out new material," Brad Sinsel states. "We headlined a lot of shows with other bands over there. One of them was Myth, which later became Queensrÿche." Once Miller had a headliner locked in, he looked to fill out the rest of the roster for the show.

"There was nothing to do at Lake Hills, so I promoted Metalfest '81 there," Brett Miller explains. "For the top band, I got TKO to do it, and I also got Babylon to do it—which was Geoff Tate's new band. Mike Wilton and Chris DeGarmo had formed a band with Scott Rockenfield and Eddie Jackson, The Mob, but they couldn't find a singer. They were rehearsing in Scotty's basement and working all these jobs. They didn't have a singer, but they believed in what they were doing. They had a really cutting edge sound at the time. I didn't even know who Iron Maiden was. That wasn't my kind of rock music. I was more into the pop/rock kind of metal at the time and power pop. But I said, 'if you guys get a singer you can play the show.' They were like, 'too bad we can't get Geoff Tate to sing with us.

THE PALACE
PRESENTS —
AN LAKESIDE ROCK SPECTACULAR
METALFEST '81
!! ROCK OUT TO 8 BANDS ON STAGE !!
"FEATURING"

TKO

BABYLON • THE MOB • OPEN FIRE
RAMPAGE • PERENNIAL • LITTLE WING
MYTH

SATURDAY — SEPT. 19th

From 12:00 noon until 12:00 midnight
Doors open at 11:10 a.m
Tickets: $5.00 with coupon and $6.00 without coupon
Tickets will go on sale September 14th. The ticket office opens
at 10:00 a.m.
THE PALACE (formerly Lake Hills Roller Rink)
15232 N.E. 8th, Bellevue, Washington 98008
(Just 8 blocks east of Crossroads Mall)

FOR DIRECTIONS CALL (206) 641-0143

This stuff is perfect for him.' They had seen him with Tyrant doing all the great Scorpions, Judas Priest, etc., tunes. So, they asked Geoff if they would sit in with them and do some of the same kind of covers he did with Tyrant, and he said he would do it."

Tate had met the guys a while before that and was also impressed with their playing ability. "I first met Chris DeGarmo in 1979 when I was 20. He was a guitarist in a local rock band. I met bassist Eddie Jackson and Michael Wilton next. They were playing in a local rock trio with drummer Scott Rockenfield. Soon, Chris joined their trio and asked me to join, too. We called ourselves 'The Mob.' We were strictly a cover band,'" Tate later said. Chris's brother, Mark, recounts seeing them play the first Metalfest at Lake Hills, as well as watching them rehearse prior to the gig: "I was there for that. I was home for summer break and I'll never forget it. But I saw them before that at a rehearsal in Scott's basement. Chris said, 'Hey man. Tate's coming over for a rehearsal. Do you want to come check it out?' And I said, 'Yeah.' They had this ridiculous... if you can imagine it, Scott's [drum] kit took up the majority of the room. The walls were knocked out and I was still literally laying on my back on an amp case, and surrounded by... If Chris turned too suddenly, he'd have hit me in the head with the neck of his guitar. Then Tate walked in and they ran through four songs. It was like... I'll never forget that moment, because it was just beyond stunning. I knew there were going to be some shockwaves when those guys went out and played as a unit."

Rounding out the bill on September 9, 1981, was Perennial (who went on to release an EP, and an album, and have a #1 requested song on Seattle's major rock station, 99.9, KISW), Open Fire (who would go on to win some Battles of the Bands at Lake Hills, the Washington State Championship in 1983, and be included on the *Northwest Metalfest* compilation in 1984), Little Wing (a Heart-meets-Led Zeppelin sort of band with female singer, Sandi Miller, and Christian Fulgham of the new wave band The Attachments) and Rampage. Myth completed the lineup and featured Brent Young (Rail singer Terry James Young's brother) on lead vocals, Kelly Gray on guitar, Randy Gane on keyboards, Richard Gibson on bass and Jimmy Parsons on drums. The core of the band were Redmond High School alumni, and who had developed their set with mostly all-orginal progressive hard rock/ metal songs like "Into The Valley", "Whales", and others. Influenced by Rush, Rainbow, Deep Purple, Yes, etc., Myth stood out in the lineup and were well-received. The Mob most definitely made a big impression with Tate fronting the band and their set list featuring covers of Iron Maiden, Judas Priest, the Scorpions, Montrose and Dio-era Black Sabbath. "It wasn't really his [Geoff's] kind of music, but he came down wearing sweats and a black leather vest at the show," Miller recalls. "Kind of like not putting on an effort. But the crowd loved him. It was huge." Geoff, of course, noticed this and was impressed by the attendees' reaction.

After singing for the Mob, Tate freshened up and then fronted his own band for the Metalfest. "While TKO played, Geoff went home and showered, and then did a set singing and playing keyboards with Babylon wearing a pink Arrow business shirt and tie, as did the whole band," Miller continues. "While The Mob did all covers, Babylon was totally original. The bass player Joe Lowery was an amazing Chris Squire-esque player, but soon after the show he left to go to college and Babylon broke up." Babylon drummer Mark Welling joined Perennial a short while later, and Corey Rivers went on to form Helms Deep with former Snowblind and Renegade guitarist Terry Gorle. Geoff Tate was left without a band.

Following the Metalfest `81 at "The Palace" (Lake Hills was renamed that briefly during that year), Rockfest 1 was held there on September 26, 1981. Cathedral, a popular progressive hard rock band, headlined over Little Wing, Tangent, New European, Myth and The Mob. Tate filled in again on vocals for the Mob, and again they wowed the crowd. Friends continued to tell him and the Mob guys how great they were together, but Geoff's heart really wasn't into the doing the heavy metal covers thing, or into that music at all. After the Rockfest was over, the Myth guys approached Tate about joining Myth as a permanent member. Young had left the band and they needed a singer. Tate liked that Myth was writing original music and were more progressive along the lines of Rush, Rainbow and Deep Purple. Myth ended up being the vehicle that Geoff Tate could truly start to develop his songwriting and stage show and presence, and continue to increase his vocal ability....

THE PALACE
-PRESENTS-
AN EASTSIDE ROCK SPECTACULAR........
ROCKFEST-1 '81
!!ROCK OUT TO 6 BANDS ON STAGE!!
-"FEATURING"-
CATHEDRAL
THE MOB •• TANGENT
NEW EUROPEAN ○ LITTLE WING
—MYTH—
SATURDAY - SEPT. 26th
FROM 12:00 NOON UNTIL 12:00 MIDNIGHT
DOORS OPEN AT | TICKETS:
11:30 AM | $5.00 W/COUPON
        | $6.00 WO/COUPON
THE PALACE   641-9143
16232 N.E. 8th, Bellevue, Wash,   98008
(Just 6 blocks east of crossroads shop. mall)

Myth was formed in Redmond, Washington, by Kelly Gray, Richard Gibson and Jimmy Parsons in the fall of 1977. Inspired by a cover band called Venus Rising that his brother Howard Dee Gray ran sound for and that rehearsed in the Gray's basement, Kelly had picked up the guitar and wanted to learn to play as well. "I got into playing when I was twelve," Kelly Gray explains. "I had a cousin who played, and I idolized him as a guitar player. His band was rehearsing at our house, and I was like a junior roadie for the band. I just picked up the guitar and started playing one day.

I really started playing a lot when the first Van Halen record came out, and latched onto that sound. The roadie work for my cousin's gig really helped me learn how to multi-task. I'm always the guy who sets things up and makes sure the sound is right."

"I dabbled in guitar when I got into junior high school," Kelly adds. "I was in a beginning guitar course, and I failed it. Six months after that, then I was totally into playing." He was influenced by a number of the popular hard rock bands in the `70s and progressive rock bands as well. "Led Zeppelin was really the first band, but then there was UFO as well," Kelly says. "Really, it was all the guitar-based guys back then—Blackmore, Deep Purple, Ozzy, Van Halen. Anything that was guitar-related. I'm actually a very unbiased listener. I like it all. Genesis, Rush, I could even play the entire [Rush] *2112* album from beginning to end."

Eventually, Kelly formed a band with friends from school, Richard Gibson and Jimmy Parsons, who were also learning to play and developing their musical skills. They started out practicing in Parsons' garage and later moved to the Gray's basement. Kelly and his brother, Howard Dee (H.D.), both went to Redmond High School. H.D. was often hanging out with the guys and eventually became a roadie for the band. They played covers of Rush, Scorpions and other bands, and it wasn't long before they had some original songs of their own.

Randy Gane joined on keyboards in early 1978 and John Monda became their first lead singer later that year. They played parties and school dances and often had a lot of people watching their practices as well. Monda left in the spring of 1979 and was replaced by girl named Lori for a short time. "Kelly was around 14, going on 15 when they really got good," H.D. Gray explains. "They didn't have a singer at first and there was this other friend from school named John Monda. He learned the songs and started playing. He jammed with them and they played in some Masonic halls and some high school shows. Something happened with Monda, and they ended up with this girl singing named Lori—I don't remember her last name. She came from far away, from Lynnwood or Seattle or something, but it just didn't work out. The distance was just too far. She was a good singer though."

Following that, they tried out a family friend of Gibson's who was an older singer. "Then there was this guy named Harvey. I wish I could remember his last name... but he was in some Rail-era band—one of those earlier ones. He was much older and brought in a lot of PA gear. He was like thirty-something years old, and he was one of Richard's family friends. Lived up the road from them," H.D. adds. "So, John Monda didn't work out, Lori didn't work out and Harvey definitely didn't work out."

They eventually found Brent Young later that year. The brother of Rail singer Terry James Young, he had previously sang for the band Shifter. Initially it was a band featuring four Young brothers – Brent, Greg, and twins Rod and Brad Young (who later played in Tyrant as mentioned earlier). Brent was an experienced singer who had opened for Rail and other band during the '70s at Lake Hills, dances, etc. "I don't remember how it came about, but Brent Young got involved then," H.D. says. "He came along when Harvey's sound system was still there. And he sounded amazing. He was like, 'this is a great operation here.' I had built a sound studio with a little mixer and microphones. Still recording everything on two microphones back then." H.D. had built much of the band's speakers and equipment himself. "Kelly didn't really have any equipment, so I built him this gear out of this junk," the elder Gray recalls. "His first rig, I got the speakers out of the trash can at this bar they were renovating, next to the auto parts store in Redmond. They were Jensens and decent speakers, so I built these cabinets for the speakers to go in. My friend, Steve Lowman, was an audio sales representative. He had this Revox Reel to Reel and turned it into this echoplex for Kelly. I still have a picture of that too with Myth painted on it."

Young's initial tenure with Myth lasted about a year. On through the Metalfest '81 and Rockfest 1 that September, and then they were without a front person once again. Myth had matured and developed and they finally talked Geoff Tate into joining their band permanently. "They played a while with Brent [Young], then that just kind of fell apart, and the [Myth] guys were kind of depressed again," remembers H.D. Gray. "They were going, 'well, there's this guy named Geoff Tate.' They had went to Lake Hills and saw him with Tyrant. They were like, 'if only we had a guy like that singing for our band.' I was like, 'why don't you ask him?' They said they could never do that. I was like, 'what do you mean?' They said he would never play with them. So, I said, 'if you don't try you will never know.'"

H.D. Gray ended up taking all the Myth guys and the band's recordings down to the house Tate used to live in on Idlewood Park on

Lake Sammamish. It was a a small boat house that he lived in with his wife at the time, Sandy. After knocking on the door and explaining themselves, Tate listened to the recordings and was impressed with what he heard. Gray said the first thing Tate said was "how did you get the snare to sound like a whip." From there, Tate decided Myth's direction was more in line with his own tastes and started rehearing with them.

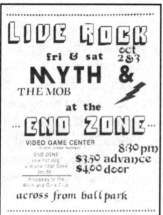

After Babylon broke up post-Metalfest, Geoff Tate bounced a bit between Myth and The Mob, fronting both groups on local bills together and separately. First up, there was a dual bill of Myth and The Mob at the End Zone in Kirkland on October 2-3, 1981, where he sang for both bands again. The End Zone was an arcade in an old grocery store that decided to build a stage and have bands play on Friday and Saturday nights to help attract more business. Culprit played their debut show there opening for TKO, and Gypsy. Rail, and even the California band Winterhawk did gigs there. Following the End Zone nights, the Mob played a party in Everett, Washington, on October 17, 1981, that featured Geoff on lead vocals again. Following that, he committed to Myth full-time and began working on more lyrics for their songs. Geoff liked Chris, Scott, Mike, and Eddie, but he wasn't into playing their type of cover songs any longer. "Geoff played a couple of parties, etc., with The Mob after that, but his heart wasn't into heavy metal cover tunes," says Brett Miller. "He was a big Peter Gabriel fan and wanted to write progressive music."

Over the next few months, Myth wrote and rehearsed material and developed a set geared toward performing local shows with Tate fronting the band. "Geoff started coming over and jamming with the band, and all of the local crowd would come over," says H.D. Gray. "It was kind of this cult underground, really, of people that would just come and listen to Myth play. That was when the band got serious about taking that stuff that was on that tape and turning it into these actual songs." Myth developed original songs such as "Iron Curtain", "No Sanctuary," "Take Hold of the Flame," "Before the Storm" and "Walk in the Shadows." Some of which would later find their way into being Queensrÿche song titles, albeit with different lyrics and music. "Those were written out of Geoff's experiences in Germany," continues Gray. "He talked to us about how he had these feelings and why he wrote this or that. Myth was really a melting pot. We listened to Marillion, Peter Gabriel-era Genesis, Rush of course… the roots of this go back to a lot [of] older bands. Pink Floyd was a big influence as well." This was where Geoff Tate started to really blossom as a lyricist, tapping into his inner psyche. It was something that he would continue to do over the years. "I did it to exorcise my demons," Tate explains. "Creating as a way of escapism and in a way, like therapy. When it was time to go on stage and present it, I was terrified. It's something I had to learn how to do. Even to this day, I still pretty much have to close my eyes to sing."

By the spring of 1982, Myth started playing local parties, dances, etc. In June, they competed in the recently re-started Battle of the Bands at Lake Hills/Crossroads. Craig Cooke, who had put on the first one in 1979 that Joker and Tyrant competed in during his tenure with Unicam, had launched out with his own booking company by now. The owners of the roller skating rink were struggling again and asked him to bring back bands to the facility. So he brought back what was popular before with the kids. Much like the previous Battle of the Bands four years prior, it featured mostly hard rock bands (as Craig was also fond of). The timing was perfect as the recent renewed interest in heavy metal and hard rock was increasing more and more (fueled by the so-called "New Wave Of British Heavy Metal", or "NWOBHM").

Myth landed a spot in the Battles and played on the third week of the competition on July 8, 1982, and faced off against Realms (featuring future Heir Apparent singer Paul Davidson), Rampage and Capt. Pinstripe. They played eight original songs during their 45-minute set— "Take Hold of the Flame", "The Warning", "Iron Curtain", "Into the Valley", "Walking the Valley", "No Sanctuary", "Lightning Chaser" and "Let Us Pray." (Three of the song titles here would later be used by Tate for Queensrÿche songs, but with different lyrics.) Myth were popular with the crowd and judges, with their original material harkening back to '70s progressive hard

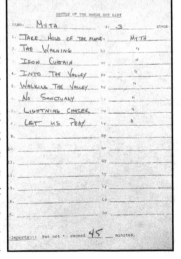

One of dozens of MYTH masks Jeff Tate tossed to the crowd at a Lake Hills Halloween Concert About 1980

Myth At Lake Hills Roller Rink

rock, and they advanced to the next round (along with Realms). "After Babylon dissolved and Geoff joined Myth, rumors began to circulate around the eastside about the source of Geoff's spectacular voice," Corey Rivers says. "Babylon had been a relatively 'closed' endeavor, and Geoff's voice was being revealed to a new, larger audience. The rumor had it that Geoff had sold his soul to the Devil in exchange for his super-human pipes. Laughable, but it had some traction in our circles. I guess humanity has a long history of wishing to credit the truly exceptional to an act of supernatural tampering."

Myth competed in the second round of the battles on July 30, 1982, against White Lightning, Stranger and Realms. White Lightning featured Scott Moughton on guitar, who would later work with Geoff Tate on his first solo album and play in his band. Surprisingly, both Myth and Realms lost to the other two bands and failed to advance, despite being popular with the Lake Hills/Crossroads crowds. Undaunted, Myth continued to practice and look for their next gig. That would happen courtesy of Brett Miller a short while later.

After the popularity of the inagural Metalfest at the now what was called Crossroads Roller Rink in 1981, Miller launched Metalfest II on August 29, 1982. TKO again headlined, with Culprit, Overlord, Realms, Kidskin and in the place of Hard Luck who canceled, Portland's Wild Dogs (their debut Northwest gig after a U.S. Metal II compilation album release concert, in San Francisco, with Culprit and label owner Mike Varney's Cinema rounding out the bill). Myth was again part of the festival, but this time Geoff Tate fronted the band. Their setlist was modified from the Battle of the Bands II version, with a powerful and haunting cover of Simon and Garfunkel's "Scarborough Fair" now included, along with their orginal songs. During this time, Geoff started to develop his command of the stage as a frontman. "You had to do that, because if you didn't people would throw things at you," Tate recalls, laughing.

Myth played their final gig with Geoff Tate as part of the first Headbanger's Ball on October 30, 1982. They opened for Portland's

Wild Dogs (making their return to Seattle after their popular Metalfest II debut) and headliners Culprit. Both of the other bands had been signed to Shrapnel Records to record their full-length debut albums and were all the buzz. Myth held their own and played a strong opening set. They looked to be the next local band to get signed with Tate fronting them, but there were other events happening to derail that. "We definitely notched it up a bit with Geoff," Randy Gane explains. "With Brent [Young], we were all kind of casual about it. We were all teenagers and having fun playing music. When Geoff joined, we

all started taking it a lot more seriously. For one, everybody wanted him in their band. The band we stole him from was The Mob, who eventually stole him back and became Queensrÿche. We always knew it was a matter of time. We knew we had limited time with him, so we really tried hard to push it. We were practicing every night for three or four hours. For no reason, you know. We played the same eight songs over and over and over again."

Following the shows with Tate in October of 1981, The Mob was back to square one again without a singer. They committed to finding a permanent one, as well as writing original material. They practiced all of the time and worked up their own songs. "Inspired by the buzz they got at Metalfest '81, the four guys in The Mob—Chris, Mike, Scott and Eddie—started a five-day-a-week rehearsal schedule in Scott's parents' garage where they had built a studio to work on writing original music," remembers Brett Miller. "It seemed like we hardly ever saw them anymore. They were so different. It was like the story of the squirrels—the one who gathered his nuts and survived the winter, and the one who frolicked and then starved. I remember us calling Mike Wilton to go party. We were twenty-one years old then. Mike told us he had to stay home and do hand and finger exercises for his fret hand. We thought he was being ridiculous at the time. Lots of times we'd call Mike or Chris to go to a great party we'd heard about and they would time and again say they had practice. We thought five times a week was excessive, not to mention obsessive, at the time. We would roll our eyes."

The Mob developed a couple of original songs by early 1982. Michael Wilton had written the music for "Blinded" and "Nightrider," and Chris DeGarmo had written the lyrics for them. They wanted to find a singer and go into a professional studio and record them. They asked a former Myth singer to do it and after some rehearsal, they went into a studio in the Wallingford district to lay down the tracks. "We put together our own demo of songs with a singer named Brent Young," Michael Wilton explains. "We recorded at Crow Studios in Seattle." Young declined joining the band full-time though and the Mob was back looking for a singer again. They also didn't care much for the recordings and felt they could do better. They did—at Triad Studios in Redmond.

Tom Hall learned sound engineering at Eastern Washington University. The school had built a full studio and he worked on recordings for Doc Rockit, Kracker, Ridge, and others, with Terry Date as his assistant. Once he was done with school, Tom took a job working in a basement studio for Heart's former road manager and did some live recording around the Seattle area in 1981. Pacific West Recording, in Redmond, changed ownership a few months later, rebuilt and renamed the facility Triad. Eager to land a more permanent position, Hall applied for an opening at Triad in the spring of 1982 and got the job. "I think my first official day of work there [at Triad Studios] was March 15, 1982," Tom Hall states. "The studio manager gave me a bunch of flyers. He said, 'Put these up around town. You can advertise yourself at being available for $40 an hour here at the studio from Midnight to 8 a.m.' I put up all the flyers at music stores around town, called everybody I knew and didn't get a single response. The deal was about to come to an end, and I got a call from this kid named Scott Rockenfield. He's like, 'Hey, is that $40 an hour deal still good?' I said, 'Unfortunately it just expired last week.' He said 'Oh, man. My band just did this recording over at Crow

Studios and we're not happy with it. We want to come in and do an EP.' I said, 'Let me talk to my manager and see what I can do.' I went in talked to Dan [Foster] and he said, 'Yeah, we can do that.'"

All four members of The Mob had worked and set aside enough money to spend the amount of time needed on the recordings, which likely helped it become the polished end product. "They all took on at least two jobs each and saved all the money for the big 24-track recording they were going to make," recalls Brett Miller. "By the time they had enough money, they booked time at local Triad Studios. I think it was five consecutive graveyard shifts Monday through Friday."

The Mob guys now had it lined up to record at the better studio, but still didn't have a permanent lead singer. They asked Tate once again to fill in, but this time in the studio instead of onstage, and he said okay. He thought it would be good experience with an eye on doing the same thing with Myth at some point. "It did not go over well when Geoff agreed to help out The Mob guys and sing on their recording," Miller says. "Geoff and the band Myth were very close, and all lived together in a ramshackle house in the rural outskirts of Redmond, Washington. But Geoff wanted the experience of recording in a professional studio and convinced Myth that in the long run it would be a net positive for all of them. He really meant it at the time."

By this time, Chris DeGarmo had written music and lyrics for another song, "Queen of the Reich," and the music for what would become "The Lady Wore Black." "There were three sets of lyrics that I wrote on the EP—'Queen of the Reich,' 'Nightrider' and 'Blinded,' Chris stated in a 1991 interview. "At that time, I was in a pretty dark state. As a young teenager, I was fascinated with Jimmy Page and all that he was into—the warlock, the castle, Aleister Crowley—it was all spinning around in my head. I don't feel the same way, by any means, but at that time it was the Dio-esque, Maiden, Page sort of blur." "Queen of the Reich" had especially dark origins. "I wrote the lyrics to this song after having a nightmare," Chris explained. DeGarmo had also just written the music and lyrics for a fifth song, "Prophecy," but it was still in the early stages and the band felt it wasn't quite done, nor the right fit with the other four songs for the EP, so it was not recorded at that time. "Geoff Tate went with The Mob into Triad Studios to cut those four original songs," Miller elaborates. "[The fourth was] a song that Chris had written the music for but had no words. Geoff wrote the lyrics that week in the studio. I was in the studio the night Geoff laid down the vocal tracks for 'The Lady Wore Black.' Geoff needed to set the mood, so he had the lights turned off and sang with a single candle burning in the studio. While waiting for his first verse to come up, he whistled along with the opening guitar, not realizing they were taping him. He told them it was a mistake, but everyone agreed it was cool, so they kept it. What a cool thing to have seen!"

Tom Hall continues the story: "The idea was that we were going to do this demo, a four-song demo, and do it over two days. Because it was a demo I was like, 'We don't have to go crazy getting sounds. Let's get it roughed in pretty good so we can get this thing done in two days.' We did the basic tracks on a Friday night and the overdubs on a Saturday night. The idea was I give them rough mixes and let me know if you want to do more with this. Well, Chris DeGarmo was like, 'This is way cooler than we ever thought it was going to be and we actually want to spend more time on this.' So they came back over the course of weekends, I think on through June of 1982, and finished and polished this thing up in early July. They were very focused about what they wanted to hear and how they wanted it to sound. There was no ambiguity about it. They were like, 'This is our sound.' Really capable musicians. Even when they were eighteen [years old]. Just ridiculously well practiced. Eddie might have been less ready than the others, but not by much. He still did a great job. And Geoff really brought it on the vocals. I'd never heard anything like that before in my life." To get the sound of the EP, Hall also explains the process: "We experimented some. We ended up with the guitars a lot louder than I would have done if left to my own devices, but it was perfect for that record. It was just exactly what it needed to be."

CHAPTER 5:
206 ON EASY STREET

The Mob now had a great sounding and well-recorded demo tape, but what to do with it? They played it for a few friends and at some local parties over the next couple months to see what people thought. "Chris showed up at a party at Brett Umbedacht's house about a week or two later acting very suspiciously," Brett Miller says. "He came over to me and quietly asked if I wanted to hear his new recording out in the car. I, of course, said 'yes' and we went out to the Ford Pinto wagon he was driving at the time. As the opening chords of 'Queen of the Reich' began with Geoff Tate's soaring wail, my jaw dropped to the ground. I couldn't believe how professional their recording was. How well thought out every part of it was down to the sequencing and segueing between songs."

Mark DeGarmo also helped his brother's band get the music into people's ears. "I took their demo tape up to Western and took it to parties. I went to Western Washington University in Bellingham. I used to wander around with records under my arm, go to parties, and take over the turntable when nobody was looking. So, I took their four-song demo up to this party in Bellingham, put it on the stereo and turned it up. The party just kind of stopped and people were coming up to me and were like, 'Who is this?' I said, 'Oh, this is an Eastside band.' At the time, they were still going by The Mob. I didn't tell people it was my brother's band. I didn't want to be that guy. I would just put it on, turn it up and people would come to me about it."

The Mob also started sending their tape out to a few record labels and received either rejection letters or no response at all. Still, the band members knew they had something. They continually played it over the summer, and everybody loved the tape. Brett Miller continues:

"Everywhere they'd go, every party someone would ask them to put their tape in. Geoff would tell people he wasn't really into that kind of music, when they would bug him at parties about how great the tape was, and how come he didn't quit Myth and join The Mob. The Myth guys actually—and with good reason—got quite insecure about The Mob." Tate had convinced his Myth bandmates that the studio experience would be good for them, and Kelly and Randy had even joined him in the studio initially, but with so many people encouraging Tate to join The Mob full-time, it caused more tensions in the band. Tensions that would later come to a head....

Heading into the fall of 1982, The Mob demo tape finally got into the hands of an interested party. Easy Street Records owner Kim Harris was a longtime record store fixture in the Seattle area, going back to running Campus Music in the University District in the 1970s. Campus was one of the first stores to start carrying import records, and Kim continued that pattern once he relocated to Bellevue in 1979. Kim had his finger on the pulse of the new hard rock and heavy metal coming out in the United Kingdom and Europe and sold a lot of those releases in his store. He had a relationship with three different distributors based in England and Germany and had made a couple trips over there to establish the relationship even more. Harris also helped supply new music of that sort to the local radio stations.

Kim Harris explains that his relationship with Queensrÿche started with Scott Rockenfield's younger brother, Todd. The younger Rockenfield would pop into Harris' store asking if he wanted to hear Scott's demo tape. "He'd come in every week or so after school and say, 'Do you wanna listen to my brother's tape?' I think I put him off for like two months saying I would get to it. He finally said, 'You really have got to listen to this, I really want your opinion on this.' I said, 'Okay fine.' So I put [the demo tape] on in the VW Rabbit convertible. I had a cassette player in it, so I put it on and actually stopped the car on my way home and said, 'What the fuck is this? They sound like Judas Priest for God sakes with a little Motley Crue thrown in.' I'm like, 'Who

Easy Street Records
Imports/Domestics
Owners
Diana Vaughan Harris & Kim Harris
15251 Bel-Red Road
Bellevue, WA 98007 U.S.A.
Phone
643-1433

are these guys?'" Kim took the tape home to his then-wife, Diana, who had a background in band management, music promotions and sales, and played it for her. She helped break Striker. Kim Harris continues: "I said, 'what do you think about the guitars?' She said, 'fuck the guitars, who's the singer?'... Well, I come to find out it's Geoff [Tate] and he had his band Myth. He was just subbing for somebody who couldn't make it."

The Harrises were blown away by the young group in their own backyard and thought they could help them with some of their connections in the industry. They took the demo tape and had copies made up, along with an info sheet and a photo. "The [Queensrÿche demo] tapes had a cover and the songs were listed on the back," says Kim Harris. "We sent them out to all the music people that Diana and I knew all over L.A. and New York, and we got nothing, no feedback."

Kim and Diana then traveled overseas to England, and Germany, for some record buying and a bit of much-needed relaxation. Diana suggested they take the band's demo and drop it off somewhere to see if they could get it heard. Kim recalled a new magazine called *Kerrang!* that was getting popular and selling out in his store. The pair tracked down their address in the West End of London and went to deliver the tape. *Kerrang!*'s office was on the second or third floor of the building. The Harrises walked in, saw one guy up front on the phone, and another further back cataloging stuff. Eventually, they got the ear of the person on the phone. "We're from Seattle and we've got this tape we want you to hear. We would love your feedback because we think we've really got something here!" Kim Harris shares. "He played a little bit of it and said, 'This is really good.' And then he put it in a stack of nine hundred other tapes and he said, 'We'll give it a listen.' I said, 'Great. Here's press and articles we wrote about the band.'" Kim and Diana gave the manager promotional materials about the band, including a picture. But it turns out they were talking to the wrong person. "We found out, after the fact, that the

guy in the back of the place went nuts when he heard the tape," Kim adds. "It was Paul Suter. We were gone by then and [apparently] he grabbed it and never gave it back. And he wrote an article that he had [heard] the future of music. They put it with that picture of the band that Diana had brought."

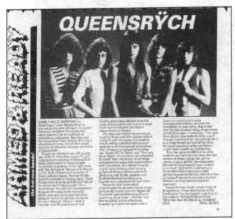

Just prior to the Harrises heading out for their trip overseas, The Mob decided to change their name. Taking it from their lead-off song on the tape, they decided to call themselves "Queensrÿch" as all one word with the umlaut above the letter 'ÿ'. Which is how the name was published in the issue of *Kerrang!* that arrived on the newsstands around late February/early March 1983.

"We got home from our trip three weeks later, and we had a great time. It was the first vacation I'd had in years," Harris says. "We walked into the record store and there was a stack of mail this high (demonstrates with his hand). People wanted to order and buy the Queensrÿche tape. What the fuck are you talking about? What tape? We had over 800 people that had written asking, 'How much? Where could I get it?' God what had we done? It was Paul Suter man. Paul said this was it."

With the overwhelmingly positive response, Kim and Diana Vaughan-Harris knew they needed to jump on this popularity quickly and ride the momentum. "We sat down with the guys in the band, and we hadn't signed anybody yet," Kim says. "We had just dropped off the tape and you saw what happened. They freaked out. Chris and Michael went nuts, Scott was overwhelmed and Eddie... was looking for pizza."

Harris remembered that Tate took the news a bit differently, focusing on the business end of things. "Geoff said, 'How much, when and what do we have to do?' The other guys were all, 'Hey this is great.' I said, 'Let's make some kind of provisional agreement and let's make some copies of this and get them out there. I'll front this from the store and see if we can get some momentum here.' That's how we started." While Tate had initially only agreed to let the band use his name and image for promotional purposes for some sort of compensation, as he still intended to stay with Myth, he eventually caved and joined Queensrÿche full time. The momentum behind the band and the recordings helped convince him it was a smart move for the future.

Tensions over Geoff Tate singing on The Mob/Queensrÿche demos had come to a boiling point by the end of 1982/early 1983. Rather than it being a positive experience, it ended up driving a wedge between the Myth members. "When the whole Geoff thing kind of reached a head ... there are these bands [in history] that aren't going to go anywhere and I believe this was one of those cases," says H.D. Gray. "Everybody kind of knew it, I think, but didn't want to admit it. These tensions always came out of that, always these little fights and things. I came over to the band house one day. The only people there were Kelly and Geoff, and they did not look happy at all. They had been in another huge band fight and everybody left. I think that's when Jimmy said, 'Forget it, I'm done with you guys.' And went off to play with Lipstick."

H.D. Gray continues: "They wouldn't tell me what happened, but I looked at Geoff and I said, 'I tried to tell you years ago and you got mad at me, but I'm going to tell you again. You have to do what you have to, to get someplace, before you can do what you want.' And he looked at me square in the eyes and said he understood that now. Then he quit the band and he joined The Mob."

The Harrises pressed up the EP on vinyl on their own 206 Records label (the area code for Seattle at the time). Scott Rockenfield's brother Todd had come up with a logo after the band had changed the name from "The Mob" to "Queensrÿche". A friend, artist Wes "Griz" Griswold (who went way back to playing in the pre-Myth band Venus Rising with Randy Gane and was a Myth crew member), did the cover art and design for the record sleeve. "The Tri-Ryche thing came from artist Wes Griswold [for the Queensrÿche EP]," H.D. Gray explains. "It was the way he always signed his artwork. I remember him doing it all the way back in high school, and it started

206
RECORDS
inc.
Management & Artistic Direction
Diana Vaughan Harris & Kim Harris
15251 Bel-Red Road
Bellevue, WA 98007 U.S.A.
Phone
643-1433

out, I think, as a peregrine falcon. But you know how big business is. They just took it and ran, and then all the credit hounds planted their flag." David Morris also comments on Griswold's importance early on: "I knew Wes [Griswold] and I think it's very important people know how much work he did, how much time he spent working with Chris [DeGarmo], on developing that [Queensrÿche] logo." A local photographer, Hans Hugli, took the band photo (which was the same one that *Kerrang!* used in their review). Just prior to pressing up the record, they also added the "e" on the end of the band's name to avoid any connection to the German Nazi party. By the time the EP was released on vinyl in April 1983, that was how the plug ran in the local *Rocket* magazine/ newspaper.

Kim Harris states: "I called the distributors I knew all over the country. The first pressing was like 2,500 copies and I called up four distributors. One in Texas, one in Mississippi that handled all the south, one in upper state New York and one in L.A. I had worked with some of these guys for over a decade and they knew who I was. If I said I was going to buy something, I bought it, paid for it on time and all that stuff. We had a trust system that actually worked. I put together a process that had never been done before. The independent working with the major distributors to get this product out, out to as many stores as possible. I worked out sale incentives for them. In Texas it went ballistic. I had a pre-order of 2,000 copies over the space of the next three weeks, and sold them all out in Dallas, Fort Worth and Houston because there were two radio stations there that were playing Queensrÿche like they were the second coming. They went nuts down there. More sales in Texas

than any other place in the country. Beat L.A., beat Seattle too. I ended up doing just over 6,000 copies of the 206 EP total."

On the first pressing run of the EP, 850 copies, a mistake in the cover had the songwriting credits listed as registered to ASCAP, while the credit below showed BMI (the correct one). This was fixed by the next pressing run of around 2,500 copies. The first run with the ASCAP mention also has the artwork a bit brighter and sharper than subsequent pressings. Word was that eventually a grand total of 14,655 copies were pressed up of the EP on the 206 label, despite Harris' claim of 6,000. It is very likely that the distributor, Greenworld, contributed to the additional copies pressed up due to demand. Another misconception is that the "206" EP sold 50,000 copies (a couple of the Queensrÿche band members have said this in interviews), but that number is likely a combination of both the independent EP and EMIs first reissue of the record.

Queensrÿche's EP quickly started getting radio play in both Washington and Oregon and was very popular, getting continual requests. Robert Newman at *The Rocket* received a copy of the 206 EP in May 1983 and wrote a very favorable review of the record for the June issue. People wanted to know who this band was. The buzz was definitely building.

Kim Harris continues: "We started getting mail with people wanting to know when the fan club was starting. [I was like] 'What the hell?

Speaking of Eastside metal, a band named QUEENSRYCH is attracting a lot of attention. KIM and DIANA HARRIS of Easy Street Records took a tape to *Kerrang!* magazine in England on a recent trip. The result was a half-page story in the most recent issue with a giant photo and glowing write-up. The band plans to release a 4-song EP soon. LOUIS X. ERLANGER

Give me a break here.' But this was where it was going. We got together with the band and said, 'If you had the choice, what record label would you want to be on?' This was when the majors called the shots. We weren't worrying about working with some rinky dink. We already had an independent label, mine. We had that if we wanted to stay put. We'd already sold 6,000 copies, and probably could have done another 6,000 no problem, but what were we gonna do then? You're gonna tour some small clubs then come home, go to school, what then? I said, 'We need a major label on this that will front us everything we want.'"

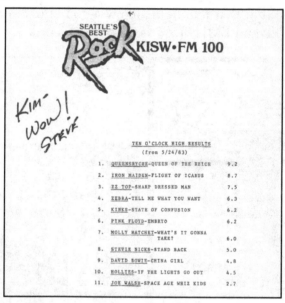

In the post-1970s record label boom, and pre-grunge days, how did you do that in the Pacific Northwest?

CHAPTER 6:
EMI COMES CALLING

Without any major record label divisions/offices in Seattle anymore, and very few label scouts focusing on the Pacific Northwest by that time (corporations laws changed, and as a result, labels tightened up their wallets and became less risk averse), the Harrises knew they would have to get one to come to them. Kim Harris explains: "We put together a plan of how Diana and I would do this. [It had multiple] pieces to it: the first one was [to] find the right record label that had total dedication to them, would listen to them and do what they wanted, as opposed to, 'sound great and go do something else.' Which happened all the time. The other parts were: we knew we needed a first class touring company to handle them nationally, not just Washington or California. I wanted someone with clout. That did more than anything else we did."

They found one fairly quickly that was very well-regarded in the industry. Continues Harris: "We wined and dined some people and we ended up with ICM out of New York—which at the time I had worked with them on some small projects for sales. When a band would come through the West Coast, we fed them and set up their records for sale and all. Nobody else would do it so we had a good rapport with them. They had two new guys who were really impressed with the band and what we did. They seemed on the same level. 'Here's what we need, here's what we will do and what do you think?' We had no separate agendas which ended up being critical. The man who ran ICM was this old pro, kind of a mobster fellow called Frank Barcelona. Frank Barcelona was probably at the same level as Clive Davis in the music industry at that time and he was that powerful. In fact, the group that he had just broken internationally, just on his word, was U2. We didn't know who they were. I'll never forget this: Warner Bros. was pushing *Boy*. It was good, new wavey stuff. It was fun, but I didn't really think it was the best thing I'd every heard personally. But it was good and solid. Frank said, 'It's gonna be huge.' That was all he needed to say and this thing went number one in a few weeks. So, we had Frank Barcelona behind Queensrÿche and we could not do anything wrong thereafter."

The pieces started to come together for their plan, but a couple were still missing. "The other two parts of this were: getting a first class music attorney to handle us and the right record label," Harris says. "First, I thought about Warner Brothers or Elektra—because they were breaking Motley Crue at the time. They were making this band huge. They were just okay really if you think about it, they were more show than play. But they were pulling it off big time. They had money and they had stature and distribution. So, Diana called a friend of ours we knew from Seattle named Mavis Brody. Mavis used to work at KOL and then started as the low rung A&R person for EMI Records down in L.A. She had moved to L.A. for business. We got Mavis on the phone and we said, 'you've got to hear this.' She said, 'are you serious? I can't get up there right now.' We said, 'wait right there and listen.' And we put the record on in the store while she listened over the phone. Before the fourth song was over she's telling Diana, 'I'll be there tomorrow.' As soon as she said that, we put together a little place where we could play, practice-wise, down in West Seattle. It had water coming down the walls on the insides. It was a mess, it was awful."

Harris continues the story: "Mavis was ready to sign that band when she saw them. They played one song and she was ready to sign them. 'How much do you want for these these guys? What do you want?' The Vice President of A&R of Capitol and EMI, who was making a name for himself, was this young kid named Gary Gersch. Mavis went to him and begged him to sign this band. He went, 'oh no, they have all these metal bands in L.A. and we've never done a band like this.' Mavis said, 'this band is going to be the biggest band we have on this label, we don't want to let them go.' She fought for them and Gary turned around and said 'fine.' He came up and saw them play and he went, 'what do you guys want?'"

At this time, Harris was already writing up the contracts for Queensrÿche and representatives from other labels, such as Warner Bros., and CBS called about the demo. After hearing Queensrÿche had interest from Mavis Brody and EMI, the other labels asked for Harris to keep them posted. "We already said that if [EMI] gave us what we want, we weren't so worried about the money at this point," Harris adds. "It was what they could do for us on the back side."

Queensrÿche had also done their first music video, "Nightrider," around that time. It was shot locally in Seattle at the KING 5 television studio. The band mimed the music and Geoff lip-synched and made amusing lip/mouth exaggerations. It was shown on local TV stations a bit and also up in Canada on the *Good Rockin' Tonite* show. "'Nightrider was the first clip we did," explains Chris DeGarmo. "It was made just after we'd done the first EP. We were only *just* a band! The cameras were all manned by interns from a local TV station, and it was far removed from the sort of cut that's the status quo these days. That was just the way we were."

Chris' brother, Mark, was a big part of that video happening: "The backstory on that is I was an intern at KING TV," Mark DeGarmo shares. "I was a broadcast communications major in the newsroom. I was working as an intern and then moved on to be a cameraman's assistant. I started out in TV news. So, I'm at channel 5 and one of the other photographers—I won't mention his name—but he moonlighted on the production side. Outside of the news. He was working on *Seattle Live*, or one of those local programs. So, I'm working at the TV station, and this photographer said to me that the company he worked for was putting together a showcase of live bands from Seattle. They were going to have a contest, and it was basically like a battle of the bands. The winner would get a free video shown on KING, and they'd get the opening slot on a $2 'Catch A Rising Star' concert at the Paramount [Theatre]. Which we all used to attend."

Mark continues: "I had this reputation sort of, as the guy who was listening to a lot of music. This guy said to me, 'We gotta find some local bands and you're kind of plugged into that scene. Do you know any bands that might be good enough to compete in this?' Again, I didn't say that it was my little brother. I said, 'Yeah, as a matter of fact, I know a pretty good local band. And I even have a demo tape out in my car. If you want to check it out, you can listen to it.' We went out to my car and he listened and he was like, 'Bullshit. These guys aren't from Seattle. We need a local band.' I said, 'These guys are a local basement band, and have never played live together.' At that time, it was still true. So, he asked me if he could take the tape and I said,

'Sure.' He disappeared for a couple of weeks and then came back. He's like, 'Dude, if you're shitting me, I'm going to kill you. Because the producers of the show love them. You're not bullshitting me, right?' 'No, I know these guys.' I didn't reveal the [family] connection because I wanted them to win on their own merit. Lo and behold, they win. They come in and do the 'Nightrider' video and get the slot on the 'Catch A Rising Star' show, and they open for Zebra."

Queensrÿche was added to the bill for two of the local "Catch A Rising Star" concerts (sponsored by KISW radio in town and KGON down south). They opened up for Zebra at the Paramount Theatres, in both Portland, Oregon, on June 29, 1983, and in Seattle, Washington, on June 30, 1983. They were finally able to show off their well-rehearsed stage show. They had around 40 minutes to showcase their material from the EP and play all four of those songs ("Queen of the Reich", "Nightrider", "Blinded," and "The Lady Wore Black"), along with three new songs: "Waiting For The Kill", "Warning" and "Roads To Madness." This would be the first time that Kim and Diana would see Queensrÿche perform on a big stage, in front of a crowd, as they never witnessed The Mob performances with Geoff Tate at Lake Hills/Crossroads, the End Zone, etc., back in 1981. "We didn't know the power of this band [live] until we did the first couple of shows with Zebra at the Paramount Theatres in '83 and we blew them off the stage," Kim Harris says. "Zebra didn't want to go on for that second show." Mark DeGarmo agrees and expands on it: "The crowd was filled with, not only our family and other families, but pretty much everybody else from the Eastside. They came out and just blew Zebra away. They got booed off the stage after the 'Ryche. And sitting behind me were seven different representatives for different record labels. I remember they had the seats behind us reserved for them, and I remember turning around during

'Nightrider' and the looks on their faces. The crowd was absolutely out of control. They destroyed the place. I always felt like that was my little contribution, as far as getting them in that competition. And then the "Nightrider" video was very influential, as far as getting them a look, and then it getting them that show. They got signed by EMI right after that concert."

Queensrÿche officially signed a seven-album contract with EMI on July 7, 1983. Following that, they went into Triad Studios again to record some pre-production demos on EMI's dime. They recorded live and then it was dumped to a second track for stereo. The songs laid down were: "Warning" (a Tate/Wilton composition), "Waiting for the Kill"

(DeGarmo), "Prophecy" (DeGarmo), "Roads to Madness" (DeGarmo/ Tate/Wilton), "No Sanctuary" (Tate/DeGarmo), "Child of Fire" (Tate/ Wilton) and "Before the Storm" (Tate/Wilton). This was sent to their producer (more on who that was in a bit) before they went into the studio to record their debut for EMI. All five members of Queensrÿche quit their day jobs on August 5, 1983. This is something the band members consider a milestone and regularly celebrated it thereafter.

Following the debut concerts, and the major label signing, Queensrÿche started getting more press in both local publications, such as the *Seattle Times*, and from sources outside the Northwest as well. First was a very favorable review of the Seattle Zebra concert in San Francisco native Ron Quintana's *Metal Mania* #12 (with photos by local fan and *Denim & Leather* zine contributor Ashly Bexton). This was followed by an article on the band by K.J. Doughton in the debut issue of a new UK publication, *Metal Forces*. *Kerrang!* covered them in a four-page spread, and also *Journal America* with a full-page piece. The first cover feature on Queensrÿche was in a local magazine, *They Entertain Us*, which landed on the stands in August 1983. On August 12 and 13, they had record release parties/signings for the 206 EP at the Penny Lane record stores in West Seattle, and Tacoma, respectively (this was part of the last pressing of the 206 Records edition done prior to EMI's reissue of it. Five hundred of the "206" EPs were signed in gold pen. Some of which were sent to fan club members for free, and the rest were sold for $10 each through the fan club merchandise list). "It was because of our friendship and alliance with Easy Street that Penny Lane Records hosted Queensrÿche's

very first in-store meet 'n greet," explains Jeff Gilbert, *The Rocket* writer, "Brain Pain" host and local record label owner. "After we finished the in-store in West Seattle, we drove with the band down to our Tacoma store on Bridgeport Way and the band did another meet 'n greet. Been friends with the [Queensrÿche] guys ever since."

MEAN QUEENS—EMI America recording artists Queensryche strike a tough pose during the shooting of their anthem "Queen Of The Reich." Pictured from left are set designer George Mitchell, director Cort Falkenberg, production assistant Kim Bellman and group members Chris DeGarmo, Eddie Jackson, Geoff Tate, Michael Wilton and Scott Rockenfield.

In the latter part of August 1983, Queensrÿche traveled south to shoot the video for "Queen of the Reich" in Los Angeles. Kort Falkenberg III directed the video, with set design by George Mitchell. Falkenberg also directed videos for Billy Idol and John Waite and later helmed the shoot for Queensrÿche's "Gonna Get Close To You" video in 1986. The "Queen of the Reich" video received some minor play on MTV and local TV stations in the Northwest on through the summer and fall that year.

It was also around this time that David Morris came on board as a guitar tech and crew member. "I started a company with a guy named Fred, called Studio Four," Morris says. "I was still doing guitars for TKO [as a tech], but we were doing lights and sound for bands at Lake Hills. For whatever band needed it. And that's when Chris [DeGarmo] came to me. He pulled up in his [Dodge] Charger and said, 'Hey Davey, hop in. I want to play you the EP of the four songs we've recorded.' Then he asked me, 'What are you doing for, like, the rest of your life?' Then he asked me if I would come over to England with them. They were going to record an album there. So that's where it all started for me with them."

Through their booking company, Queensrÿche got on a leg of Quiet Riot's national tour, who were riding the success of [what would become] their #1 platinum album, *Metal Health*, and a well-received opening slot on the U.S. Festival in May of that year. It kicked off with a show at the Memorial Hall in Kansas City, Missouri, on September 14, 1983. They opened for Quiet Riot for a total of ten dates on through September 27, 1983, at the Memorial Auditorium in Burlington, Iowa. "We went on tour for ICM with Quiet Riot, who we hated," remembers Kim Harris. "[Queensrÿche] hated it. The bass player, Rudy [Sarzo], was a great guy though, like a lost brother. That guy was full of heart and love, caring. But the lead singer of the band, what's his name? Kevin DuBrow. He was an asshole. His own band members came up with ways to hang him."

"I did the dates with Quiet Riot in the summer," David Morris says. "Rudy Sarzo was really nice. Axe was on that bill for some shows. Accept too. That was when I came on board. I remember going down to Texas for those shows. I was blown away by Accept. It was a couple of shows with them. Good stuff."

A high point was the show in San Antonio, that was the largest gig the band had played up to that point. "We did [this huge concert] with them in San Antonio, Texas," Kim Harris shares. "Nobody knew what to expect. They were going to play to an 11,000-seat audience. They went from playing at the Paramount, which is 2,900 seats, to the Country Club which was 1,100 - 1,200 people, to Texas which was 11,000 people. Mavis and Gary Gersch called all the people in all the local areas of EMI-America and told them that they [had] to see this band. We had A&R and salespeople from all over the Midwest who didn't know who the band was, or their music. They were just label people—they didn't listen to the stuff. They said, 'Show us whatcha got.' I'll never forget. In Texas, when the lights went down, it was black. Couldn't see anything. The place lit up with lighters. I had never seen so many lighters at one time and [I] had been to shows where there were 200,000 people. Nothing like this. Everybody in this place stood up and Queensrÿche came out and played two or three songs and the place erupted, they went nuts. I'll never the forget the label guys turning around and asking, 'Where in the hell did you find these guys?' I found them in a record store, what can I tell you? We made them believers and the call went out to L.A. from them and they said, 'We don't care what you do, but we want to be a part of this band period. Give them anything they want.'"

During Queensrÿche's time opening for Quiet Riot, EMI reissued the Queensrÿche EP and pressed up 35,000 copies for stores. Radio play continued, as well as some video play. The record hit #81 on the charts

and continued to sell well over the years, eventually being certified by the Recording Industry Association of American (RIAA) as Gold and Platinum (for 500,000 and 1 million units being sold, respectively) by 1991. Queensrÿche newsletters were also made up in the "tabloid" newspaper style to help promote the band. They featured press clippings, photos and other information. One was done just after the EP was reissued and another one just before *The Warning* came out in 1984. The newsletter was in most of the retail record stores and was a freebie by the door you could take. "We helped them out with what we could do from an advertising standpoint," Harris explains. "Diana put together a newspaper format that went over really well. It was dirt cheap to produce and they made about 100,000 copies of this thing. They worked so well that EMI turned around and used the same format for seven other bands, including Great White. The singer, Jack Russell, said to me one time that these helped break his band with these newsletters."

EMI also created film can test pressings of the Queensrÿche EP in 1983. These special pressings (housed in a circular "box" containing the recording) were sent to all of the radio stations in the U.S. and Canada that played hard rock. At the time, there were 204 stations in the U.S.

and 25 in Canada, and that total number (229) is generally accepted by collectors as the approximate number of film cans pressed. The label on the U.S. test pressings are white with handwritten numbers "1" and "2." The Canadian test pressings use the same type of film can with a black and gold sticker, but the label is the same as the retail versions of the EP sold in Canada. The Canadian test pressings also came with a small press release printed on pale yellow paper, dated August 26, 1983, giving a small description of the early praise Queensrÿche had received.

"The Lady Wore Black" also received a 7" vinyl test pressing from EMI. It was likely made at the same time as the EP film can test pressing. For fans who have never heard "The Lady Wore Black" 7", it features an edited version of the song (it is missing the intro) on both sides. These test pressings are extremely rare, with approximately 10-15 in existence.

Following the jaunt through the Midwest with Quiet Riot (Florida band Axe was also on the bill for some shows), Queensrÿche returned home to Seattle to open for former Rainbow and Black Sabbath singer, Ronnie James Dio, on his first solo tour. They played the Paramount on October 1, 1983, to a large crowd. The band's stage set included Scott's gold chain drum set, and a backdrop including the "coat of arms" crowns from the EP. It was designed by their friend Matt Bazemore, who had continued his new career path as an artist. Queensrÿche enjoyed playing with Ronnie and his band, and it was the start of a relationship with Dio that would last until his tragic passing in 2010. The band was treated with respect, given ample soundcheck opportunities and shown "the ropes." Kim Harris elaborates: "Ronnie was fine. I helped him out with some things. It was nice. We had a great rapport and that's why we ended up going through Europe, England, Ireland and Scotland on that huge tour over there. Ronnie liked what he saw with us." Queensrÿche opened for Dio two more times in California. The first was on October 4, at the Memorial Auditorium in Sacramento, and the second was on October 5, at the Civic Auditorium in San Jose. (Another gig was scheduled and announced opening for Dio, at the close to 1,000 person-capacity Starry Night club in Portland, Oregon, but Queensrÿche canceled and Portland's Wild Dogs opened instead.) Dio also gave them a bit more time as the opener and they were able to expand their set list to 10 songs. "Prophecy", "Before the Storm" and "Child of Fire" were added to the set list, from the previous Zebra show in June, and gave the crowd more of a taste of what would end up on Queensrÿche's first full-length album.

On October 9, 1983, Queensrÿche played their first headline gig, in Reseda, California, as a showcase for EMI's new act. "When we got down to L.A., the label had put together a showcase show at the

Country Club, as I remember," Kim Harris shares. "It was about a 900-seater, a big rock club and it was low key, low promotion. The record company called a few people in the business to come check out our new signing, [saying] 'We think they are going to be huge, this new band from Seattle.' The place was sold out, packed. In fact, I got into trouble with the fire marshals because we were over the amount of people. So, I'm already learning how to pay off people in the business. Seriously. The people in the business said that they had never seen as many musicians in one place, at one time as that show in L.A. ever. You name a rock band from L.A., or the vicinity, and they were in the audience. It was unbelievable the people that were there. Queensrÿche ran into some technical difficulties on the first song, someone had sabotaged us on the back side and pulled out some plugs on one half the stage at the beginning of the first song and they were freaking out. I walked up on stage and told them to keep playing, don't stop for nothing, but I'm ready to shoot people. We got it set up. Seemed like hours, but it was only six minutes trying to figure out what was wrong. But they pulled it off. The label said, 'If they can handle this, they can handle anything.' From there they had a meet and greet at the tower, the

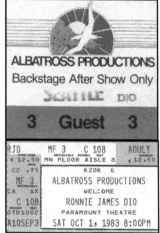

[Capitol Records Building]. They did another secret show down in the studio for the people from the label. They did a few songs for the people there and everbody loved them. They did not have anybody else like them on their label. This was all new to them."

The Harrises also continued to help out other bands as they could, both local and national touring acts. They had their eye on expanding their management company, and were frequently receiving tapes from bands around the Seattle area. But Queensrÿche's rapid climb curtailed that quite a bit. "At that point, I had met Kim Harris and he wanted to take us on," Heir Apparent guitarist Terry Gorle explains. "He had already done the Queensrÿche EP and they were starting to get

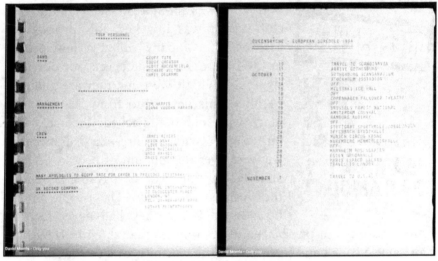

some attention. Having Kim and Diana Harris to manage our band made it easier to get people to join up for that type of commitment. To actually rehearse and work on things for a while. We recorded our five-song EP in the first week of July 1984. Just a couple of weeks before that, Queensrÿche was off and running to Japan and they didn't want Kim and Diana's attention on anything else. I'd already booked the studio and made that committment to Triad, so I scrambled for a week or two and ended up borrowing a few thousand dollars from my parents."

Despite pulling out of managing other Seattle bands per Queensrÿche's wishes, Kim Harris still tried to help others along the way. "I did typical managerial stuff," says Kim Harris. "Not just with Queensrÿche, but with other bands that I helped, other managers who needed help.

If Queensrÿche was in the studio, I would get a call from guys with Iron Maiden's stature that we got along with. 'Can you take Dokken out on the road? I've got twelve shows to do and I need someone to take care of them.' Sure!"

Other musicians in the scene noticed Queensrÿche's quick ascent up and out of the local area, and looked to use that as a blueprint for their own bands. "I decided I needed to come back here [to Seattle from L.A.] and put together this vision I had, which became Fifth Angel," says guitarist James Byrd. "I modeled the idea basically after what I had seen Queensrÿche do. Which was rather than expending energy playing gigs and trying to get record executives out to see the band, we'd hole up and self-finance a fully produced album and shop it. That was my big plan. And that wasn't a common plan in 1982. Very few people were thinking along those lines. Everybody wanted to get noticed playing live."

After the Los Angeles visit in early October, Queensrÿche headed back out on the road with Twisted Sister. They opened for them for fifteen dates at clubs and theaters starting on October 12, 1983. at the Uptown Theatre in Kansas, and wrapping it up at Le Spectrum in Montreal, Canada on November 6. "To watch

congratulations!

for your first Album on the EMI label

engineered by Tom Hall
recorded at : TRIAD STUDIOS

them grow and go through so many phases was cool from my standpoint," David Morris shares. "The other one that was pretty cool was the Twisted Sister tour that we did, with Queensrÿche opening for them. We had a tour bus and they didn't. They were traveling in a van. We did shows as far north going up into Nova Scotia with them, and it was getting really cold. The band members could sleep on the tour bus overnight if they wanted to. In fact, every one of Twisted Sister's band members came and slept on our tour bus except Dee [Snider]. He was the only one who didn't take them up on it. That guy is an interesting guy, because he was completely straight. He never drank or whatever. And they treated [Queensrÿche] very well. I had so much fun on that tour. Man, in fact [Twisted Sister] took me out for my birthday and got me laid at a strip club. Really fun guys."

This would also mark the first time they played the popular Harpo's club in Detroit (on October 19, 1983), that they would return to the following year for a radio broadcast show. "I remember going to Baltimore, and all around the East Coast," David Morris relates. "Playing Hammerjacks and a lot of well-known places that have since been shut down." After that, the Queensrÿche members all went back home for the Thanksgiving holiday, and some much needed rest after the whirlwind of that year. Then came their first trip out of the United States....

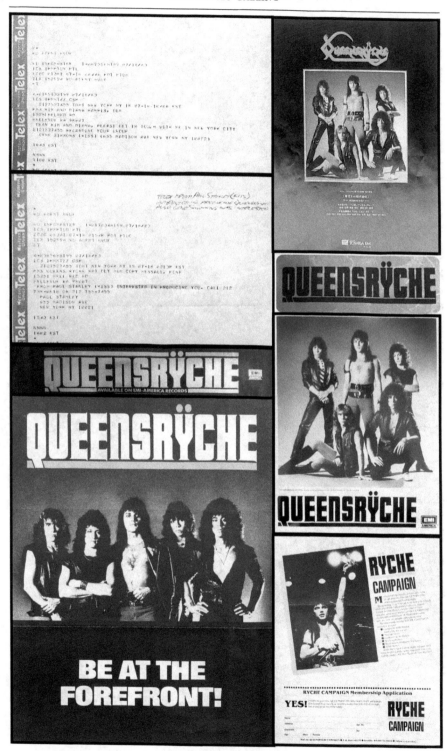

PHOTOS BY RICHARD GALBRAITH

PHOTO BY RICHARD GALBRAITH

PHOTO BY RICHARD GALBRAITH

CHAPTER 7:
ENGLAND'S WARNING

After the break, Queensrÿche headed overseas to record their first full-length album. They had chose to work with Pink Floyd producer James Guthrie at the famous Abbey Road Studios in England. Initially, EMI had wanted the band to record a few more songs to expand the 206 EP to a full-length but that idea was quickly nixed by the Harrises. "They wanted us to go into the studio immediately and record more songs to add to the EP," Kim Harris explains. "We said, 'No. We want it to be a separate thing, keep it special. We don't give a shit; you can sell it for $3.95. We don't care, but it will be a separate thing. This is their stuff they put together.'" Queensrÿche already had new songs at the ready for a new record and wanted to do the album in England. The label, Harris says, had other ideas. EMI expected Queensrÿche to go to Sunset Studios in Los Angeles, spend two weeks, and hand the new songs to an engineer to combine with the EP. But Queensrÿche had a different plan."

"These guys have an idea to make a conceptual album," Harris says he told the label. "I started interviewing producers and engineers. I went through everybody in the business that was heavy. They ended up with a guy they fell in love with who was the lead engineer and producer for Pink Floyd. He had his own studio in Sheppard's Bush [in London, England]. He was married to one of the gals in Bananarama."

Queensrÿche had continued to write material the summer and fall of 1983, for what would be called *The Warning*. They were inspired by current world events and George Orwell's 1949 novel, *Nineteen Eighty-Four*. They set out to create, lyrically and musically, a statement about the human condition in the face of uncontrolled technology and political tyranny. The band wanted to retain its metal roots, as well as stretch out and experiment. All five members of Queensrÿche were big Pink Floyd fans and very excited for the opportunity to work with James Guthrie at this next level. In London, these five young men found a strange new world of cultural diversity and overt political strife which was very different from that of their homes in Bellevue. A Libyan embassy just a few doors down from the studio was even bombed during the time they were recording. These events would help shape the sound of the album. David Morris traveled over with the band to act as the only tech person for them. He remembers fondly the experience: "It was just me, Kim and Diana, and the band. We got three flats in downtown London at a place called Notting Hill Gate. Right by the Piccadilly Circus [public] square. Cool spot. Kim and Diana had their own flat, and upstairs it was Geoff, Chris and Eddie. Downstairs I was in a flat with Mike and Scott. We stored everything at this place called Botanica Row that was owned by Pink Floyd. James Guthrie, the producer, of course had connections with them."

The Warning featured progressive elements, incorporating keyboards and sampling to push the music to a more futuristic sound than that of the EP. Tate took on a significant lyric-writing role for Queensrÿche, and along with DeGarmo, the duo would be credited for most of the band's lyrics during the pair's time together. One song of note, "Deliverance," was written entirely by Michael Wilton, lyrics included. The band was introduced to Michael Kamen at this time, who provided orchestration to album and would play more of a role in the band's evolution in the years to come. During the time they were in the studio, they were surprised by visits from Pink Floyd drummer Nick Mason, and Led Zeppelin guitarist Jimmy Page. Chris DeGarmo was especially thrilled to meet Page—his longtime hero. They also met other legends during their time over in the U.K. According to David Morris: "We went to see David Gilmour after recording one day. James Guthrie asked us if we wanted to see David and we were like, 'Fuck yeah!' He was playing at the Hammersmith Odeon. So, we go down and that night we watched the show. When it was done, we went backstage, and it was so full of people. But we met David and he said, 'Do you want to meet my friends?' And he turned, and it was Jimmy Page, Mick Ralphs of Bad Company, and Roy Harper all standing there. And Gilmour was so nice. He took [the Queensrÿche guys] and really made everybody feel comfortable. Didn't treat them like a new band or anything. James Guthrie also made it a point to introduce

them as Queensrÿche, like a band that was already established, not as a new band. James was really an incredible individual."

Geoff Tate expanded on the trip to England: "We went to London and made our first record. We were in amazement at the amount of money they paid us, how much fun we were having and how long we got to spend on the record. We were living in London for seven- or eight-months making music. It was a dream come true really."

Their managers were a bit more stressed about how long it was taking and how much it was costing. "When we were over in England, we were there for a few months at the label's expense," Kim Harris says. "We rented out a flat for everybody at eleven hundred pounds a week when they were putting together [*The Warning*]. I remember that we were using four different studios for rehearsals, because time and money was so tight then in London. We had to share studios with eight other groups. So, it was like 12 a.m. until 2 a.m. at this one, and then the next night from 8 p.m. until 11 p.m. You are paying for that time and the engineers are ready to go. We were doing a lot of late-night stuff with regard to recording."

The recording, tracking and mixing of the album proved to be both frustrating and rewarding to the band. It was definitely an educational period. Harris explains: "Every argument they had internally had to do with the guitars not being loud enough. I always sided with the guitar players because I thought that was the driving force behind the band. They were looking for this sound that was sort of layered and deep and heavy. One of those, we are doing things that we know are going to happen like, Scotty's doing underwater bells. They spent like $28,000 doing this whole thing and only used four notes, under water. Four notes... Took them a week and a half. I was like, 'You can't do this guys, this is screwing, killing me.' The label was pissed until they heard some of the songs. I used to have a tape of the rough demos of the finished songs. They were very powerful."

As mentioned above, the recording took place at four different studios—Abbey Road, Mayfair Studios, Angel Recording and Audio International—and went over budget by $300,000. Time was short as the band had headlining gigs, in Japan, in August. EMI took it upon themselves to finish the mixing and mastering of the album while Queensrÿche was away. Val Garay was credited to the mix, and often blamed for the final outcome, but Kim Harris says that wasn't the case. "It wasn't Val Garay, so much as it was Harry Maslin who was doing the mastering. Garay mixed it, which was good, but Maslin fucked it up. I remember when we first were listening to the finished product and it had been out of our control. We were [back from Japan and] all sitting in the same place, at my house, and were listening to it. 'What in the hell? Where's the guitars?' It was muddy. Condensed. The only way I can describe it was there was no thrill. The passion was out of it. The songs were good, but this wasn't what we finished with when we left for the Japanese tour." The dual guitar sound that was part of the band's sound, and was more up front in the mix originally, was now buried.

Geoff Tate feels the same on it: "We went $300,000 over budget and the label took the record out of our hands and gave it to someone else to mix. The guy that mixed the album had no clue what Queensrÿche was. He never listened to hard rock music and didn't take input from anyone in the band. He just mixed it according to how he thought it should sound. No one in the band could listen to that record. We all hated it."

The sequencing was also changed on the album before it was finalized, changing the flow and concept Queensrÿche had for the record. The song "NM 156" was to open the album originally with its staccato, mechanical riffing. Additionally, the title track was intended to precede the final track, "Roads to Madness", with the same intro note/effect ending the album. Creating a "circular" connection. And two additional songs—"Deliverance" and "No Sanctuary"—were flip-flopped so that the former preceded "Take Hold of the Flame". All done mainly so that the lead single, "Warning", would be the lead-off track.

During the time, the label was trying to speed up the process and sidestep the band and their managers. Queensrÿche played a handful of dates in Japan from August 4-7, 1984, (with two shows on the 5th). "When Mr. Udo came calling, he owned a whole city block in Tokyo. It was his. The entire block. Seriously," Kim Harris states. "He came to us. He got ahold of me on the phone through two intermediaries, [asking] 'How much do you want for the band if I bring them here and do eight or nine shows?' We did a total of eight shows. Three shows in Tokyo, shows in Kyoto and I forget where else. It was on the fly, it really was. We didn't have any sets, we had nothing. We made it up when we were over there. But Udo turns around and says, 'You do the whole tour and I'll give you $200,000 U.S.'"

Harris and Udo "negotiated" further, with Udo offering to put the band up in five-star hotels and provide travel arrangements for the band members' families to fly over. "We were being treated like kings and queens," Harris adds. "We had fun."

David Morris accompanied the band on the road and shares memories of that time: "I did the Japan tour with them and then the whole European tour. I watched quite a few things take place in Japan. It was really interesting. They created a podium that kind of reminded me of Hitler and the Nazi Party. Geoff had it constructed for him for the song, "NM 156", and he would come out for it and stand behind the podium. That song, by the way, started out as a completely different one before we hit England. It was James Guthrie [who] should get a credit, his name should also be on that song, because he was the one that came up with that whole concept and the synthesizer sequencing. So anyway, in Japan, Geoff was kind of like this dictator in this song. Kind of a Pink Floyd kind of trip. I wonder if anybody got photos or video of it?"

The first "tour program" was also created for Queensrÿche during the tour in support of *The Warning*. It was designed by Robert Ellis (also including photography by him), with artwork by Garry Sharpe and additional photography by Ross Halfin. The tour program noted that Queensrÿche's first EP had sold over 350,000 copies by that point in 1984.

Following the successful Japan concerts, Queensrÿche went out on a trek with Ronnie James Dio again. This time it was for 39 dates on through the United Kingdom and Europe. It went from September 4 through October 30, 1984, and included three nights at the famous Hammersmith Odeon in London. Queensrÿche had established themselves as a strong opening act that could help pull more concertgoers. Kim Harris explains: "What worked before and for several decades was: You had a headliner, a major band, and before the tour, the company would sit down with the label, figure out how many records they could they sell, and how they were selling in certain areas. So, if they were making the jump to major clubs like in the Midwest, like the 1,200 seater clubs and theaters ... not like the ones we have in Seattle, but first class clubs, they could make as much as $15,000-$20,000 as headliners in a club in Pittsburgh. But when they jumped to the 15,000-20,000-seat venue [size], [the band] would have to figure out how many tickets they could they sell. If they could sell 70 percent [of the tickets in a venue], they would try to find another band that could guarantee them 20-25 pecent of sales. So they could get to the rubber ball and make some real money. That's how they did it. Queensrÿche proved themselves so quickly, that they were the number one in regards to getting the calls to be an opening act and I made sure that they were paid more than any other opening act in this country."

Harris continues: "The average price for an opening act at that time was between $2,500-$3,500 and I was saying that we wanted at least $5,000. We got it up as high as $6,500 across the board, which meant the label didn't have to front them so much money for touring. The band could handle literally paying their own way, and the crew was making a lot of money too. If they wanted to stay in hotels on an off night, they all could. I made sure they had the funds to fly out their parents and girlfriends if they wanted to. We had the money in the bank."

As Harris tells it, this helped the band immensely. Major clubs from New York and the east coast would call to book Queensrÿche for weekends, and Harris would tell them $20,000, which the promoters agreed to. "We were selling those kind of places out," Harris adds. "That's how I broke this band."

While they were on the tour with Dio, *The Warning* was released on September 7, 1984. It hit #61 on the Billboard 200 in America, #42 on the Swedish LP charts, #91 in Canada and #100 in the UK. The title track, "Warning," was released as a single in the U.S. A special promotional 12" single with the studio version, and the live version from the Japan shows, was sent to radio stations. A 7" single of the title track backed by "Deliverance" was additionally released in Japan. "Take Hold of the Flame" was released in the UK and Europe and was also a hit in Japan. The album cover also features artwork by the band's friend, Matt Bazemore. It was inspired by Matt's interpretation of Queensrÿche's lyrics. Early stages of the artwork showed a cloaked mystic holding an infinity tarot card, but it was modified for the final cover.

"It wasn't long after [Queensrÿche] had returned from their first real touring experience, that I received a call from Chris DeGarmo asking me to create a color comp for a cover design," Matt Bazemore explains. "He described an ancient mystic or 'Druid guy' burning a tarot card in a candle, while crouching over the 'Book of Centuries' [from *The Prophecies of Nostradamus*] all contained in a large pentagram on the floor. I saw it as an infinity cover, where the image of the old man burning the card appears in miniature on the card he is burning, and so forth. It would have been very cool, but as it came to pass it evolved into something quite different, and I think even better. My first rendition of the cover, that you would recognize today, occurred when I presented the tarot cards on a table facing the viewer with a spotlight on the cards—as if you're having your fortune told. When Chris looked at it, he exclaimed, 'It looks like a planet in outer space.' In the blink of an eye, and the length of a thought, all the previous concepts were gone from memory. *The Warning* cover, visually, was going to go

out to the whole earth. The green laser lights pouring out of the eyes was inspired by the lyrics [of "Child of Fire"]—'light tracers follow me farther.' The storm forming in the ocean was to illustrate "Before the Storm."

Following the couple of months on the road overseas, Queensrÿche returned home to start a lengthy tour with KISS throughout North America. The first leg went from November 15-December 30, 1984, and they moved from larger clubs and theaters, to arenas and stadiums. During this time, Queensrÿche headlined another show at the popular L'Amour club in New York City (Brooklyn) on November 30, 1984, and also headlined a show back at Harpo's, in Detroit, on December 10. Local band Halloween opened (Geoff thanked them during the set) and it was broadcast on the radio there (and has been a regular soundboard-quality "bootleg" release ever since). "At the end of the tour, I just basically stayed home on sabbatical," David Morris says. "Because the drugs were getting pretty heavy. That's why I didn't continue on [with Queensrÿche]. Then I went down to L.A. and got hooked up with Ratt. That was even more fucked up with those guys (Laughs)."

The impact of Queensrÿche's success was still being felt in the Pacific Northwest in 1984, as other aspiring bands were looking to break out, and managers looking to help them achieve that goal. That it was possible to record great music and get signed to a major label, get out on big tours, and garner a fan base, was obviously appealing. Groups such as Metal Church sprung loose from the attention Seattle bands received due to Queensrÿche's "overnight" success. "I wasn't thinking of releasing *Northwest Metalfest* nationally, just something we'd sell at Penny Lane. Kim Harris was doing killer business with the first Queensrÿche EP, so it was the logical next step. We needed a "label" to put it on, so I suggested Ground Zero, a military term that meant where an explosion occurred on or near the surface. Seemed appropriate. That, and it sounded cool," Jeff Gilbert (*The Rocket* writer, "Brain Pain" promoter, and local record label owner) says. "It was in that context I was introduced to Metal Church. The band's founder and guitarist Kurt Vanderhoof came in with a demo tape and it was clear after listening to it they were in the same league as Queensrÿche. Really powerful riffs and songwriting."

Triad Studios, where Queensrÿche cut its EP, also experienced an upswing. They soon had the reputation of the place to get that "polished" heavy metal sound, and many bands would make the trip over the bridge to Redmond (or in some cases travel up from Oregon or California) to work with Tom Hall, or his protegee Mike Tortorello. That said, not everybody felt that sound was right for them, despite Queensryche's influence. Jeff Gilbert continues: "I really didn't have long-term plans for the [*Northwest Metalfest* compilation] album, but taking Kim Harris' lead with Queensrÿche, Willie Mackay and I thought we should do an entire album with Metal Church. Elektra became interested in Metal Church after they saw Capitol Records' success with Queensryche and contacted Willie. Metal Church needed to get in a quality studio, so we went to see Tom Hall who engineered the first Queensrÿche EP, over at Bellevue's Triad Studios. We sat in the control room and Tom played some stuff for the band. I could tell by looking at Kurt Vanderhoof's face he didn't much care for Tom's highly polished style. I think it was Willie who found Terry Date and played Metal Church's demo for him." Despite Metal Church's going to another studio, many other bands such as: Century, Cyperus, D.C. LaCroix, Gargoyle, Hammerhead, Kil D' Kor, Lipstick, Lookout, Rail, SATO, Shock Treatment, Xanadu, and the aforementioned Heir Apparent, all recorded at Triad in the 1980s.

After a couple of days off from the December 30, 1984, show with KISS in Milwaukee, Wisconsin, Queensrÿche headlined ten club shows in the Northeast with Fates Warning, Assassin, Paradoxx and others opening from January 4, 1985 – January 16, 1985. Then Queensrÿche were fortunate to be able to support Iron Maiden for four dates at Radio City Music Hall from January 17-20, 1985. "The most memorable shows we opened were the seven shows we did with Iron Maiden in early 1985 at Radio City Music Hall in New York," Scott Rockenfield adds. "It was a very exciting week of metal!" Somebody else was impressed by the young band with the vocalist with an air-raid siren for a voice. "Bruce [Dickinson] was knocked out," Kim Harris recalls. "He was standing on the side of the stage, next to me, when he heard Geoff hit those high notes. It scared him that Tate could hit them so easily. This guy was killing his voice every night and Geoff was just singing away."

Post-Maiden shows, it was back on the road with KISS for 25 more dates before wrapping it up on March 3, 1985, at the Corral Arena in Calgary, Alberta. During that last leg, on February 13, Queensrÿche was back in Seattle with KISS for a triumphant hometown return at the Seattle Center Coliseum. It had been around 16 months since their last show there with Dio, and they had played approximately 130 shows during that time. Many of the band's family and friends attended the concert and had their first taste of a big arena event thanks to Queensrÿche. Local reporters were there interviewing attendees and asking them their opinions on the biggest band out of Seattle since Jimi Hendrix and Heart. Queensrÿche's set drew from songs from the EP and the new album, included the unreleased song, "Prophecy," and closed with "Take Hold of the Flame." Queensrÿche was tight and even more experienced from being on the road. Everyone seemed to know the material and was singing along during their set. The band left the stage to a thunderous ovation. In the backstage area, the members of Queensrÿche were welcomed to a room full of admirers and news cameras. There was food and drink and excitement in the air. The band looked like they were on a high and feeling very accomplished. They had toured the world and arrived home the victors. Cameras flashed and reporters interviewed the band and others. Friends and family congratulated the members of Queensrÿche. A KOMO TV reporter asked Scott Rockenfield's dad, "How did you manage having the band practicing in your basement?" He responded with, "Three or four years in our basement. It was nothing... just pain and self-denial!" Many of the assembled fans likely realized after this show that their local heavy metal band really did belong to the rest of the world.

During their time on the road with KISS and the other bands, a home video concert from two of their shows in Japan (August 4-5, 1984) saw release on Laserdisc in Japan toward the end of 1984, and on VHS and Betamax cassettes in the U.S. in early 1985. UDO Artists Entertainment company filmed *Live in Tokyo* and EMI financed it. This was fairly unprecedented at the time for a newer band to do something like this. "We taped three of the shows for the video, and of course we weren't ready to do videos," Kim Harris says. "We didn't know what we were doing, but we thought

'what the hell.' The label said we had $85,000 to do it.... This was a huge opportunity for a band this young to not only headline a series of shows in Japan, but also have the opportunity to record them for a home video release."

After the KISS tour was done, the Queensrÿche guys went back home for a much-needed break. Geoff Tate was invited by Ronnie James Dio to take part in a special charity project he was working on called, "Hear N' Aid." It was to be an album to raise funds to help with famine in Africa. Dio wrote an original song for the album, "Stars," and invited a large number of musicians from the heavy metal and hard rock bands popular at that time such as: Rob Halford (Judas Priest), Don Dokken and George Lynch (Dokken), Dave Meniketti (Y & T), Kevin DuBrow (Quiet Riot), Buck Dharma (Blue Oyster Cult), Yngwie Malmsteen, Vivian Campbell (Dio), Brad Gillis (Ozzy Osbourne, Night Ranger), Neal Schon (Journey), Paul Shortino (Rough Cutt), and many others. His own band played the rhythms along with Dave Murray and

An All-Star Album For Famine Relief

Adrian Smith of Iron Maiden. It was recorded at Sound City Studios and A & M Studios in Los Angeles from May 20-21, 1985 and released on January 1, 1986.

Following that, Tate's Queensrÿche bandmates joined him in New York for two nights headling L'Amour in Brooklyn, New York, on May 31 and June 1, 1985. Then a bit more time off and back down to Southern California for shows at the Hollywood Palladium (with Carmine Appice's King Kobra and Leatherwolf in support) on July 12, at the Irvine Meadows Amphitheater on July 13 (with Accept and Keel), and at the California Theatre on July 15, in San Diego (with Keel opening again). The shows in Hollywood and San Diego were notable, as Queensrÿche would road test a new song they had been working on called "Neue Regel." The band took a bit of a break following the gigs and then began rehearsing and writing music for their follow-up full-length album....

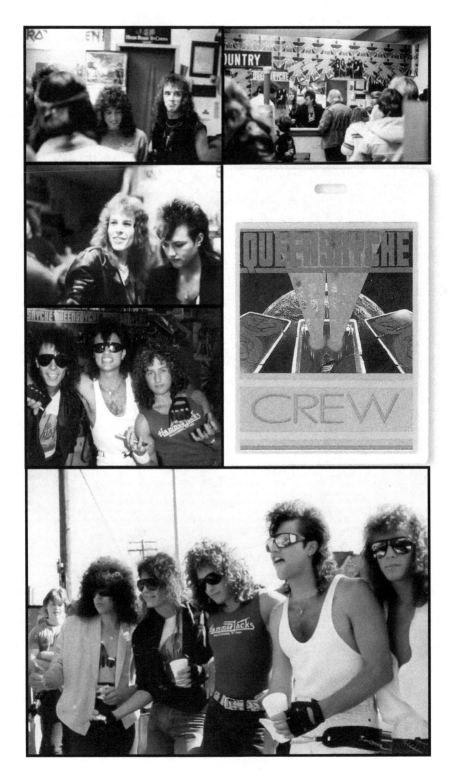

CHAPTER 8:
SCREAMING IN DIGITAL

A fter *The Warning* tour finally ended in July 1985, the guys took a month or so off before heading back into the studio. After their previous experience with the album being taken from them, remixed and re-sequenced without their input or approval, they all vowed to not have that happen again. Their management had confronted the label and enlisted guarantees that the Queensrÿche camp would have final approval on the mix of the next album.

Kim Harris explains: "The label really screwed it up and I made sure that they owed us bigtime (laughs). I said, 'Here's what we're going to do for the next record. We're going to have total control of this product. I don't care how long it takes or how much it costs, but we are going to do it our way and you're going to take it when it's done. Or I'm going to start [telling] some people in this business about what you did to that record.'"

For the producer of what would become *Rage for Order*, Queensrÿche chose Neil Kernon. Originally from London, England, Kernon had started out at Trident Studios (working as an assistant on various albums by Queen, David Bowie, Marc Bolan, Elton John and others). By the early 1980s, he had become a producer and engineer of note having worked on gold and platinum records by Yes, Kansas, Judas Priest, Hall and Oates, Bow Wow Wow, Peter Gabriel, Dokken, Helix and others. He had heard Queensrÿche was looking for somebody, and he put his name in the hat. "When I first heard Queensrÿche, I was really impressed," Kernon says. "It was a different sound and I was thrilled by that. So, when I heard they were looking for a new producer, I was very interested."

"We were looking for a very live and aggressive sound," Scott Rockenfield states. "We finally found a huge stone warehouse. It was a business park. We brought up Le Mobile, which was a mobile recording studio, and spent about five days getting the drum tracks." Based out of Los Angeles, Le Mobile was a state-of-the-art recording studio housed inside a ten-wheel GMC van. The $1,000,000 roving studio had updated audio and video equipment at that time, including twin 24-track digital tape decks. Guy Charbonneau was the owner/operator and on the road ten months a year, recording artists. He had previously recorded Dire Straits, Pat Benatar, David Bowie, Dolly Parton, and the Live Aid festival in Philadelphia. In 1986, Le Mobile was in Bellevue to record drum and bass guitar tracks for *Rage for Order*. Queensrÿche rented a vacant Bellevue office building, the old CMC International headquarters, and used various sided rooms to get just the right sound from the instruments. While there were other mobile sound studios back then, "Charbonneau's is the best in the world," Neil Kernon says.

To get a guitar sound that Queensrÿche were happy with, DeGarmo and Wilton used a couple of old Marshall amps with a Variac voltage transformer that caused them to work harder (a technique pioneered by Edward Van Halen of using the Variac to starve the tubes to get his signature "Brown sound"). Michael Wilton elaborates: "We must have tried about 50 different speaker/amplifier combinations. We finally ended up using these two old Marshall amplifiers which were on the verge of exploding. That gave us this edge and tension for the album."

Queensrÿche also recorded at Mushroom Studios in Vancouver B.C. (where Heart recorded in the 1970s) and did some additional recording at Yamaha Studios in L.A. It was a research and development center for the Japanese instrument company back then. There they were able to create some of the futuristic, industrial sounds and effects for the album.

Another interesting effect used on the album was Michael Wilton yelling into his pickups on one of the songs on *Rage for Order*. Neil Kernon says: "One of my favorite [moments] was in recording 'Chemical Youth.' While Whip and I were tracking his lead guitars, I had told him that shouting through the guitar pickup could make an interesting sound. So, once the [lead guitar] had been completed, we set about tracking some shouting through the amp via the pickup. Michael, in his inimitable way, decided to do an impression of Vyvyan from *The Young Ones* and started shouting 'Neil, you bastard!' at the top of his voice, while I recorded the result onto some blank tape for use at a later date. He was crouching on the floor screaming this insult over and over again when the door burst open and in rushed several of the studio staff, the studio manager and receptionist, etc., all looking very alarmed. We just looked at them standing there, and they

just asked 'Err…is everything ok? We thought there was a fight going on' (laughs)."

Queensrÿche had written most of the material for the new album before entering the studio. Again, they were being influenced by the experiences of world travel and experiencing things that they had only read about or had seen on television. The band was no longer naive. They had become a bit worldly. They found the world colder and crueler than what they had been exposed to in Bellevue and the Pacific Northwest. Social-political strife, governmental intrusion and artificial intelligence were the lyrical themes of the album. This was also reflected in the music that became *Rage for Order*. Kernon's wish was to create a sound that was, "uncompromisingly cold, sonically." The album was a turning point for the band. They had left many of their old influences behind and became the band they were going to be. The music is very atmospheric and industrial in sound. Big guitars and drums laced with keyboards, played by Tate and Neil Kernon, gave the band a "techno-metal" sound. In the July 1986 Queensrÿche campaign newsletter, Geoff mused, "*Rage for Order* is a more mature approach. We're trying to get more texture into our music and more dynamics. Queensrÿche is a very modern band, modern as in technical. Technical, as in high-tech, high-tech and art. The machine moves with real precision, that's how I envision what we are doing, but with an angry feel, a rebellious sort of future." Chris DeGarmo adds, "It's a statement-oriented album, a complete concept. It's very much like the world is right now—a kind of chaos search for direction."

Rage for Order also continued the pattern of Queensrÿche linking lyrics thematically, that was started on *The Warning*, but this time it was expanded. It employed a three-tiered approach—personal, political and technological order—with "order" being the link between the three. The album's lyrics are ripe with references again to George Orwell's dystopian classic *Nineteen Eighty-Four*, as well as from Anne Rice's first couple "Vampire Chronicles" novels (*Interview with A Vampire, The Vampire Lestat* and *Queen Of the Damned*). "That was our delving into vampirism," Chris DeGarmo explains. "By day we'll live in a dream / Walk with me, and we'll walk in the shadows.' It's talking about joining the dark side. This song is also about infatuation. It's speaking to a woman: 'You're through with me, I'm not through with you / We've had what others might call love / You can't stay away, you need me like I need you / When the fire starts, the pain's too much for your mind.' We were all reading *The Vampire Chronicles* around that time. Our music has always had a sort of dark flavor to it. Even when we write a love song, it's usually obsessive in nature." All of the songs on *Rage for Order* consist of social commentary and observation, personal experience and fictional accounts that tie in with the sub-themes of the album. The album title itself is a contradiction in terms, pitting the word "rage" against its polar opposite, "order." This type of songwriting was way outside of what most contemporary heavy metal bands were coming up with at that time. Most were continuing to mine the "pop/party metal" that Van Halen had made popular in the late `70s/early `80s (later referred to as "hair metal")—not the intelligent, thought-provoking lyrics and challenging musical compositions that Queensrÿche created.

Some tracks recorded during the sessions for *Rage for Order* were not used on the album. "Prophecy" (which was originally written back in 1982 and first recorded during the EP sessions, and also included in the pre-production demos for *The Warning*, but not used on either record) was re-recorded by Kernon. It was included on the soundtrack for the  film *The Decline Of Western Civilization II: The Metal Years*. "Once we'd gotten the drum sounds—Scotty ended up tracking all his drums in just over a day—and we were satisfied that all the tracks were solid, I suggested we cut any other things we could (without wasting expensive studio time learning them of course)," Kernon recalls. "We had quite a few other things to cut, namely 'Scarborough Fair', the song 'Rage for Order,' and 'Prophecy', the last one suggested. It was being considered for inclusion in *The Decline of Western Civilization Pt. 2*. Ironically, there was a mammoth cockup and the wrong version was sent to mastering. The demo [was] done at the same time as the self-titled EP. So, when the EP was re-released on CD [in 1988], our new version of 'Prophecy' ended up being included on that instead."

The Simon and Garfunkel cover of "Scarborough Fair" had been a popular staple in the Myth setlist and was suggested by Tate. (It was not included on the album, but would later be used as a b-side for the "Anybody Listening?" single in 1992.) Charles Russell, a longtime friend of the band, shares a fun story about the recording of it and Chris DeGarmo: "During the pre-production for *Rage for Order,* Chris called me up. There was a guy named Mike that had a sitar, and they were going to record the 'parsley, sage, rosemary and thyme' song ("Scarborough Fair"). We picked up the sitar and Chris quickly learned how to play it. I mean like in an hour. Then we decided to have a little fun and make a show of it when we went to Triad Studios. We tie-dyed a huge t-shirt, slicked back Chris's hair, put a red dot on his forehead, grabbed the sitar and then headed to the studio. We giggled like 13-year-old girls hoping to shock the hell out of the band when we walked in. And we did. We went in and everyone said, 'Hi Chris. Let's record.' (Laughs) Nobody knew of the hours of preparation we put into his look, nor mentioned it."

"Prophecy" was also included as the b-side of the "Gonna Get Close to You" single from *Rage for Order* in Europe. Other songs Queensrÿche had demoed for the *Rage for Order* sessions, such as "From the Darkside" and "The Dream" remained demos. The band had also intended "Rage for Order" to be the title track. Although it was not included on the album, the main riff from this song was worked into an instrumental piece played during some shows on the tour in support of this album, and eventually morphed into the instrumental track "Anarchy-X" on *Operation: Mindcrime*, released in 1988. "The song 'Rage for Order' had a pretty interesting rap-type vocal," Kernon continues. "It was very unusual, but the music was pretty much exactly how 'Anarchy-X' turned out." One of the other interesting stories around a song that did make *Rage for Order*, is about what is being said in the vocal effects used within "London." Charles Russell explains: "In the song 'London', during the line where Geoff says, 'I don't remember your name...' and then there is a bunch of whispering... that's every girl Chris and Geoff 'met' on their first two tours whispered. I was with them when they took a sheet of paper and wrote down all of the girls' first names. We were laughing our asses off. I think this is a secret, but not so secret. (Laughs)."

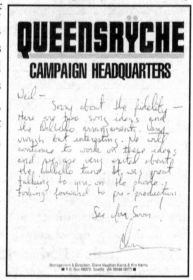

Hanging around with the guys at the studio during the recording of *Rage for Order*, Charles was also drafted into service. "We did 'gang' vocals following a night of heavy drinking in Vancouver, Canada," Russell says. "We went into the studio the following morning. We all sang backing vocals. Of course, they didn't want to credit it on the album for 'gang vocals', so Neil Kernon called the gang vocals 'The Taiwonon Minions.' Slaves to a hangover!"

The band recorded complex and dynamic songs like "Chemical Youth (We Are Rebellion)" "Neue Regel" (which Queensrÿche had written on the road during *The Warning* tour and as mentioned earlier even debuted it in rough form during some shows) and "Screaming in Digital." These songs had the hallmarks of (what would later be termed) the genre of "progressive metal." The band wanted to create a dark and cold sounding record, but EMI-America wanted the album to be radio friendly to some degree. The song "Gonna Get Close To You," written by Canadian songwriter Lisa Dal Bello, was recorded to be the first single instead of "Walk in the Shadows." While the band felt that they had found their sound with *Rage for Order*, their appearance took a drastic detour. It was suggested by their management that their provocative new sound required a look to match. The look was inspired by some of the subterranean dance clubs the band had been hanging out in during the European tours. They wore full length jackets, theatrical make up and highlighted hair. Perfect Harmony designed the wardrobe for the four musicians of the band, while Michael Murphey (who went back to being part of the Seattle glam/drag troupe Ze Fabulous Whiz Kidz, as well as did clothing for Led Zeppelin and others) did Geoff's outfit. The video for "Gonna Get Close to You" shows the band in their new dark wave glam attire and Geoff stalking a model in a neo-gothic setting (playing off of the vampire theme on some of the album and this song with Tate and the model's flashing red eyes).

Queensrÿche intended for the album cover art to be done again by their friend Matt Bazemore, but that didn't happen. "After producing the stages for *The Warning* tour of Japan and Europe in 1984—which you can still see during the track "Prophecy" on the *Building Empires* Video/DVD, or on the now hard to find *Live in Tokyo* video—I began to design the next album cover," Bazemore says. "*Rage for Order* was described to me as a musical and visual departure from the previous album. Geoff described it as needing to be 'stark, machine-like, and futuristic.' I had taken the band to see Fritz Lang's 1926 masterpiece film *Metropolis*. I wanted to connect the look of the album cover to the live show staging. They got it. Unfortunately, the powers that were EMI-America didn't."

Bazemore continues: "Knowing I had Geoff Tate's direction, I pursued a design that incorporated machine louvers and factory-inspired steam vents. I used the colors of the Nazi dress flag in an attempt to reach the audience subliminally, based solely on the album title. I thought the result was sophisticated and powerful. I remember putting all the possible solutions together over a period of four or five months. I used Roman letters to reflect timeless totalitarianism and red, white, black and gold for a more recent totalitarianism, all intended to be subconscious. When it came down to the deadline, I was told that EMI had told them, 'don't hand us this guy.' They wanted their own graphic staff to get the credit for the cover, and put it in terms of the band 'needing to get behind their label.' Well, of course I was really disappointed, because I feel the covers I had conceived were as sophisticated as the band and their music. As it came down [to it], the band was given a proof sheet of several solutions by EMI-America and was asked to pick one. Not one solution was 'stark, machine like, or futuristic', but every solution on the page was red, black white, and gold. [The label] had no intention of giving me any credit, but they thought enough of me to copy my color scheme outright. I don't blame the band at all. EMI controlled it and that was it. I was vindicated by the band when we built the staging for the *Rage for Order* tour, and we set Scotty's drums up with corrugated pvc piping and ran fog through it. It looked just like the film *Metropolis* and reached full effect during songs like 'Gonna Get Close to You' and 'Screaming in Digital' with their industrial sonics. It was fantastic, but alas it didn't have much to do with a seventeenth-century nautical map superimposed beneath a life-preserver."

The *Rage for Order* album cover was eventually credited to Henry Marquez for art direction and design by Glenn Parsons [both label staffers], but left out both Bazemore's contributions and artist Garry Sharpe-Young's (with only Bazemore thanked in the credits of the album for "his support."). Garry had come up with the ring cover artwork for a proposed 12" picture disc and that was used by EMI instead of Bazemore's mockups. A few thousand copies of the cover feature a

bluish silver ring. Later it was changed to black as the label felt it was harder to read at first. The original cassette release also had all the gold accents on the cover changed to white.  The first release CDs bearing the blue/silver ring cover are even more rare. Only a few hundred copies were made before the switch to black.

SYMBOLICALLY SPEAKING: THE EVOLUTION OF THE QUEENSRŸCHE TRI-RYCHE

By Brian L. Naron

The Tri-Ryche is a symbol synonymous with Queensrÿche. The iconic image, like the band, has changed and evolved since its inception. The Tri-Ryche began as a pencil doodling of local artist Wes Griswold. He would sign his artwork with a  winged-shaped image depicting a peregrine falcon. Wes was Geoff Tate's roommate at the time when the band decided to put out its first record. The singer asked him to design the 206 EP sleeve. His Tri-Ryche symbol became the "crown" of the band photo on rear of the sleeve. Wes also designed the QR "coat of arms" which adorns the rear sleeve.

As mentioned earlier by H.D. Gray, the Tri-Ryche symbol was a creation of artist Wes Griswold. It was the way he always signed his artwork. "I remember him doing it all the way back in high school, started  out I think as a peregrine falcon," said Brett Miller, a high school friend of the band.

Surprisingly, the Tri-Ryche had not been trademarked by Queensrÿche until recently, due to a long-standing controversy over who created the symbol. Todd Rockenfield (the brother of Queensrÿche drummer Scott Rockenfield), who designed the *logo* of the word "Queensrÿche" on the front and back of the EP, claimed the design of the Tri-Ryche in its eventual form was his, and the band acknowledges his role in the development of the Tri-Ryche.

The next step in the evolution of the Tri-Ryche came when guitarist Chris DeGarmo commissioned Matt Bazemore to create the painting that would become the cover of *The Warning*. Matt incorporated a modified version of the Tri-Ryche symbol into the playing card design for the album art. Bazemore designed and created, with help of his mother and her sewing machine, banners that would adore the backline for Queensrÿche's stage during the band's early live shows. He included crowns with the Tri-Ryche on top of them and Wes' coat of arms on Scott's kick drums.

On *Rage for Order*, the Tri-Ryche took a quantum leap forward. Matt Bazemore was again tapped to create some artwork for the album. He designed three pieces and submitted them to the band and the label. The color scheme of each piece featured the colors of the German flag: red, black and gold. One of the  submissions included flags that had an expanded Tri-Ryche on top of the planet Earth. His designs were rejected in favor of the label going with an in-house designer. EMI-America's design team ultimately came up with the *Rage for Order* cover, creating a version of Bazemore's planet Earth version of the Tri-Ryche and used his same red-black-gold color palette.

Geoff Tate told *Eye on Queensrÿche* in July 1999: "I believe it was Henry Marquez who first brought the Tri-Ryche into the forefront with his beautiful *Rage for Order* cover art. The look of the Tri-Ryche has evolved over time as well as the symbolism we have attached to it. It has followed us all these years wanting to be what it has become, the symbol for Queensrÿche."

 The Tri-Ryche would again evolve during the *Operation: Mindcrime* era as a skull and EKG wave. It was elongated like a dagger for *Empire*. *Promised Land* featured the symbol as a totem pole. It appeared as an ancient sketching of a bird on *Tribe*. As time went on, it would appear on numerous album covers, singles, posters, stickers, jewelry and even guitars. Like the band, the Tri-Ryche continuously morphs and reinvents itself.

When it came to releasing *Rage for Order* and expectations for it, Queensrÿche's managers also had their challenges with the label. Kim Harris explains: "When we got to the *Rage for Order* record, I had some major battles with the record label about sales because all of their numbers showed that this band would only sell 360,000 - 375,000 copies total in the U.S. They figured they would have advanced sales pre-orders of around 30,000. These are the numbers their sales division came up with. I was sitting in a meeting with these guys in L.A. and New York and I'm telling them that we can do better than this. I know we can. I laid out an entire program. Additional billing, longer dates, discounts and promotions. I came up with the numbers I thought we could do. I thought we could do 80,000 in pre-orders. They started laughing at me. I'm in a room with 12 guys who have been doing this for something like twenty years. I told them that we were going to sell close to a million of these records, *Rage for Order*, before this is all done. We sold 89,000 copies in pre-orders and the label went nuts."

The album was released on June 26, 1986, and immediately sold better than its predecessor. "Initially it was 486,000-487,000 copies," Kim Harris recalls. "Then it jumped up to gold at a half a million and stayed there for a while." *Rage for Order* hit #47 on the U.S. Billboard charts, #58 on the German charts, #31 on the Dutch charts, #47 on the Swedish charts, #66 in the UK and #85 in Canada. "Gonna Get Close To You" went to #91 on the UK singles charts and had frequent radio and MTV play as well.

Queensrÿche kicked off the *Rage for Order* tour on July 31, 1986, in New Orleans, opening for AC/DC. The band employed a sixth musician into the touring band, keyboardist Randy Gane from Myth, to play Neil Kernon's and Tate's album parts. Geoff even played some rhythm guitar to bolster the guitar sound. Scott Rockenfield's drums feature "high-tech" tubing wrapped around the kit and set was lit with louvered lights, as envisioned by Matt Bazemore. They played 14 dates with AC/DC on that tour leg (mostly in the Midwest and West Coast, with a three-city jaunt up in Canada), ending on August 29, 1986, in Minneapolis, Minnesota. This included shows

in Portland, Oregon, at the Memorial Coliseum on August 18 and the Tacoma Dome in Washington, on August 19. At the Tacoma stop, they did an in-store appearance at Tower Records earlier in the day, which some fans who attended stated that most of the band seemed "smug and full of themselves." They also were supposed to have a backstage meet and greet at the show that night, but nobody but touring member Randy Gane showed up to announce the band was "too tired." The grueling road life, or the trappings of success, depending on your opinion, was starting to take its toll.

Following that, they joined Ozzy Osbourne for 25 more arena shows, starting on September 4, 1986, and concluding on October 8. These were mostly on the East Coast, from Florida, through the Carolinas, Philadelphia, New York, Rhode Island and so on. Queensrÿche jumped off the Ozzy tour to headline eight shows of their own from October 10-October 22, 1986, in Texas, Arizona and California with Keel, Black N' Blue and others opening for them. After that, they headed overseas to open for Bon Jovi for around 20 dates in the UK, and Europe, concluding on December 8, 1986. After a break for Christmas and New Year's, they opened for Ratt for five shows starting on January 24, 1987, in Mississippi, Tennessee, Texas, and Oklahoma, and headlined four nights at both L'Amour clubs in New York. This concluded the *Rage for Order* tour on February 21, 1987. One of those shows made a big impact on a local musician who would go on to make a huge impact himself. "I saw Queensryche and Fates Warning play together [at the L'Amour club in New York]," recalls Long Island native Mike Portnoy (ex-drummer of Dream Theater, and current drummer for Liquid Tension Experiment, Sons of Apollo and a number of other bands). "I was drawn to Queensrÿche because they combined the metal of Judas Priest with the theatrics of Pink Floyd. And the way Fates Warning was doing an Iron Maiden-meets-Rush – these were all favorites of mine at the time, and those bands had an immeditate impact on me."

Queensrÿche had been on the road, or in the studio, nearly non-stop since mid-1983 and was ready for a break from the grueling schedule. They wanted to reconnect with family and friends, and to energize their creativity for their next crucial, "make 'em or break 'em" fourth record.

The continual life on the road had started to take its toll on the Harrises as well. Says Kim Harris: "We were touring everywhere. In a two-year period we did the two KISS tours, AC/DC, Ozzy, the list went on and on. I was burned out and I was killing myself. When the band finished [touring for *Rage for Order*], I went out with Judas Priest. I went out with Iron Maiden, with the Scorpions in Europe. I was still doing drugs at the time and was starting to crash and burn, which I did. I was going into blackouts and so on... I have 31 years sober now, but it didn't happen overnight. They had to drag me off a tour bus, and pronounce me dead on the way to emergency to get me there."

The first casualties in the Queensrÿche family were logged as the band continued to ascend the ladder of success. "I stepped down. I couldn't handle it," Harris continues. "My relationship with Diana... Literally, we were ready to kill each other and I was never home, really. I was on the road 280 days a year. Two hundred and eighty! I didn't even know what city I was in most of the time. It was just a blur. I finally said I just couldn't do this anymore. The band deserved better than that. I was fortunate enough to hire some really good people. Real pros, and I paid them a bloody fortune. They literally handled the group because I could not do it. I wanted to, but I couldn't. I couldn't even tie my shoes or find the door knob. I was laying in the hospital and I could not do a damned thing. I was out, and I was gone."

It should be noted that toward the end of the *Rage for Order* tour, Chris DeGarmo took over booking some shows for Queensrÿche. The guitarist pulled double-duty, both as a performer, and helping out on the business end as Kim Harris' ability to keep up waned.

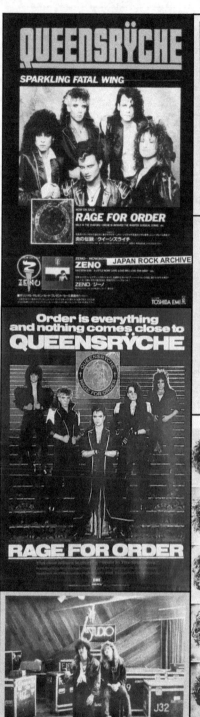

CHAPTER 9:
EVOLUTION CALLING

During the time off that winter/spring of 1987, Geoff Tate spent some time in Montreal, Canada. He found himself in an old catholic church, and then later met the leader of an anarchist-type group in a bar. These eventually became the seeds of a storyline for a concept album. "We had been on the road with *Rage for Order*, and Chris and I had been talking about trying to write a conceptual piece," Geoff Tate explains. "We didn't quite know what it was, but we had some music that ended up being 'Suite Sister Mary.' It was sort of a long involved piece and we were working on this on the road and talking. When the tour ended, I went up to Montreal to live for a while. I was staying up there and I met some people and I hung out with Quebec separtists. I can't remember how to describe them; there's a name for it. These people were trying to separate Quebec from the union of Canada. They were pretty interesting, although pretty extreme. So, I met and associated with them. And I was tossing around the experiences of the last tour. One night, it was snowing and I had run out of cigarettes, so I got on all my heavy clothes to walk down to the corner and get some smokes. When I got there, I bought my smokes, came outside, unwrapped them and was having a cigarette when I saw this Catholic church across the street. And I had this really strong desire to walk in there. So I did, and I sat down, and I was kind of looking around and sinking into the vibe when all of a sudden I started getting this musical idea in my head. It got very strong, and all these words started swirling around and I had the idea. I raced home and I just started writing, and in about three hours I had outlined the entire story and written the first verse and chorus to the song, '*Operation: Mindcrime*.' And that just got the ball rolling."

Tate continues: "When I got back to Seattle in March, I presented the idea to the band and none of them really got it. They didn't like it at all, and I was really upset because I really thought this was a strong idea and I really wanted to pursue it. The next day Chris called me up and said, 'You know, I've been thinking about that idea. I think what we need to do is talk more about it. Come over to my  house and maybe we'll write some stuff.' I did and we started talking about it and the idea started rolling out. Chris and I really came up with some musical ideas at that point and we honed in on the storyline with a little more detail. And then with him and I presenting it to the rest of the band again, they all bit on it and we started working on it."

"Eyes Of A Stranger" and "The Mission" were a couple of the earlier songs developed, along with "Operation: Mindcrime" and "Anarchy-X"—the latter of which evolved out of the instrumental recorded first in embryonic stage during the *Rage for Order* sessions. The pieces were starting to fall into place. The album's plot revolved around drugs, murder, sex and corruption. The cast of characters included the mysterious underworld revolutionary figure named Dr. X, who manipulates a drug addict named Nikki and a nun, Sister Mary (who had been a prostitute earlier in life), into a scheme of political assassinations and political anarchy. The album storyline pulls the listener into the characters' desperate plight. The connection between Nikki and Mary grows and Dr. X orders Nikki to kill Mary and the priest, fearing they know too much about the anarchist's plans. When Mary does die, the listener is left pondering her demise. The clues are subtle and leaves one unsure if Nikki, Dr. X, or someone else had killed her. The music and lyrics link together to tell the dramatic tale that Geoff Tate had dreamed up the year before in snowy Montreal.

"*Operation: Mindcrime* was a whole other scenario, because it was a story," Chris DeGarmo stated a bit later on. "The point of the story was denial; that's the best way to describe it. *Operation: Mindcrime* is a whole series of stories, just in case you didn't catch that. It's about mind control. It's named like a military operation, like Operation Desert Storm. It's about brainwashing. There's a character named Dr. X who is this brilliant, demented person who sees a better way, in his mind, of changing the government. He decides that he's going to recruit heroin addicts, who he can control through their addictions, to carry out these assassinations on people he wants eliminated, so he can replace them with his own. Nikki is this street kid, this junkie, who buys Dr. X's plan, and Sister Mary is this street kid who gets taken in by this corrupt priest. This stuff was written around the time that all these preachers were sort of falling from grace, if you will. Some of these characters are based on people we've met while out on the road and what was happening around us. Geoff pretty much came up with the idea of the whole Mindcrime album."

DeGarmo continues: "A concept album was something the band had fancied doing for some time and was extremely challenging to put together. We wanted the music to paint a picture. We had a vision and worked very hard on the segues... The story is set in contemporary times and there is a bit of finger pointing at certain things going on in America. It has a cynical edge to it, but disguised in a fictional tale. Geoff Tate is responsible for the lyrics which reflect what we see going on. It's not a 'let's go to the beach and party record,' that's for sure. But we're not unpatriotic. We just like to write dark, twisted tales that make you think. The first piece is a flashback for the character Nikki, a street kid gone wrong who has a heroin addiction and is pretty unmotivated as far as life and goals go. He becomes the subject of manipulation by Dr. X who wants violent political change. He is used as a hit man to eliminate people. 'I Remember Now' begins this wild roller coaster ride with Nikki having a flashback as he comes out of a coma, watching himself on the news, seeing the horrible crimes he has committed."

Neil Kernon was originally slated to produce Queensrÿche's third album, but was unable to do it because of other commitments. "I was supposed to do *Operation: Mindcrime*, but my schedule got screwed up working with Dokken, so that ended that dream," Kernon says. The band ended up using Peter Collins, who had worked with Gary Moore, Billy Squier, and Rush, amongst others. That latter band, especially, appealed to the Queensrÿche members as they had been fans of Rush from way back in the 1970s. James "Jimbo" Barton and Paul Northfield were tapped as the engineers. They all entered into the Kajem/Victory studios in Philadelphia, Pa., to begin the recording of *Operation: Mindcrime* with Collins. Michael Kamen was back on board for orchestral production (Choir and Cellos). Recording continued at Le Studio, in Morin-Heights,

Quebec—the same studio used by Rush, The Police, David Bowie, and other notable artists. The album was recorded in about three months and mixed by James Barton at Wisseloord Studios in Hilversum, The Netherlands.

Queensrÿche also tapped others to voice the characters in the story and help bring it to life. English actor Anthony Valentine (from the TV shows *Callan* and *Colditz*) played/voiced Dr. X, Debbie Wheeler played/voiced the Nurse, and Scott Mateer was Father William. NBC News anchorman Mike Snyder's voice was used on the album as well. Seattle singer Pamela Moore played/voiced Sister Mary. Moore went way back in the local scene having had success playing the club circuit and had also released a couple of albums in the early 1980s. Chris DeGarmo had seen and heard her doing commercials for a music store she worked at part-time. The audition happened quickly as he called her about it one day, and the next she was flown to Montreal to sing on the album.

Operation: Mindcrime was recorded digitally on a Sony 24-track digital tape machine. The album was also mixed and mastered in the digital format. It was one of the first records to be done that way instead of on analog tape. Compact discs had just started to be produced in the United States (after previously being made over in Japan and Europe only) and that format was starting to gain popularity.

After some searching, Q Prime was landed as the new management team that could help take Queensrÿche to the next level of superstardom. Ran by the team of Cliff Burnstein and Peter Mensch, they have helped guide the successful careers of Metallica, Dokken, Scorpions, Tesla, Red Hot Chili Peppers and many others. Peter Mensch started out working as a tour accountant for Leiber-Krebs in the 1970s, and was assigned AC/DC as his first client as a manager. He was friends with Burnstein at Mercury Records who asked him to sign Def Leppard when they were having problems with their first managers. Due to a falling out with Leiber-Krebs over royalties for the band, Mensch was fired and he started his own management firm with Burnstein. By 1987, they had built one of the most powerful artist management firms in existence, and one with a reputation for taking care of their talent. "When Peter and Cliff stepped in, they stressed that the creativity should continue to come from us," DeGarmo states. "They just contribute their advice and they don't interfere. We submit everything to Cliff and Peter, and it's them who talk to the record company."

All of the pieces were in now in place. After just over a year of conception, writing and recording, *Operation: Mindcrime* was released on May 3, 1988. Promotional singles of "Revolution Calling" and "Breaking the Silence" had some radio play, but neither one charted. Queensrÿche also recorded a promotional video of the song "Speak", but it just used some live footage of the band playing and didn't include any of the album story concepts or characters. An interesting side note about "Speak"—it was musically written by Michael Wilton, but the guitarist also came up with the lyrics of the chorus, and the song's title: "Speak the word. The word is all of us." The critics responded favorably to the album with very positive reviews in *Kerrang!*, *Metal Forces*, *Raw*, *The Rocket*, and others, but the album didn't quite grab the public initially past the Queensrÿche fan base, at least in America. It was a slow burn on *Operation: Mindcrime* to start, but it would eventually catch fire. "It wasn't really well received at the time," Geoff Tate explains. "It sold exactly the amount that our previous album had sold... It kind of hit the wall sales-

wise. And [EMI-America] were happy with that. They said, 'Okay, we have time to make another record.' And in between the time they said that and the time we actually started making another record, we got an invitation to make a video. MTV called, one of the guys there was a fan, and they said if we made a video, they'd play it. So we put all of our money into making 'Eyes of a Stranger' and it just became a big hit. Immediately the album went gold, then platinum, then double platinum, and it's just been selling ever since."

Q Prime was also instrumental in helping break Queensrÿche on a larger scale by being able to get them on big tours with other bands they managed that were huge. "Q Prime were capable of putting us on any stage in the world," Tate says. "And that's what they did." Queensrÿche started out their tour for *Operation: Mindcrime* opening for Def Leppard on their *Hysteria* tour, on September 7, 1988. They did twenty dates with them through mostly the East Coast in Florida, Georgia, Pennsylvania, New Jersey, Massachusetts and Michigan, ending on October 2, in Wheeling, West Virginia. They jumped onto Metallica's "*Damaged Justice*" tour following that and ended up doing over 100 shows with them, starting with 18 gigs from October 13 – November 5. During this time, the video of "Eyes of a Stranger" was getting a large amount of rotation on MTV, and also significant radio play, and the general public finally started to catch on to the record – especially in the United States.

Due to their larger popularity in England, Queensrÿche jumped over to headline three shows in Hanley, Nottingham, and London, on November 7, 8 and 9, respectively. Then it was back to Europe to continue to the tour with Metallica. They completed 22 more shows with them, before headlining a triumphant New Year's gig at the Seattle Center Coliseum, with Metal Chuch supporting. Queensrÿche performed most of *Operation: Mindcrime* (aside from "Suite Sister Mary," "My Empty Room," and "Waiting for 22"), and it was broadcast live on Z-Rock. They also had a nice Christmas gift from England around that time. By the end of 1988, *Kerrang!*

magazine had ranked *Operation: Mindcrime* at #2 in their "Album Of The Year" poll, and *Sounds* put it at #26.

Following that Seattle New Year's Eve show, it was back out on the road with Metallica for 63 more shows. By then, all the members of both bands had gotten to know each other pretty well and there were some fun antics. "The first night we became friends with Lars, we told him to come on our tour bus, and that was a big mistake," Michael Wilton laughs. "Lars came on with a bottle of *Jägermeister*, which is their

drink of choice. It's got some sort of opiate derivitive in it. We were sitting in the front lounge of the bus, and the whole bottle was gone in three minutes. Then he brought in another one and drank that. Pretty soon, he had his clothes off and was running through the bus." Queensrÿche eventually had to ban the Metallica drummer from their tour bus. "We couldn't invite him back on the bus," says Geoff Tate, smiling, "because he'd come in and pee all over our bathroom and then deny it the next morning." Metallica was notorious for hazing their opening bands and for the final show with Queensrÿche, they said bon voyage in grand fashion with a bevy of male strippers dancing on stage behind their opening band. It was all in good fun though, as Metallica also gifted the band with an opportunity to record the behind the scenes on the road on film. "When we finished the Metallica tour, the band gave us all Sony Minicams as parting gifts. So we've got lots of tapes and footage," Tate relates.

They also saw an old friend, Brett Miller, now in a band named October, on the road during that lengthy tour and showed him some kindness. "In what I believe was 1988, Queensrÿche opened up for Metallica and they got us backstage," Miller says. "We gave Chris DeGarmo our tape, and he literally walked right over and gave it to an A & R lady and asked her to listen to it. We never heard from her after that, but it was still really nice of him to do that."

After 103 shows with Metallica, Queensrÿche finally jumped off for good with a final show in Bloomington, Minnesota, on April 21, 1989. Following that, they headlined the Hammersmith Odeon in London, and the Aardshock Festival in Germany. Then they played the Metal Hammer Festival with Ozzy, performed five more headline solo concerts in Japan from May 4-8, and then finally wrapped it up in California with headlining shows in San Diego, San Jose and at the Irvine Meadows. Following that, they took some much needed time off to recuperate and start work on their next album.

While they were still out with Metallica in April, *Operation: Mindcrime* finally went gold and had sold over half a million copies. By August 1989, it was reported in *The Rocket* that they had sold close to a million copies. The album would go platinum and then eventually double platinum. In September 1989, Queensrÿche released *Video: Mindcrime*, a VHS and Laserdisc (and later DVD) compilation of eight of the songs from *Operation: Mindcrime* (which would also go gold and platinum very quickly and was certified by the RIAA in November 1989). Queensrÿche were finally superstars.

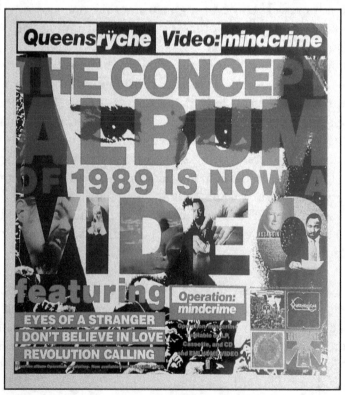

VIDEO: MINDCRIME

 Released on September 26, 1989, on VHS tape by EMI Video in the U.S., and by Picture Music International in the UK and Europe. Also released in Japan on Laserdisc by P.M.I. (Later included on DVD as part of the deluxe *Operation: Mindcrime* box set released by Capitol Records in 2006 and again on the 2021 box set release of *Operation: Mindcrime* in 2021.)

Directed by: Chris Painter and Mark Reshovsky ("Eyes of a Stranger")

Executive producers: Julianna Roberts (for the Foundry), Matt Murray (for EMI).

Executive producers: John Signvatsson and Tim Clawson (for Propaganda Films).

Design by: Reiner Design Consultants.
Management: Q Prime.

Producer: Friend Michael Wells.

Art Direction: Peter V. Sparrow.

Edited by: Lewis Weinberg, Aaron Landry and Tom Acito.

Post-production by: Ute Leonhardt and Steve Lavy.
40 Minutes.

(*Some copies of the tape had a hype sticker on the VHS sleeve and a lyric booklet.)

CAST:

Queensrÿche: Geoff Tate, Chris DeGarmo, Michael Wilton, Eddie Jackson and Scott Rockenfield.

Newscaster: Ron Blair

Police Detective: Paul Greenstein.

Nikki: Dennis Henning.

Father William: Ray Jarris.

Dr. X: Milan Melvin.

Orderly: Said Naber

Sister Mary: Chantelle Sims.

Police Detective: Friend Michael Wells.

Nurse: Sandra Lee Williams

Federal Agents: Jeff Brown, David Garrison and Patrick McArdle

VIDEOS:

"I Remember Now"
"Anarchy-X"
"Revolution Calling"
"Operation: Mindcrime"
"Speak"
"Breaking the Silence"
"I Don't Believe in Love"
"Waiting for 22"
"Eyes of a Stranger"

After the *Operation: Mindcrime* album had finally caught fire and took off, due much in part to the "Eyes of a Stranger" video in heavy rotation on MTV, Queensrÿche had options. The band could use the budget EMI was providing (amount unknown) to finance another video or two, or they could use the money to shoot a long form home video using mostly live footage that would be performed at one location and be spliced with some conceptual footage to tie it all together. The band opted for the latter, and *Video: Mindcrime* was born. The songs chosen from the *Operation: Mindcrime* storyline were performed using scenes and images shot with actors playing the characters from the story such as: Nikki, Sister Mary and Dr. X. That footage is mixed with images of riots, war and other historical events. There are also words flashed on the large video screens, when the band is shown playing on stage, that help the viewer get an idea what is going on in the storyline.

The video opens with "I Remember Now" playing while it shows Nikki laying back in chair, in a dark room, with two hallways running opposite directions. It almost looks black and white the way it was shot. It next goes to "Anarchy-X" and shows a collage various images of war, riots and other historical events as the credits roll. This continues through "Revolution Calling" as well. "Operation: Mindcrime" shows Dr. X recruiting Nikki to carry out his nefarious plan. Images of Dr. X handing Nikki a white folded envelope package (likely photos of who he wants assassinated, money or drugs) and then showing him the gun, loading a bullet into the chamber and playing "Russian Roulette" is especially effective. "Speak" continues the storyline and shows images of Nikki lighting a candle, waiting by the phone in his apartment and reflecting on what Dr. X hired him to do. A shot flashes on the screen of a newscaster and somebody in a photo with the word "Assassination" next to it. It ends with a shot of somebody painting "Revolution = Power" in paint on a wall. The next video, "Breaking the Silence" was shot live and just shows the band on stage. Following that, "I Don't Believe in Love" shows a considerable amount of imagery of Nikki in the interrogation chair with a voice-over saying accusingly, "Why did you do it?" As the song continues, the video shows Nikki flashing back on the events that led to him being there. Sister Mary lighting a candle in church, turning around with a knife in her hand and dead on the pulpit with a bit of blood on the side of her lips. It also shows Dr. X approaching Mary with Rosary beads in his hand, Nikki sitting on the concrete and writing "Love" in chalk and then crossing it out, and various shots of Nikki, Mary and Dr. X interspersed throughout. "Waiting for 22" features shots of the band performing live combined with footage of Nikki remembering the events leading up to this point—kissing Mary, the aforementioned interrogation, images of Mary as a prostitute working the streets, and finally, Mary with a knife in her hand, and Nikki discovering her on the floor of the church, dead. The video concludes with "Eyes of a Stranger" depicting Nikki being wheeled into a hospital with a Nurse looking at him and Dr. X turning around dressed as a doctor. It flashes multiple images of Mary, Dr. X and Nikki throughout the video and those speed up quicker as the story concludes.

Even though some songs and vignettes from the album were left out ("Spreading the Disease," "The Mission," "Suite Sister Mary." "The Needle Lies," "Electric Requiem" and "My Empty Room"), it still works as an abridged way to tell the story. There is enough imagery and key scenes included to help illustrate the concept from *Operation: Mindcrime*. It likely would have improved the video to have included those additional tracks with more images and scenes with the actors interspersed throughout, but that was not the case. As it stands, many Queensrÿche fans still identify the faces of Nikki, Sister Mary, and Dr. X with the actors that portrayed them in the music videos here.

Notable on *Video: Mindcrime* was also a clue (answer) to the demise of Sister Mary. If you watch past the credits, an alternate version of the "I Don't Believe in Love" video appears. Toward the end of the song, as Tate sings "the pain that you feel," the word "suicide" briefly flashes on the screen, following an image of Mary lying dead on the floor. It is the only time the word appears and disappears rapidly.

Much like Pink Floyd, who had huge mainstream success with a dark and complex concept album in *The Wall*, Queensrÿche managed to hit a nerve with the public with their own foray into that realm. They were able to fuse progressive rock into heavy metal and make it accessible without compromising their sound or style or heaviness to gain acceptance. As time went on, *Operation: Mindcrime* would be considered one of the best albums of all-time, ranking high up in many lists in various publications such as: *Kerrang!*'s "The 100 Greatest Heavy Metal Albums Of All Time" (#34); *Kerrang!*'s "100 Albums You Must Hear Before You Die" (#70); *The Top 500 Heavy Metal Albums Of All Time* – By Martin Popoff (#7); *Terrorizer* "The Most Important Albums Of The `80s" (no order); *Classic Rock* "The 100 Greatest Rock Albums Of All Time" (#42); *Decibel* "Hall Of Fame" (#80); and *Rolling Stone* "The 100 Greatest Heavy Metal Albums Of All Time" (#67).

PHOTOGRAPHER UNKNOWN.
FROM THE COLLECTION OF BRIAN HEATON

QUEENSRYCHE LIVE, 1988-1989.

FROM THE COLLECTION OF BRIAN HEATON.
UNKNOWN IN-STORE EVENT FROM 1988-1989.

Queensrÿche

MARY X-MAS AND HAPPY HOLIDAYS

Queensrÿche

Operation:mindcrime

"Queensryche are not only one of today's most creative bands but also one of hard rock's most consistent live performers."

"Metal music needs Queensryche!"

"...Metal you can believe in."

"Queensryche have pushed forward the parameters of rock music..."

"...metal with muscle—Music that is designed for staying power."

THE NEW SINGLE AND VIDEO
I DON'T BELIEVE IN LOVE (50014)

DON'T MISS QUEENSRYCHE'S "OPERATION: MINDCRIME" HOME VIDEO.
AVAILABLE THIS JULY!

DEMAND QUEENSRYCHE NOW!

EMI

Queensrÿche   Operation: mindcrime

REVOLUTION CALLING

REVOLUTION CALLING

Queensrÿche
Operation: mindcrime

REVOLUTION CALLING

REVOLUTION CALLING

Queensrÿche

SPEAK THE WORD.

Queensrÿche Operation:mindcrime

CHAPTER 10:
BUILDING EMPIRES

After the success of *Operation: Mindcrime*, Queensrÿche started work on their fourth full-length album. Having finally broke through with a big hit album, the pressure for most bands was usually on to continue that trend. But by then, the band had established a level of trust with their management and record label that left them free to explore and come up with a great follow-up. Thanks to *Operation: Mindcrime*, the Queensrÿche back catalog continued to sell and everybody was reaping the benefits. Chris DeGarmo on their relationship with EMI-America by that point: "They're cool. They just want us to make a good record. It's kinda nice to have a relationship like that. I think the days where record companies played God are over. EMI doesn't hurry us. They did get involved early on in our career, but now the deal is that if the band and management are happy, then they don't mess with things."

Queensrÿche started working up new material in the fall of 1989. As usual, DeGarmo and Michael Wilton mainly composed the music, and Tate most of the lyrics, but this time Eddie Jackson and Scott Rockenfield started bringing more to the table. They co-wrote "Another Rainy Night (Without You)" and "Della Brown" (the latter thought of by many as Queensrÿche's take on the blues) respectively. Rockenfield had previously written the music to the segue piece, "Electric Requiem," on *Operation: Mindcrime*, but this time his contribution expanded to a full song. DeGarmo was especially prolific and steered the direction of *Empire*, writing or co-writing nine of the 11 songs on the record, as well as "Last Time in Paris," a non-LP song that originally appeared on the soundtrack for *The Adventures of Ford Fairlane*, which hit theaters on June 12, 1990. Queensrÿche actually submitted "Empire" for the film, but the studio thought it was "too serious" so the band sent them "Last Time in Paris." The majority of the album was produced again by Peter Collins with James "Jimbo" Barton back as engineer. The song "Empire," was recorded first at Triad Studios and produced by Paul Northfield. Tom Hall assisted on the boards. The rest of the record was recorded at the Vancouver Studios in Canada. Michael Kamen returned to help with orchestration. *Empire* took around three months to make and was completed in late spring 1990. It was mixed by Jimbo Barton at Royal Recorders Studio in Lake Geneva, Wisconsin, and mastered again at Masterdisk in New York by Bob Ludwig (back from his work on *Operation: Mindcrime*).

When they were all done, Queensrÿche had a more commerical-sounding release, and one that showed huge growth for the band. The musical performances and songwriting were more refined, but maintained a level of technicality, excitement and energy the band always seem to generate. Lyrically, the songs on *Empire* showcased the band's social consciousness. Some of the songs reflected the mood of the post-Reagan Administration country. Tales consumed by gun control, drugs, violence ("Empire"), the environment ("Resistance") and homelessness ("Della Brown") peppered the record. Other songs were more personal in nature, relating to life after stardom and the pursuit of dreams. "Silent Lucidity" featured the string orchestration of Michael Kamen. This helped create an ethereal mood to a magical song. The band had created an album full of songs that were much more accessible than those they had written before, and yet they did not fall into the category of "selling out" to achieve this new level of success.

"We didn't want to repeat ourselves [with *Empire*]," Chris DeGarmo elaborated at the time. "It cheapens the original to sit there and do a sequel, so to speak. So we just thought we'd leave *Operation: Mindcrime*'s story where it is. And the idea of doing a completely different concept didn't sound too appealing, as we didn't want to get stuck doing different concept records for the rest of our lives. So we chose to make a record that took a different approach in the way it was composed, like the fact the lyrics aren't in sequential order, like on *Mindcrime*. It was really a matter of wiping the slate clean and getting to the next step. There are songs that deal with social issues and songs that deal with personal relationships. We tried to write things that are interesting. One thing about *Empire* is that it's more diverse. *Mindcrime* was slower to change direction, with the mood set up on side one that just slowly wrapped around to side two; the first five songs were just in your face. With this record, we're just showing the light, shade and contour of the band much more. It's also more of a dynamic record in showing the different styles that the band can do. From a melodic standpoint, we're becoming better songwriters."

Empire was released on August 20, 1990. It landed at number nine on the Billboard charts and sold well from the start. This time, EMI-America really got behind Queensrÿche and pushed the record right out of the gate. The title track was the first single released from the album and hit #22 on the single charts in September. It got very good radio rotation and the video a lot of play on MTV on *Headbanger's Ball* and so on. The label did a lot of print and radio advertising around the album and it started to build much quicker this time. They headed out on tour in support of *Empire* starting October 29, 1990, in Dublin, Ireland, with Lynch Mob opening for them. They played 27 dates on through the UK and Europe on through December 6, 1990. A break for the holidays after that and then on to the Rock In Rio Festival on Janauary 23, 1991, along with: Guns N' Roses, Megadeth, Billy Idol, INXS, and Run-DMC. Following that, Queensrÿche headlined five shows in Japan with dates in Tokyo, Osaka and Yokohama from January 29 – February 6, 1991. It was during this Japan run that vocalist Pamela Moore would make her live debut with Queensrÿche, reprising her role as "Sister Mary." Following the Japan leg, the band took a couple of months off, and would kick off its U.S. tour in mid-April.

During this time (February 1991), "Silent Lucidity" was released as the second single from *Empire* and shot up the charts to #1. A very Pink Floyd-esque ballad written by Chris DeGarmo about lucid dreaming, it broke through to the pop markets and fans not normally into heavy metal or hard rock music. "The song is about dream control, which is something I've really gotten into the past few years; the ability to realize that you're dreaming, recognize it, and actually participate in the dream, shape it, change it," DeGarmo explained at the time. "I had never had the opportunity to present it in song form, to talk about it. It required much more immense production, simply because I wanted it to take on the scope of a dream; this limitless landscape that was changing as it approached- what I call the dream sequence. It starts turning into a nightmare, with these intense audio images coming at you from different sides, just like a dream. Lyrically, it's about a little child who has a nightmare about someone close to him dying. He wakes up completely emotionally shaken and crying, and a parent figure comes in and tells him, 'Hush, it's just a dream/Wide awake you face the day/The dream is over, or has it just begun.'"

Queensrÿche finally had a chart-topping song. Subsequent single releases from the album also charted well with "Best I Can" hitting #28 in June of that year, "Jet City Woman" making #6 in August, "Another Rainy Night (Without You)" charting at #7 by November and "Anybody Listening?" landing on #16 in February 1992. Almost two years after *Empire* was released, Queensrÿche was still having singles fom the album do well. This also pushed the album itself up higher in the Billboard charts to #7 as it's final ranking. *Empire* was certified gold and platinum by the RIAA on January 7, 1991, and double platinum that December. It would eventually be certified triple platinum by October of 1994. It also helped boost sales for the band's back catalog and their previous releases all went gold or platinum by 1991 as well.

It was during this tour that Chris DeGarmo and Michael Wilton debuted their signature "Tri-Ryche" guitars from ESP.

QUEENSRŸCHE AND ESP GUITARS

By James R. Beach

ESP (Electric Sound Products) was founded by Hisatake Shibuya in Tokyo, Japan, in 1975. It was first launched as a shop that provided custom guitar replacement parts. They expanded shortly after that to making guitars under the ESP and Navigator brands. In 1983, ESP was introduced to the United States and began making custom guitars for musicians such as: Bruce Kulick (KISS), George Lynch (Dokken, Lynch Mob), Page Hamilton (Helmet), Vernon Reid (Living Colour), Vinnie Vincent (KISS, Vinnie Vincent Invasion) and others. James Hetfield and Kirk Hammett of Metallica also became sponsors in the late 1980s.

Michael Wilton and Chris DeGarmo had previously played various Fender Stratocasters, Kramer "Super Strats", Gibson, etc. They both started to use ESP guitars around the time of the *Operation: Mindcrime* tour, and became endorsed by ESP in early 1990. Hammett and Hetfield were using ESP by that time and encouraged Wilton and DeGarmo to check them out. They purchased their first ESP guitars while playing in New York. The Queensrÿche bandmates helped design their own special, custom-made guitars that were made for both, for the *Empire* tour. A white, single-necked, strat-style model was produced for Chris with a Tri-Ryche logo underneath the lower pickups and bridge (The Empire-D model). A reverse black model was created for Wilton with a light grey Tri-Ryche symbol in the same place. A special double-necked model with 12-string and 6-string necks was also done for DeGarmo for the *Empire* tour.

DeGarmo would additionally use a special multi-colored "Andy Warhol" model, and a guitar with a body in the shape of the Tri-Ryche symbol.

It is also notable that around the time that DeGarmo and Wilton started their endorsements with ESP, they also changed their amplifiers and effects from their Marshall JCM 800's and various pedals, as well as Celestion Vintage 30 Speakers, to Bradshaw rigs and Yamaha rack-mounted digital effects processors—which likely helped give them a "warmer tone" overall on *Empire*. Soldano amplifiers were also utilized at that time. In later years, Wilton switched to Krank amps (around 2009) and by 2020 was using the Kemper amplifier processer on tours.

Wilton has continued to use ESP guitars over the years and has had a number of different models with one with multiple Tri-Ryche images on the body, and the popular "Skull" model MW-600 (featuring multiple skull images on the body that glow in the dark on the signature models). Many of the different types have been made available to the public for purchase over the years, including a 25th Anniversary ESP *Empire* model in 2015 (with the classic Seymour Duncan pickups and Floyd Rose locking tremelo system).

After their time off, Queensrÿche started their North American tour with Suicidal Tendencies in support. They played 69 shows total with them from April 15, 1991 (starting in Amarillo, Texas) and wrapping it up on July 31, in Hartford, CT. Following that, it was back overseas to be part of the famous Monsters Of Rock Festival for 17 dates on through Europe, and in the UK at Castle Donnington. AC/DC headlined it with Metallica, Motley Crue, and the Black Crowes joining Queensrÿche on the bill. They wrapped up the huge concerts in September, and then it was on to Oakland, California, with Metallica for the "Day on the Green" show (with Faith No More and Soundgarden rounding out the lineup) on October 12.

Queensrÿche then continued on their headlining tour on through the United States and Canada with Warrior Soul joining them as openers. They played 31 dates with them starting on October 17, and continuing on through December 15, 1991—which included three nights at the Long Beach Arena.

During this time, Queensrÿche released the *Operation: LIVEcrime* box set on November 5, 1991. This included the complete album the band had been performing live during this tour. It was taken from three dates earlier that year (May 10-12) in Madison, Milwaukee and LaCrosse, Wisconsin. It was rumored that the band was so dialed-in, that they could have used any of the three performances by themselves for the release. The only miscues during the three nights was Wilton breaking a string, and Geoff flubbing one line of lyrics.

The original packaging of *Operation: LIVEcrime* was a box set that included a CD or cassette, a VHS videotape and a special libretto. (It was later released as a standalone DVD/CD in 2001.) It went to #61 on the Billboard charts and was certified gold, platinum and then double

platinum by January 1992. Wayne Isham—who had done videos for David Bowie, Def Leppard, Motley Crue, Michael Jackson and many others—directed the film. Pamela Moore also joined the band onstage for these performances. "I think the first time we ever sang the song "Suite Sister Mary" together was when I toured with them on the [Building Empires] tour," Moore says. "Nothing can ever compare to the adrenaline rush you get singing in front of so many fans. It was then I realized how fortunate I was to have been able to participate in something so special."

Queensrÿche concluded their *Building Empires* tour in the Pacific Northwest from December 28, 1991 through January 3, 1992. Gigs took place at the Pacific Coliseum in Vancouver, B.C., the Memorial Coliseum in Portland, Oregon, back-to-back nights at the Seattle Center Coliseum in Seattle, and at the Spokane Coliseum in Spokane, Washington. The Spokane show was a bit different. Being the last full production of the tour, Queensrÿche filmed footage for the "Anybody Listening?" video at the show and performed the song five times. As a result, "Della Brown" and "Last Time in Paris," which had been in the encore during the latter leg of the tour, were dropped from the setlist.

Local band Sweet Sister Sam (featuring keyboardist Randy Gane, ex-Heir Apparent singer Steve Benito, ex-Fifth Angel guitarist Kendall Bechtel and Uncle Sam/Pistol Moon bassist Tim Johnston) opened for Queensrÿche for the five dates on through January 3, 1992. "We were very happy to see *Empire* received so well, and we enjoyed touring off it," Chris DeGarmo beams. "We were out on tour for 14 months, and could've gone on longer, but I think that we were getting a little burned out. I know that it wasn't the longest tour in the world, but when it starts grinding a bit..." He pauses, "It was fun, but we just got to the point where we decided to stop because we were ready to come home and do something else."

Post-tour, Queensrÿche made an appearance at the Grammy Awards in February after being nominated for two Grammys that year. They had already celebrated winning a "NW Area Music Choice Award," Concrete Music's "Best Hard Rock Band," and an MTV "Viewers Choice Award" the previous year. In April 1992, they did the *MTV Unplugged* show with an all-acoustic set. Queensrÿche performed eight songs, but only six were aired to fit within the show's time length. "I Will Remember", "The Killing Words", "Della Brown", "Silent Lucidity", "Scarborough Fair" and "The Lady Wore Black" made the cut and some were performed multiple times. "Anybody Listening?" and a cover of Neil Young's "Rockin' In The Free World" didn't get aired.

The show found the Queensrÿche guys in good spirits, with the band joking and goofing around. Chris DeGarmo teases playing "Suite Sister Mary" while Geoff Tate goes wide-eyed and fakes leaving the stage. The performance of "Anybody Listening?" didn't seem to be planned. Video bootlegs of the raw gig footage showed the band trying to figure out what else to play, with Eddie Jackson hesitant to play "Anybody Listening?" After some cajoling by the fans in attendance, Ed agrees to come in on the parts that he remembers. They start the first take, and Michael Wilton plays the wrong part, getting everyone to laugh. Stopping and restarting, Queensrÿche completes the song and receives a raucous ovation. The show was very popular and continued to fuel sales for the band.

Queensrÿche's last show for 1992, and what would also be their last show for a couple of years, was the Rock & The Environment benefit at the Gorge Amphitheatre in George, Washington, on June 6. They joined Heart, Alice In Chains, Metal Church, War Babies, The Walkabouts, Bananafish and Rumours of the Big Wave. The highlight was members of Queensrÿche performing renditions of the Rolling Stones "Gimme Shelter" and the Beatles' "Revolution" with members of Heart, Alice in Chains and War Babies. Queensrÿche also included some rarely-played songs in their set such as "No Sanctuary," and "The Killing Words." They added "Anybody Listening?" as well.

Another long form video was also created, titled *Building Empires*. The release was a compilation showing Queensrÿche's evolution over the last decade through videos and live footage and some of the *MTV Unplugged* broadcast. Mary Lambert (*Pet Sematary*) directed the in-between commentary of Chris DeGarmo, Geoff Tate and Michael Wilton. "I don't think it was designed as any sort of lure to catch people who just stumbled across us," responds Chris with his usual honesty. "I don't think that any of our videos have been like that. We decided to put it out mainly because we had such a wealth of film just lying around, including some that we hadn't included on… *LIVE:crime*. But we didn't want to rip our fans off just by putting out a couple of tunes and nothing else. We tried to put as much as possible on there, making it a bit

more collectible." Fans seemed to agree. *Building Empires* was initially released on October 20, 1992, and it sold very well. It was certified gold by the RIAA on January 4, 1993. It was also reissued on DVD in 2001, and the 30th anniversary edition of *Empire* released in June 2021.

After two years on the road, Queensrÿche had become big stars, but it came with a high cost....

VARIOUS EMPIRE-ERA PROMOTIONAL ITEMS

Various Empire-era Cover Stories

CHAPTER 11:
ROAD TO THE PROMISED LAND

Almost every big success comes with a high price. Queensrÿche was very much feeling this after their two-year album and tour cycle around *Empire*. Their time on the road increased with every record and by 1992, it had started to take a toll on both the band members themselves, and their relationships. There were rumors that Queensrÿche might break up, and Tate said he had thoughts about leaving the band at that time, as did DeGarmo. Although the band started coming up with song ideas and writing toward the next album as early as the summer of 1992, *Promised Land* wouldn't be completed until the late spring of 1994.

"It wasn't planned, it just kinda happened," Geoff Tate explains. "After the *Empire* tour we all went our separate ways for a while. Before we knew it eight months had gone by. *Empire* bought us a lot of time, really. Before that album it had been just a hectic schedule of recording and touring. Its success allowed us to have a nice break, something we hadn't known until then." At the time, Tate had changed his look by cutting his hair short and growing a beard during their furlough. "It was strange taking time off," Geoff continues. "I think it was at that point it dawned on us that we'd achieved all the goals we'd set. It was actually kinda difficult to know which move to make next."

The music scene had changed drastically during the time Queensrÿche had released *Empire* in 1990 and toured around the world for it. The so-called "Grunge" music that had launched out of Seattle into the public consciousness, had started to wipe away most of the polished, glam-type metal and hard rock coming out of Los Angeles, and would eventually bury it. It was now about dressing down, detuning, and deconstruction, and darker and more introspective subjects about depression, drugs, abuse and how we fit into society (or don't). Alice in Chains, Nirvana, Pearl Jam, Soundgarden and Mudhoney (and to a lesser degree Gruntruck, Love Battery, My Sister's Machine, Sweet Water and others) had shot out of Seattle and helped erase the good time, L.A. party vibe of style over substance.

Members of Queensrÿche were dealing with some of their own demons around that time, which helped fuel their next album. "The thing is," Geoff Tate reflects, "after years of struggling you suddenly have this success, money and everything that you'd think would make someone happy, but it really doesn't. When I get stuck into a project I become so obsessed with it that everything else in my life falls apart. I got to the stage where I really wasn't very happy. I realized that everything I'd been working for musically I'd accomplished."

Scott Rockenfield had his own relationship problems at the time. He had just split from his wife, Cara Kaye Whitney—who he had dated for five years during the mid-1980s, and eventually married on September 28, 1991 (they divorced a while later in 1996). Scott had moved into an apartment in downtown Seattle and was back to the single life. A Porsche 911 Carrera helped soften the blow there, despite the painful breakup. "It was a goal!" Scott laughs. "I always wanted to have one. The insurance costs a fortune, but I wouldn't part with it!" Tate had his own relationship struggles as well. "Before we had the time off, I never realized how little time my wife and I spent together," the singer explains. We had this long-distance relationship which worked fine, so being around each other so much it was almost like we had to re-discover one another again." Despite the positive outlook there for Tate, he and his wife Suzanne (who he based the lyrics of "Jet City Woman" on), would split up before long. His wife divorced him and Tate ended up broke and living on his boat. She was awarded all of his songwriting royalties on up through the *Empire* album—likely a sizable amount back then given how popular Queensrÿche was at that time, and how well their albums were still selling. It was rumored DeGarmo even helped Geoff keep a roof over his head during this time by paying his rent, or letting him stay at his house, or both.

Michael Wilton, like Tate and Rockenfield, also felt the strain on his personal life. "I think I got a little burnt from touring," he admits. "I felt consumed by the entity that is Queensrÿche. I love playing on stage, but everything else that goes with touring wreaks havoc after the first six weeks. I felt I had to re-discover myself a little." Chris

DeGarmo had his own issues around their success: "I don't think of myself as an unhappy person, but you think that money might limit the struggle. The thing is, I was so passionate about what we were doing that I never noticed we were struggling anyway! If anything, I think I'm more appreciative of the personal time I get to spend with my wife and daughter." Wilton had other problems with investments in chocolate and coffee companies that went south, and he was also trying to recover from some dependency issues (Michael had an alter ego called "SPIKE" back in the day that reared its head when he had consumed too much alcohol. On the *Promised Land* tour, he had a statement, "SPIKE IS DEAD," on his guitar picks). Eddie Jackson also saw the videogame stores he invested in fail and close down.

While DeGarmo was the most stable of the five members, he felt the strain of being out on the road most of the time, and had missed his wife and had not been able to see his kids growing up very much (which would inspire one of the most popular songs on *Promised Land*, in part). So, he worked very hard to make sure the time spent with his family was quality. He also earned his pilot's license during the time off, which would later become very significant. Chris was the glue that kept them together at this time and eventually corralled his bandmates back into the studio. Without him pushing, it's very likely the record would not have happened...

Even though the members of Queensrÿche were on hiatus in 1993, they still managed to stay in the public eye with a song contributed to the soundtrack of the Arnold Schwarzenegger film, *The Last Action Hero*, which was released on June 8, 1993. Titled "Real World," there isn't any info on when the song was actually recorded, other than saying it was during the sessions for *Promised Land*. More likely it was done during the *Empire* sessions, or shortly thereafter, as Peter Collins produced it and it was co-written by Michael Kamen. Neither one of those guys worked on *Promised Land*, so it seems more like that was the case. "Real World" was released as a single (one of five released by a variety of bands from the popular soundtrack) in advance of the film on May 31, 1993, well before the band members started recording material for their next album. The song itself did very well for Queensrÿche and hit #3 on the Billboard charts.

What the members of the band were going through, with adjusting to the price of fame and success, helped shape what became the "theme" of *Promised Land*. They started working up ideas separately before going into a studio to record the album. "Once the tour had ended we worked on stuff at home," Geoff Tate states. "We'd all invested in this home studio gear, and it was a very creative time, so we were able to tape every idea that came into our heads. We were on a roll. Previously, we'd made very inaccurate sketches of what we'd wanted to do before recording. This gave us a real opportunity to experiment." DeGarmo continues: "We just kept saving all the noodling that we did on tape at home. I'd put together this network of portable digital recorders that allowed us to send our ideas back and forth and add to them. As things began to develop, we'd get together and record over at Scott's parents' place to get the rhythm section worked in." The old "Dungeon" practice room in the Rockenfield's garage, that Queensrÿche had initially formed and developed in, was still set up and served as a convenient location for both rehearsing and recording. Triad Studios was also utilized for some recording with their old friend Tom Hall assisting. "We tracked some piano that was never used and also did some editing," explains Hall. "We also ended up doing lots of post-production work at Scott's parents' house, in Redmond, between tracking the record on San Juan Island and mixing at Studio X. Triad was only a couple of miles away and was convenient if we needed tools that we didn't have at the Rockenfield's."

Eventually, Queensrÿche had enough material worked up to go into the studio and lay down the tracks. "It probably took between eight to twelve months before we finally had what we wanted to go with," recalls Tate. "Finally, we pooled all our studio equipment together and had it built into this huge log cabin that we'd found up in the San Juan Islands, north of here." James "Jimbo" Barton once again was tapped to help them capture the music on the boards and this time he served as co-producer with the band, and head engineer.

As they had developed the music and lyrics, Tate and DeGarmo recognized the theme running through the songs. "We'd all begun to look at our lives, ourselves, and began wondering who we were and where we were at," states Tate. "Because *Empire* was such an economic success it changed our lifestyles dramatically. It was a difficult thing to get used to. We'd all come from backgrounds where money was tight. Suddenly you're in the high tax bracket and people are treating you differently. It was a very strange thing."

"There were a couple of tracks that I had written, and Geoff had begun writing lyrics for, where we hadn't really talked about what we were going to do, but we noticed there was this sense of introspection becoming evident," reveals DeGarmo. Rockenfield also continued his recent trend of bringing more to the songwriting table with the music for "Dis-con-nec-ted", the intro piece "9:28 a.m.", and co-credits on the title track and "My Global Mind." "Dis-con-nec-ted" was written on keyboard and had a shuffle beat. DeGarmo took the idea and translated it to guitar for the version of the song that landed on the album. Chris states on Scott: "Scott's a real creative force in this band, especially on the last couple of albums he's really started to take off. He's set in his mind he's going to be a writer now." Jackson also came up with parts for some of the songs and landed a co-credit on the title track as well. Michael Wilton, who had always been a major contributor in the songwriting for the band, was left out a bit on this one. "The way we set it all up was really innovative and allowed us to be more inspired, but a lot of the songs I came up with didn't get finished, because the album kinda went in a different direction," Wilton says. "It was actually a bit more left-field to the way I think, but once I saw how things were going and heard the finished record, I realized that it was a really sensitive, special recording. Geoff really opened himself up. It was a cleansing for him in a sense." Tate's lyrics for the song "Damaged" were very personal and at the time cathartic. "That's really what [that song] is about, recognizing where I've come from as a person and what's shaped me," Tate explains. "Through finding out who you are as a person, or where you've been, helps you figure out where you are going to go."

Then there is "Out of Mind," where Tate talks about a childhood experience visiting a mental hospital. During a Tate solo acoustic show in March 2017, the singer revealed the genesis of the song, explaining to the audience that his mother worked in a mental hospital when Tate was a child, and often took him to work with her (she was a single parent at the time). As a result, Tate observed a lot of interesting behavior from the patients. During the *Promised Land* sessions, Tate told the story to DeGarmo, who according to Tate, was so inspired by the story, he came back the next night with "Out of Mind" completely written.

The "cleansing" for Tate on "Damaged" also applied to DeGarmo in some of the songs such as, "Bridge," which deals with his father leaving his mother when he and his brother were very young, and then showing back up much later on. This unresolved situation fueled the song, along with missing his own family out on the road, which asked the question of, "How can there be a 'bridge' between two people in a relationship that was never built?" DeGarmo later said he was able to resolve it to some degree with his father before he passed away, but it was something many people were able to relate to in the world. "Someone Else?", which ended up being the last song on the album, is a haunting, powerful piano-led song that was quite personal to Tate as well.

The album version of "Someone Else?", however, didn't materialize until most of the record had already been completed. Initially, the song was a full band effort, running over seven minutes in length (Queensrÿche had become known for their epic album closers over the past few records). At the end of the *Promised Land* sessions, DeGarmo had come up with the alternate piano take of "Someone Else?", and Tate's vocals were spliced from the original version (cutting out some verses) and put on top of it. The band felt the stripped-down version better fit the vibe of the record, so it replaced the original full band recording. "Someone Else?" was issued as a promotional single in late 1995 (perhaps to start hyping the *Queensrÿche's Promised Land* CD-ROM game that would follow in 1996), with both versions of the song on the CD.

Another tune often asked about is "Dirty Lil' Secret" which appeared initially as a b-side on the import CD single version of "I Am I." Written by Chris DeGarmo and Geoff Tate, "Dirty Lil' Secret" is an enigma—not much is known about the track. Although it was included on the remastered editions of *Empire* over the years, "Dirty Lil' Secret" first saw the light of day in 1994. The song was likely written and recorded around the same time as "Real World." Once the recording was done, it was mixed by Barton and the band at the Bad Animals Studio in Seattle in the summer of 1994. Bad Animals was formerly Steve Lawson's studio—where Metal Church, Fifth Angel, Sanctuary and many others had recorded—before Heart's Ann and Nancy Wilson bought in as partners and renamed it. *Promised Land* was mastered by Stephen Marcussen at Precision Lacquer (later renamed "Precision Mastering" in Los Angeles). Don Tyler helped with some digital editing and effects. Hugh Syme (Rush, Fates Warning, etc.), did most of the album artwork. The striking Tri-Ryche totem pole, however, was created by Harold Alfred, an artist from Victoria, British Columbia, Canada.

On the evening of October 10, 1994, the members of Queensrÿche stepped out of a Cessna prop plane, piloted by guitarist Chris DeGarmo, onto the tarmac at Boeing Field. The band hosted what was likely the quietest record release party ever. Their new album, *Promised Land*, was scheduled for release on the following Tuesday, but this Saturday evening, 1,500 Queensrÿche fans RSVP'd to get on the guest list for this unique event. The listening party was held at Seattle's Museum of Flight next to the airfield. The eager guests were handed a folded CD lyric sheet for the new record and directed to headphone listening stations throughout the museum. Once the music began, fans quietly listened while the new music played in their ears. An occasional gasp, "Ooh" and other more colorful euphemisms were uttered during the listening portion of the program. When the final strains of "Someone Else?" faded out, the cavernous room erupted in cheers and clapping. An announcement was made that the band would be hanging out awhile for a meet and greet and that all who attended "could keep the headphones!" MTV's *Headbanger's Ball* host Riki Rachtman asked Eddie Jackson what he thought about the new album. Eddie jokingly stated, "It's better than CATS!" (Referring to the popular Broadway show.)

Promised Land was released finally on October 18, 1994. It sold briskly and entered the U.S. Billboard charts at #3, the highest the band had charted so far. It also landed in the top-20 in the European, UK and Japanese charts as well. "I Am I" was the first single off the album, and received considerable radio play and hit #8 on the single charts. According to *The Rocket*, it was #2 on the local store sales list. By the end of the year, the album had slid down to #78 on the Billboard charts supposedly (according to *The Rocket* again), but it was still in the top-20 for local sales and would be certified both gold and platinum by the RIAA on December 13, 1994. Not bad for a band that had went back to the darker, progressive style of their second album, *Rage for Order*, as well as embraced the brooding introspection and heavier, down-tuned groove of the modern local music. Some fans who had discovered Queensrÿche during the success of *Operation: Mindcrime* and *Empire* had trouble relating to the more complex and proggy album, but many long-time Queensrÿche fans embraced the record. The second single, "Bridge," helped alleviate that some with a ballad that many connected to, much like they had with "Silent Lucidity", and that song charted a bit higher at #6 in early 1995. "Dis-con-nec-ted" was also issued as a single. "Someone Else?" was the final single released during 1995, and charted in the U.S. Top 40 again at #32. *Promised Land* also did well elsewhere and went gold in Canada, and charted in the top 20 in the UK, Europe and Japan.

Queensrÿche headed out on the road in support of *Promised Land,* kicking it off with the first show on October 20, 1994, at the Astoria Theater in London. The gig was reported in

Kerrang! magazine to have sold out in a few hours after being announced about a week or so before. They played four more shows that month, including a showcase for their record company, and some special live radio broadcasts in Italy and Sweden. The band then took the holidays off to spend some time with their families before heading out for the main tour. Starting on February 9, 1995, they played 23 dates in the UK and Europe, with Static-X and others opening. Then they headed over to Japan for seven dates booked by their old friend Mr. Udo. Following that, it was back to England for a shoot in the MTV studios there for their "Most Wanted" show, and then a landmark concert at the famous Royal Albert Hall.

Then it was back to America to continue on the road. Former Carnivore singer Peter Steele's brooding, goth-metal band, Type O Negative, opened for them for 69 dates from April 14 on through July 27, 1995. Although a heavier group than the headliner, they certainly harkened back to Queensrÿche's goth-prog masterpiece *Rage for Order*. Type O Negative had recently broken out with their third album for Roadrunner, *Bloody Kisses*, in 1993, which catapulted them to triple platinum status as well. A popular cover of the Seals and Crofts

hit, "Summer Breeze," helped them achieve their success, along with the hit "Black No. 1." The set for Queensrÿche on this tour consisted of huge video screens, live-projection laserdisc technology and a set change to a bar backdrop where the band played on a small stage in the corner and Tate portrayed a drunk while he sang "Promised Land." Various fans (mostly from the band's fan club) were allowed to come up on stage and be some of the bar "patrons", as well as photographers and reporters chasing Tate around during "I Am I." The setlist consisted of a significant portion of songs from the new album, as well as selections from *Empire, Operation: Mindcrime*, and a couple older tracks from *Rage for Order* and *The Warning*. Of note, Queensrÿche performed abridged versions of "NM 156" and "Screaming in Digital," helping fuel the fan discussion that the two songs were intended to be linked, thematically. In addition, a third version of "Someone Else?" was born—a hybrid between the full band and album cuts of the tune. Queensrÿche closed the show with song, beginning it with just DeGarmo on piano and Tate on vocals. Slowly, the other band members would come out, with Wilton adding an emotional lead guitar, Jackson slowly strumming his bass, and Rockenfield on percussion. During the trek on through the United States, Queensrÿche stopped in the Northwest, playing the Gorge Amphitheatre, in George, Washington, on May 26, 1995 and the Memorial Coliseum in Portland, Oregon, on May 27. The show in George was especially significant for one member of the band, as Eddie Jackson used the opportunity to propose on stage to his longtime girlfriend, Theresa Golden. She said yes.

Queensrÿche also had plans to capture the Road to the Promised Land Tour on video. Throughout the tour, the band had "taper's sections" established, so fans who wanted to record video and audio had a dedicated place to set up their gear. The idea was for fans to submit the recorded material to Queensrÿche and at some point, professionally combine and render the footage into some sort of live album release. A ton of live Queensrÿche shows from this era found their way into the hands of fans. Unfortunately, however, Queensrÿche never did release anything official to commemorate the tour.

During the recording of *Promised Land,* the band had hired Chris DeGarmo's brother, Mark, to direct behind the scenes video footage for a special project, which finally came out in 1996....

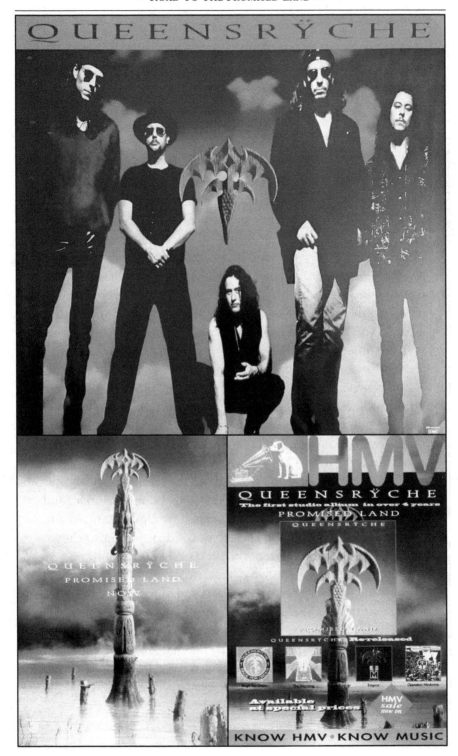

Queensrÿche's Promised Land CD-Rom

In 1996, EMI, in conjunction with Media X and Virgin Interactive, released a special interactive *Queensrÿche's Promised Land* PC CD-ROM game. Personal computers were starting to be a household fixture by then, and videos and other supplemental multimedia materials were being added to album releases on compact disc. *Queensrÿche's Promised Land* CD-ROM was one of the first band-related videogames of its type, with only a couple of other artists predating them (Todd Rundgren was the first with his interactive album, *No World Order,* in July 1993, followed by Peter Gabriel with his interactive CD-ROM game, *Xplora1: Peter Gabriel's Secret World*, released in late December 1993).

Queensrÿche's Promised Land game includes 23 mini documentaries on Big Log Studios and production of the *Promised Land* album, with interviews with the Queensrÿche members and producer/engineer James "Jimbo" Barton. Three music videos play within the disc. The "I Am I" video was directed by Wayne Isham and produced by Curt Marvis, the "Bridge" video was directed by Matt Mahurin and produced by Louise Feldman, and the "Dis-con-nec-ted" video was directed by David Barnard and produced by Perry Joseph. These music videos were also shown on MTV, etc. in promotion of the *Promised Land* album.

The "game" features five distinct worlds where players can explore the personalities of each band member. Along the way, users must solve riddles and search for pieces of the Queensrÿche totem pole depicted on the *Promised Land* album cover. If you succeed in beating the game/winning the challenge, and collect all the pieces of the totem, it plays a video for a special non-album acoustic song, "Two Mile High." Queensrÿche also provided the musical score for the game.

"EMI and Capitol, they wanted to jump into this new format, and we said, 'Hey hey hey, pick us, pick us! We're into this stuff, you know, we're computer literate. Give us a chance, we'd like to do that,'" Michael Wilton said in 1995, prior to the release of the game. "This whole CD-ROM venture has been very informative for us, seeing how it works and how it's developing in the beginning stages, QuickTime motion and memory. It still has a long way to go as far as I'm concerned. I'm still edgy around some of the movies, and the standard has to be brought up so that it gets run on faster machines. But I really think CD-ROM is going to be a viable part of the market in the near future, based on the sales of computers and CD-ROM apparatus. I think it's good—I think it's trendy in a way, but then I think there's going to be some really interesting information you can get on a CD disc."

The idea at first was more of typical band making the record in the studio type film, but the concept evolved. "The whole -2020162671 *Promised Land* CD-ROM was brought up to first do just an informative documentary," Wilton explained. "So, in recording *Promised Land* at Big Log Studios off the coast of Washington, we filmed it all. ... Chris DeGarmo's brother, Mark DeGarmo, filmed it. We digitally rendered the film in a three-dimensional format, and began placing everything that was in the log cabin back, so that you could have full screen. You can wander around through the log cabin, click certain things and find certain things, and bits of information will pop up. Basically, the first disc is going into the recording studio, clicking things and finding things, finding interviews and documentary footage. But then on the second disc, we decided, 'Let's make something for the fans. Hey, this is CD-ROM, and you know there's a CD-ROM market out there, and there are people who are CD-ROM-heads—I mean, they're into this stuff. So let's give a little visual interpretation of Queensrÿche, and give a little gaming element into it as well.' So if the user chooses, he can venture outside the log cabin into our forest, which is kind of the magic forest where things happen, and as you wander around, you find ways to transport yourself to different worlds. There are five worlds, representing the ideas and beliefs of each band member. As you venture through these five worlds, you have the choice—or it's inevitable, basically, that you'll trip a natural disaster. You have time periods and certain maneuvers that you have to do to clean up the disaster that you tripped, or else something really bad happens."

Wilton continues: "So thus, it has kind of an ecological theme to it, taking care of certain situations, teaching the user to be responsible and think things out. As you venture from each of these worlds—which, by the way, are all very different, Eddie's is like a game show, mine is my brain, they're all very drastically different—after you've ventured through all of them, and successfully tripped and solved all the things you need to solve, you find your way to this place where we come out and play a track on the computer, live. It's a track that will never be released on album. I don't know, if you spend a lot of time on it, you could probably do it in a couple weeks, three weeks, maybe. If you're just a casual user, then it's three months. Some of it's challenging, but then again we didn't want to make it so hard that it would piss people off. There are some gaming elements, some gaming puzzles are harder than others in certain worlds."

As Wilton mentioned, Chris DeGarmo tapped his brother, Mark, to direct the video footage for the project. But he was reluctant to accept at first. "It's a funny story because I actually turned them down," Mark DeGarmo shares. "The thing was, I never do business with family. It's a recipe for disaster. Christopher had been trying to get me involved and I said, 'Hey man, I don't want to put our relationship at risk.' Because there were four other guys in the band, and if somebody didn't like something, or whatever... But on the *Promised Land* thing he said, 'Look, I need you to come live with us. We don't feel comfortable bringing in a stranger. The guys all want you and I want you.' And I had just had my first child. My son had just been born. And it was four months of being gone, and my poor wife puts up with my lifestyle already. Then it's like, 'Hey honey,

I'm going to go live with a rock band for four months.' So, at first, I turned him down. I was heartbroken. But then Chris called my wife Kelly and she was like, 'Look, you need to go do this.'"

Work started on the interactive game in 1993, during the recording process of the *Promised Land* album at Big Log Studio in the San Juan Islands. Mark DeGarmo goes on with the story: "Chris said, 'We want a behind the scenes thing. You can pretty much do what you want and tell us what you need.' At first, I wanted to shoot with film, but the budget wouldn't allow it. So, we had to look at a lower cost alternative. Because even doing video was still a lot of money. But it was me and Jeff Hoien—the sound guy. We went up early because we were most concerned with the audio, believe it or not. I wanted the board output as they were recording tracks, so I could sync. I just wanted everything to be not a lot of overdubs. That I was getting live stuff as it was happening. All the talk back between Jimbo [Barton] and the band and Tom [Hall]. The engineers and what not. I wanted to hear the banter. I wanted to hear them. And Chris was kind of, um, demanding shall we say, and I wanted to capture some of his... The way they would sort of hammer away. And give Scott and Eddie a bigger presence. They cut those drum tracks first and I wanted to capture that as it happened. We lived up there for four months in the San Juans [Islands]. We'd just follow them around all day shooting what they did. What they ate, if they had coffee, etc. And obviously all the tracks. As they happened in the various rooms of the cabins we lived in."

"Probably the most challenging part of that was the aerial thing," Mark DeGarmo says. "Since we were going to rent a helicopter, and get the thing all rigged up with cameras, I wanted to do a little lifestyle thing with each one of them. Whatever their passion was, you know? Just something. Chris, at the time, was a burgeoning pilot, so he was pretty easy to figure out. Scott and Geoff and Eddie and so on. Michael... I just said, 'What do you want to do?' Scott had his convertible and Eddie had his jet ski. Geoff had his sailboat. Just coordinating that day... Because we literally started up on the island and flew with Christopher for a bit. And then raced down to Seattle and got some of Geoff. Of course, this was before cell phones, so it was interesting to coordinate all of that, but we pulled it off without a hitch. We actually had good weather, which was another miracle."

The elder DeGarmo continues: "It took about four months of living with them. And then it was the whole summer of post-production. I just locked myself in a bedroom with 34 Betacam SP 30's and logged all of it. I did the post-production here in Dallas. I live in Ft. Worth, but there was a post-production place there with Mark Worthman, who assisted me. Then it was working with the interactive guys – David Traub was his name. I had to understand what it was they were doing. He gave me sort of a diagram of how the CD-ROM would work, The idea was we would have these video rewards for navigating through, you know, the *Promised Land* environment. And obviously each song had its own thing. [I] wanted to show a little bit of what the raw tracks looked and sounded like. Where they were recorded. Then the complicated part was I needed to create 19 individual little 30 second, or one-minute bits. Then if they hit 'Couch Potato' mode, it needed to all become one linear video."

Work on the assembly and creation of the CD-ROM, post-video shooting, took a bit longer to do. Media X eventually completed the discs in late-1994/early-1995, and it was slated for a release that year, but didn't come out until 1996.

Before the release of the *Queensrÿche's Promised Land* CD-ROM, there was some speculation going around that clips from the game might be incorporated into the video projection on the tour, but it didn't happen. Wilton explained at the time what was behind the idea and why it didn't happen. "That was a wish from the people at Mediatrix. They wanted to somehow promote it, and they saw the perfect opportunity up there, but they don't know the logistics of, and cost involved in, trying to transfer that onto a laserdisc format that's already been done, burned in. So no, as far as that being incorporated in our live show, we can't do that. The only thing we've done is at a couple shows, we've had media rooms set up for people, and we've had the alpha disc there, and they can mess around and maneuver their way through it." EMI did team up with a company at that time called, RockOnline, that put up a website on the Internet with some samples from the CD-ROM to promote it.

The *Queensrÿche's Promised Land* CD-ROM was eventually released in March 1996 and sold pretty well. It received positive reviews at the time, and people continue to find the game 25 years later and review it online. Other heavy metal bands such as Iron Maiden followed Queensrÿche with their *Ed Hunter* CD-ROM game, released in 1999, and had success as well. The technology, of course, is a bit dated now on *Queensrÿche's Promised Land* CD-ROM (as it is with other releases of that time), but you can still play the game and watch the behind the scenes video and so on. And Queensrÿche showed that they were still looking to push the boundaries, try new things, and embrace new ideas.

Credits:

- Released in March 1996 on EMI Records in
  conjunction with Media X and Virgin Interactive.
- Game created by Media X, Inc.
- A Tri-Ryche Corporation Production.
- Executive producers (EMI): Henry Marquez, Larry
  Braverman and Don Harder.
- Produced by David C. Traub (Media X producer).
- Co-producer and technical director: Matthew
  MacLaurin.
- Co-producer and technical director: Gaben Chancellor.

- Music, score to opening animation and soundscape collaboration by Queensrÿche.
- Sound design by CS Audio Visual, Inc.
- Engineers/designers: Josh Beggs and Reid Ridgeway.
- Video direction by Mark DeGarmo.
- Location sound and field assistant: Jeff Hoien.
- Editor: Mark Boardman.
- Blue Screen direction by Gaben Chancellor.
- Management: Q Prime, Inc.

(Press release – early 1996)

Queensrÿche's Promised Land, the first ever full-length Rock and Roll CD-ROM adventure game, created by multi-platinum recording group Queensrÿche, will be released March 1996 by EMI Records, Virgin Interactive Entertainment (VIE) and CEMA distribution. This two-disc adventure evolved from their 1994 platinum audio CD release and includes not only the *Promised Land* game disc but a second disc, Big Log, which explores the log cabin studio where Queensrÿche lived and worked during the eight-month long recording session for the *Promised Land* album.

Queensrÿche's Promised Land was conceived by the band and designed in conjunction with Media X, Inc. (Santa Cruz). Flying over a small island in the Pacific Northwest, the Queensrÿche Totem separates and scatters in five pieces. Players must explore the five bandmembers' worlds within the beautiful, digital forest, solving three-dimensional puzzles and thought-provoking ecological challenges, as they attempt to find the pieces necessary to recreate the Totem, avert ecological disaster, and win the game. Those who triumph over the game are rewarded by a previously unreleased bonus audio track, "Two Mile High," written specifically for *Queensrÿche's Promised Land*.

The game features two thousand photo-realistic, raytraced images, over 70 diverse computer-generated digital worlds, and a hundred minutes of digital video and music. Queensrÿche wrote and performed the haunting ambient soundtrack for the CD-ROM. Soundbites from their album *Promised Land* are scattered throughout the game as well as the documentary disc, Big Log. *Queensrÿche's Promised Land* is a hybrid disc that is compatible with Macintosh, Windows and Windows '95 at a suggested retail price of $49.95.

Despite the success of *Promised Land,* there were signs Queensrÿche was starting to slip as a priority. MTV had supported the band with a large amount of video play for *Operation: Mindcrime* and *Empire,* but didn't give much rotation to their videos from *Promised Land.* The music scene had changed drastically by then. "Heavy metal" music was proclaimed dead in favor of the "grunge" movement that originated in Seattle, and efforts were being made to help bury heavy metal by the music industry itself. The band also had its share of personal issues that had happened and caused some strain between members.

The question was: would Queensrÿche survive all of this?

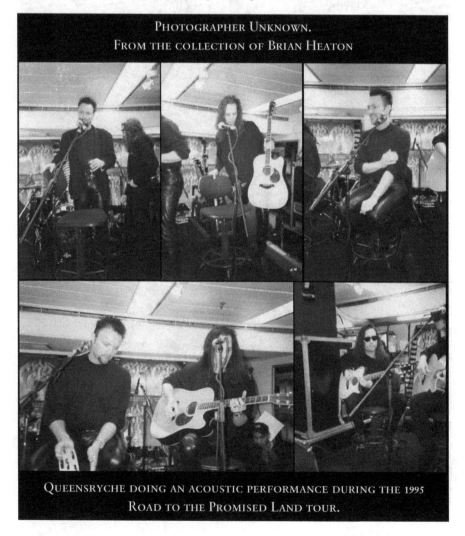

PHOTOGRAPHER UNKNOWN.
FROM THE COLLECTION OF BRIAN HEATON

QUEENSRYCHE DOING AN ACOUSTIC PERFORMANCE DURING THE 1995 ROAD TO THE PROMISED LAND TOUR.

PHOTOGRAPHER UNKNOWN.
FROM THE COLLECTION OF BRIAN HEATON

PROMISED LAND IN-STORE, CHICAGO-AREA, ILLINOIS, 1995.

PHOTOGRAPHER UNKNOWN.
FROM THE COLLECTION OF BRIAN HEATON

CANDID SHOTS FROM THE ROAD IN SUMMER 1995.

QUEENSRÿCHE

EMI Records

Michael Wilton

Geoff Tate

QUEENSRÿCHE

EMI Records

QUEENSRŸCHE: PROMISED LAND ERA

VARIOUS MAGAZINE AND PUBLICATION COVERS FROM THE PROMISED LAND ERA.

Queensrÿche: Promised Land Era

Various Magazine and Publication Covers from the Promised Land Era.

Chapter 12:
Some People Fly

After the tour cycle was over for *Promised Land*, the record company wanted Queensrÿche to get started working on another album in 1996. Although not the success that *Empire* was, a platinum album was still a platinum album, despite some feeling that a decline from the heights of the predecessor signified some sort of failure. The question was really if Queensrÿche could weather the change in the music scene. Heavy metal music had most definitely fallen out of favor as the '90s continued. The popularity of the so-called "Grunge" and "Alternative" music had caused a number of metal and hard rock bands to fold up their tents. On the other hand, progressive rock and metal was having a bit of resurgance in that decade. Fates Warning had continued to evolve from their Iron Maiden-influenced roots to a more polished, Rush-inspired band with Terry Brown even at the helm. Dream Theater had also blown everybody away in 1992 with their second album, *Images and Words*, showing that you could combine the heaviness of Metallica, the complexity of Rush and Yes, and the accessability of Journey, and have popular success. Heavy metal and hard rock music was certainly not dead, it had just evolved. The question was, where did Queensrÿche fit in?

Rather than showing disdain for the newer music to come out of Seattle, as many of the metalheads and rockers of the '80s did, members of Queensrÿche embraced it, and it would influence their direction for their next album. "Out of all the bands from this area the one I have the most affinity with is undoubtedly Alice in Chains," Geoff Tate stated at the time. "I like the music they do the best, because it's heavier and darker and I kinda like that." The singer also liked Soundgarden, as did other members of Queensrÿche. "I think their last record was very good," Tate adds. "They're a good band and I'm happy for their success. Ben Shepherd is a neighbor, so we hang out when we're not busy working." Chris DeGarmo was also a fan of Alice in Chains and had gotten to be friends with the band, especially with guitarist Jerry Cantrell and drummer Sean Kinney. Michael was into some of the newer bands such as Sevendust and the dark, moody, alternative progressive band, Tool.

EMI was gung-ho for another album, but not everyone in Queensrÿche was motivated to start that process. Some of the band members were focused on relationships and had significant events in that department. In post-divorce messiness, Tate married his girlfriend Susan Saunders. He had met her in 1994 and they started dating and fell in love. Susan had moved to Seattle from Colorado in 1987 with her best friend and roommate Misty, who would later marry Scott Rockenfield. Prior to Susan's relationship with Geoff, she had been married to Jason Ames Saunders, who fronted the bands Mama Troll and Tea for Twelve (with Scott Moughton of White Lightning on guitar). Susan also dipped her toes into the management world by handling her husband's bands back then. Misty started dating Scott Rockenfield and before long, on June 21, 1996, they welcomed their second child, Navee Dae. Both women, especially Susan, would become significant in the Queensrÿche story as time went on. On top of that, the Geoff and Susan were also expecting their second child that year and Emily Tate was eventually born in May 1997. Eddie Jackson would spend the year making plans with his fiancée, Theresa, toward their impending nuptials. Michael Wilton also continued working on his marriage with Kerrie Lynn, after a rocky period a couple years prior. Chris

L to R: Chris DeGarmo, Michael Wilton, Geoff Tate, Ed Jackson, Scott Rockenfield

DeGarmo was right back in the same position of rallying his bandmates together to get back in the studio.

DeGarmo ended up writing most of the music on the album that would ultimately be called *Hear in the Now Frontier*. DeGarmo had sole music credits on 11 of the tracks, and co-credits

on two more with Eddie Jackson. DeGarmo also wrote the lyrics to seven of those songs and Tate wrote the lyrics to the remaining seven tunes. Wilton is credited with writing the music on just one song, "Reach." Overall, the project was not as much of the collaborative effort as past ones had been, as far as the writing was concerned. An additional song was written by Scott Rockenfield (music) and Geoff Tate (lyrics), "Chasing Blue Sky," but it just appeared as a

b-side at the time and was later included on the reissue of *Hear in the Now Frontier* in 2003. "Chasing Blue Sky" was re-recorded by Rockenfield and Paul Speer in 1997, with a different vocalist, for their *Televoid* soundtrack project (which would go on to garner a Grammy nomination). Wilton contributed a second song, "Tomorrow Begins Today", that wasn't used for the album. He ended up giving it to another local artist, Aury Moore (Pamela Moore's sister), who re-wrote it and re-titled it as, "Breakin' Me," and it was included on her solo album. "The attitude is certainly far more 'up' than *Promised Land*," DeGarmo explained, "which I think naturally followed the flow of our lives. As we were coming off of the life segment that led into the recording of that album, with its introspection and heavy ponderings, the music reflected that. This time, there was a fresh energy. It may have been simply that the things that were going on in people's lives had been sorted out. But we could tell as we shared ideas that there was a more upbeat tone to everything."

Lyrically, the record reflects DeGarmo's sentiment. While the lead single off *Hear in the Now Frontier*, "Sign of the Times" was clearly social commentary, much like *Promised Land*, many of the song lyrics were still introspective and personal. "Get a Life" (lyrics by Tate) was rumored to be pointed at a family member. "Anytime/Anywhere" is focused on sexual desire. "Some People Fly" talks about taking a chance and reaching for your dreams. While the "Thinking Man's Metal Band" moniker was still around, those thoughts focused more inward the past couple of albums in comparison to Queensrÿche's output in the 1980s.

Peter Collins was brought back as the producer, with a new engineer, Toby Wright, at the controls. Toby was an A-list engineer and mixer in Los Angeles at the time, having worked on records by the Bullet Boys, Cheap Trick, C.O.C., Fishbone, Sammy Hagar, KISS, Metallica, The Nixons, Slayer, The Wallflowers, and many others. Alice in Chains had worked with Toby on their two songs for the *Last Action Hero* soundtrack, their *Sap* EP, their self-titled album, and their *Unplugged* record, and guitarist Jerry Cantrell had spoken highly of Wright. DeGarmo especially was looking at a more "stripped down" approach for the new album, and Wright's work especially on the acoustic-based *Sap* appealed to him.

Eventually, Queensrÿche convened in the late summer/early fall of 1996 at Pearl Jam guitarist Stone Gossard's Studio Litho in the Fremont district in Seattle, to demo most of the songs. Typically, Queensrÿche had done a lot of pre-production work prior to laying down the actual album tracks, working over each song extensively. This time, they elected for a looser and "natural" feel. Working faster likely was part of the motivation behind the change in approach, but the music scene had also changed so much. The 1990s were the "unplugged" generation. Retro sounds and instruments were in vogue and informed much of what was being created at that time. DeGarmo and Wilton were also caught up in the "vintage" vibe using some of their old guitars and equipment on the album. "Chris and Michael have been collecting vintage guitars for years and really wanted to try them out," Geoff Tate said. "So, the whole album has a sort of vintage sound because of these old instruments, amps, mics and consoles."

After the songs were fleshed out a bit, Queensrÿche traveled to Nashville, Tennessee, to start work at Sixteenth Avenue Sound. Chris, Scott and Eddie worked with Peter Collins and Toby Wright on the basic tracks starting on October 7, 1996, and spent a few days on those. Then it was back to Seattle and Chris and Michael laid down the guitar parts there from October 21 through October 31. For most of November, Geoff and Chris did the lead and backing vocals before going back to Nashville for the final mixing. That was done from December 1 – 21, 1996.

There are some interesting facts about *Hear in the Now Frontier*'s development in the studio. The sound effect of someone taking a picture at the end of "Get a Life" was misplaced. It was supposed to be at the beginning of the song. In addition, the ending violin part on "Sign of the Times" by David Ragsdale of Kansas was originally supposed to be accompanied by a final lyric: "See it all burning to the ground."

Geoff Tate explained the violin and lyric part of "Sign of the Times" to a South American reporter in December 1997: "Originally there was a lyric that ended the song. It was 'see it all burning to the ground.' The song is talking about how the level of decadence in our country, America, has risen to an extreme. So we thought, 'see it all burning to the ground,' and we were reminded of the story of Nero, who was emperor of Rome and he played a violin supposedly while Rome burned, and we thought a violin would sound great. So we brought in a violin. But then, after we put in the violin, we decided not to include the lyric line."

Following completion of the album, they took time off again for the holidays with their families. "That was the fastest recording we've ever done," DeGarmo stated at the time. "Fourteen songs in six weeks, with another three weeks to mix. We didn't do it fast in a "non-caring" way, but we approached it in a way that was not as elaborate, from a production standpoint, as some of our other projects. It made for a minimalistic approach, which fit in well with how Toby Wright, our engineer, likes to work."

Once the new year kicked off, plans were made for the forthcoming release of *Hear in the Now Frontier*. Artwork was commissioned by Hugh Syme, most known for his work with Rush. The striking front cover art was adorned with cut-off ears in or around jars in a Salvador Dali-esque type surreal landscape, and the "ear" motif was very present in the booklet interiors and promotional materials as well. The lead single, "Sign of the Times", was

dropped to radio stations in February 1997, and it hit #3 on the singles chart after favorable response. Geoff, Chris and Scott joined local DJ Scott Vanderpool in the KISW studio on the morning of March 7, 1997, to promote the impending release. Tate and DeGarmo had just gotten back from a promotional press junket for the album in Europe, hitting seven countries, and were a bit jetlagged, but still in a jovial mood. "Sign of the Times" was played, as well as "Hit the Black", "Anytime/ Anywhere" and "Some People Fly." Following that, KISW sponsored a laser show Queensrÿche listening party at the Seattle Science Center Laserium with other band members in attendance.

Anticipation built for the forthcoming release with interviews and reviews in advance of the drop. In a March 1997 interview, Chris and Geoff were asked about how the so-called "Seattle Sound" had influenced them and the new album. "Well, we thought, 'shit, we better get with it too,'" DeGarmo said and laughed. "We are from Seattle and we do make sound. They actually sell the Seattle Sound now in the stores. I bought some, took it home and sprinkled it on my creations." The sound of the album was sparser and rawer than previous efforts. Chris employed slide guitar for a few songs, "The Voice Inside" and "Hero" being two such examples. *Hear in the Now Frontier* was also DeGarmo's debut as a lead singer, as he stepped up to handle the main vocals on "All I Want." "'All I Want' is me singing!" Chris happily admits. "I did all the [lead] vocals, and it's the first time in seven albums, even though I've done backing vocals before. I'd certainly written song lyrics before, but this time I really wanted to sing them as well. Geoff was totally into it and he said go for it. Without meaning to, I felt it ended up with kind of a Beatle-esque vibe. I wasn't trying to make it that type of song, but I think it shows something that I always believed in, which is the things you grew up with eventually show up in your work in some way."

Hear In the Now Frontier was released on March 25, 1997, and debuted at #19 on the U.S. Billboard charts. "You" followed as the second single and landed at #11 as well. "The Voice Inside" and "spOOL" were also issued as promotional singles for the record. No videos were made for songs from the album, but the lack of support from MTV for the previous album likely contributed to that. *The Rocket* ranked it as #5 on their local "Top 20" sales chart in they and reviewed the album favorably. Radio stations had the first two singles in heavy rotation.

Signs were there that *Hear in the Now Frontier* was going to do well with a continued push behind it, and the positive initial support from radio stations and the press. Sadly, that didn't happen....

Just prior to the kickoff for their *Hear in the Now Frontier* tour, Queensrÿche appeared on KISW DJ Bob Rivers radio show, "Bob's Garage", on June 3, 1997. They performed three songs "unplugged" ("Bridge", "Silent Lucidity" and "Some People Fly") live on the air and it was engineered by Kelly Gray, an "old friend" from the Myth days who would figure into the picture more prominently for Queensrÿche before long. This was the first of a few more acoustic on-air appearances that summer. Two days later, they performed a "secret" show at the Very Large Array (VLA) in the desert of Socorro, New Mexico. This promotional appearance was designed to show off Queensrÿche's new stripped-down sound to MTV contest winners in attendance. Fans who attended the show received special certificates signed by the band. The setlist included a mix of songs from the new album, along with classic Ryche tracks on a bare stage, juxtaposed with the beautiful desert landscape behind them. The live concert went out on the air to 200 radio stations.

The stage production for the Hear in the Now FronTOUR as it was known, had fewer working parts than tours past, but the band's performances were high energy and professional. The concerts were typically close to two hours in length and about half of the new album was played live in rotation (about six songs were included in the set with a couple changing up here and there with others). The stage featured two large inflatable video screens in the shape of a human ear and a stone wall. Images of the band and pre-recorded video vignettes were projected so fans could again be closer to the band/see them better at a distance. These inflatable screens posed some challenges with outdoor stages and unpredictable winds.

The tour began in earnest on June 17, 1997, in Rapid City, South Dakota. It was followed by a show at the Boise State Pavilion on the 19th and then an appearance at the Rose Garden, in Portland, Oregon, on the 20th. Geoff Tate humorously acknowledged the weird ear on stage by saying it was "part of the Mike Tyson fight if you know what I mean," referring to the infamous bout between Tyson and Evander Holyfield, when the former bit off part of the latter's ear.

Queensrÿche was playing to smaller crowds in many of the same arenas they had visited on the Road to the Promised Land Tour, with

many of the venues only at half or three-quarters capacity. At the band's "hometown" show on June 21, 1997, at the Gorge in George, Washington, the inflatable ear screen was nearly lifted off the stage by the wind—perhaps foreshadowing some difficulties to come. Some fans were also starting to clue into problems with the band.

Longtime Queensrÿche fan Doug Wirachowsky relates: "My friend and I had pre-show passes [for the Portland show] and third row seats. The atmosphere during the pre-function show was different than any other pre- or post-show ones we'd been to. All of the Queensrÿche guys were low key, and kinda quiet as fans milled about and chatted up their favorite band member. Chris was especially quiet and not very outgoing, as he normally was during these events. He stood in one place in a distant corner for 45 minutes, choosing not to mingle like the rest of his bandmates. He looked distracted and his normally wide, beaming smile was reduced to thinly curled lips. He was polite and answered questions when asked, but he seemed somber. We talked with Chris the most and he signed some stuff for us. He and the band went out and performed a fantastic show, but throughout the course of the evening the rumors were flying that EMI had gone bankrupt and now the rest of the tour was at risk. We knew that without the label, no record promotion or support would happen. If the album took off on the radio that would help, but that and fan word of mouth probably wasn't enough. After the show was over, I looked at the large print of the band I had autographed, and I noticed that four autographs were in metallic gold ink, but Chris's signature was in black. The irony of this would not hit me until a bit later...."

EMI-America did in fact go bankrupt just two days after that Portland show on June 22, 1997, and by the end of the month, Virgin had absorbed the label. The support behind the album had stopped after the initial push in the spring, and it had quickly slid off the charts and disappeared out of stores. Nobody was pressing more copies, nor putting the promotion behind the release. *Hear in the Now Frontier* had only sold 330,000 copies as of 2006 (including the 2003 reissue sales). Queensrÿche was forced to dip into their own pockets to cover the expenses on their U.S. tour and their proposed jaunt to Europe was now off the table. They only played just over two months and 42 concerts total that summer, their shortest trek in a long time. To add insult to injury, Tate got a very bad summer cold and blew out his voice in July at a show in Columbus, Ohio, on July 19, 1997. By the fifth song, he walked off stage and the band stopped playing. After a few minutes, Chris DeGarmo apologized and explained Geoff was sick and they would not be able to continue. Two shows after that were canceled in Dayton and Cleveland, the first time the band had canceled any concerts in their career. They finally played the second night show in Cleveland on July 22, but it featured a shortened setlist. It took over a week before Tate fully recovered for a regular set at the Jones Beach Amphitheater on Long Island.

Despite the black cloud looming over the band during that time, there were still some good shows and the band was always appreciative of their fans' support. Superfan/collector Rick Moore shares one such moment: "I had seen the band a couple of nights prior in Florida during the *Hear in the Now Frontier* tour and had promised Chris that I had 'something' for him. I went to the soundcheck for the Raleigh, NC, show in the middle of the day. I brought a notebook and gave it to Chris. The notebook was full of newspaper and magazine clippings about the history of the band. He was very surprised and happy to receive it. He told me that he would 'give me a guitar if he had a spare.' He hooked me up with tickets and passes for the evening's show. Then I presented the band with a Rubbermaid tub full of Queensrÿche live bootleg CDs that I had accumulated from Queensrÿche collections that I had obtained over time. I let the band pick through the tub of CDs, and they were like kids with a candy jar. They picked the tub clean. Then Chris asked me, 'You're a drummer, aren't you?' I said, 'Yessir.' 'Wanna jam?' said Chris. 'What song do you want to do?' My request was, 'Eyes of a Stranger'. Geoff said, 'It's pretty early in the day for that one,' but did accommodate and I counted off and the band broke into the song. We played the first two verses and the chorus before Geoff gave the 'cut' signal by moving his index finger across his throat."

Although not part of the regular rotation, "The Killing Words" was a surprise addition to the setlist on July 29, 1997, at the Darien

Lake Amphitheater, in Buffalo, NY. As the story goes, during a promotional appearance prior to the gig, a fan had requested the song, and Queensrÿche decided to add an acoustic version of it to its next show. It marked one of, if not the first time the band had played the song in-concert (not counting the *MTV Unplugged* session in 1992). Another show of note on the tour was Queensrÿche's show on August 16, 1997, at the Starplex Amphitheater in Dallas, Texas. The gig was the first time a Queensrÿche concert was broadcast live on the internet.

Once the short tour was over, the members of Queensrÿche went their separate ways for a few months. It was sometime during this break that Chris DeGarmo decided to leave the band. It was presumably for a few different reasons, as Chris has never publicly revealed his reasons for leaving. For many close to the band, it appeared that nobody else was really helping with the load, as far as running the business of the band, as well as the creative side. Chris had driven the last two albums with a major portion of the songwriting and development of the recording, as well as wrangling the rest of his bandmates to the studios. Tensions had built up between him and Geoff over the last few years, which resulted in a deterioration of that relationship.

Add to that, Geoff's new wife had just taken over the fan club from Michael's well-liked mother, Martha "Metal Sushi" Wilton, and some rumors were that Chris was wary of the issues that could create in the future. As president of the Queensrÿche corporation, it was also assumed by the other band members that Chris would handle the negotiations with Virgin to try and see if they would retain the band. Shortly after Chris announced his intentions to leave Queensrÿche, their

A HOMEMADE "EAR IN JAR" FROM THE COLLECTION OF BRIAN L. NARON.

management company, Q Prime, which had helped guide them to super-stardom for the last decade, unceremoniously dropped the band.

Wilton later revealed in 2012 some additional factors that likely contributed to the increasing strain between band members, and DeGarmo's decision to quit. "During the recording of *Hear in the Now Frontier*, personal things changed," Michael stated. "Because of a divorce battle between Geoff and Suzanne Tate, band members were subpoenaed and were put in the middle of a personal fight that ended up causing a large amount of resentment and hurt amongst the band members. It was at this point that tensions became higher and resentment over royalties became a big issue. Now the demand to be a writer on future Queensrÿche songs started to erode the friendships. The dynamics of the band had changed." Wilton continues: "It was at the end of our tour for *Hear in the Now Frontier* that Chris DeGarmo left the band. The songwriting chemistry of Tate and DeGarmo may have run its course, but moreso Geoff's demeanor with Chris had terminated the relationship. I was saddened to see him leave and have remained a close friend to him over the years. Q-Prime also decided to drop the band due to Chris's departure."

Chris DeGarmo had been having thoughts on leaving the band since the *Empire* days. As revealed to Malcolm Dome around that time (which Dome chose not to publish until 2014 in *Classic Rock* magazine), he expressed doubts about his ability to continue on with Queensrÿche. The stress of trying to be the one rebuilding the band, coupled with tensions in the band and his continuing desire to be present for his family, as well as the changing musical landscape and uncertainty of the future, likely all pilled on and finally drove him to the point of finally quitting the band he helped form when he was a teenager.

After DeGarmo's announcement to his bandmates, Queensrÿche played six final concerts with him in South America in December 1997, helping the band fulfill its contractual obligations. After that last show on the December 13, 1997, Chris DeGarmo unplugged his guitar and walked off the stage and that was the last time he would ever perform with the band live. In February 1998, an official announcement was made that he was gone and an era had ended. Queensrÿche would never be the same after that....

WELCOME...TO THE INFORMATION AGE

By Brian J. Heaton

Information saturation today comes in the form of Twitter, Instagram, Facebook and a variety of other internet-based social platforms that deliver news and interaction on a global scale. Thirty years ago, however, before the internet took hold in the mainstream, Queensrÿche fans who wanted expanded coverage on the band had limited options.

Usenet groups and Internet Relay Chat (IRC) existed as a precursor to Web-based discussion forums, but in those early years of connectivity, most fans were limited to Queensrÿche periodically appearing in magazine articles and the occasional fan club newsletter. But it was email lists that really helped unite the fanbase on a more regular basis during the early stages of the digital revolution. The most famous being *Screaming in Digital*.

Founded by Daniel "Shag" Birchall in October 1991, *SiD* lasted for more than a decade, providing Queensrÿche news, tour dates, stories and discussion to the band's rabid fans across the world. Although it wasn't the first email list on the band, it was likely the most popular, with a subscriber base that ultimately ballooned to just under 2,000 people before Birchall transitioned *SiD* to a dedicated website in 1997.

Birchall explained that he started *SiD* chiefly because he felt the Usenet groups at the time for "metal" and "prog" weren't overly welcoming of Queensrÿche. He said that many in those groups would argue over whether Queensrÿche "belonged," and it spurred him to create the initial *SiD* email list. Hand-edited, organized by sections, and sent out weekly for the first few years, Birchall is most proud of the fact that *SiD* was driven by the Queensrÿche community.

"I wrote the first short issue, and I organized all the others and edited them for spelling grammar, but there were hundreds, maybe even thousands of Queensrÿche fans around the world over the years who contributed content to it," Birchall said. "I rarely had to ask anyone for material—it was propelled by the fervor of the fans. Hundreds of them even bought t-shirts and made themselves walking advertisements for it."

SiD was popular with fans, but it received a big public endorsement in the mid-1990s by Queensrÿche guitarists Chris DeGarmo and Michael Wilton, who spoke highly of "Shag" (Birchall's nickname given to him by school classmates who likened his appearance to that of "Shaggy" from *Scooby Doo*) in the January 1995 issue of *Guitar World*. DeGarmo told *Guitar World* that the fans' speculation on *SiD* was "entertaining" as contributors to it would often try to decipher what Queensrÿche's songs meant.

SiD wouldn't be thought of as "speculation" for long, however. Following the article, Queensrÿche's publicist got in touch with Birchall, opening a small window into the band. Birchall recalled he had the email addresses for Wilton, DeGarmo, and Scott Rockenfield, and got backstage for various tour dates. But other than receiving news and press releases like the media, Birchall was happy to keep things at arm's length and retain his independent status.

Although officially "unofficial," fans who were avid readers of *SiD* often looked to Birchall for hints and clues about Queensrÿche and its music—and he delivered the best he could. For example, in issue 263, published on February 29, 2000, Birchall authored a piece that examined possible reasons why Chris DeGarmo had left the band in late 1997. He cited "sources close to the band" to help explain why the guitarist may have moved on. With DeGarmo's continued silence on the matter, even now, 21 years later, Birchall's article is still referenced by many (including this author) when writing about DeGarmo's departure.

SiD may have been unofficial, but its presentation and Birchall's professionalism were the epitome of the classy image Queensrÿche portrayed through the 1980s and 1990s. It was a list, and eventually a place, that was much more than an information hub and e-zine—it was a trusted community of like-minded fans. And that was all made possible also due to the standards and welcoming nature Birchall set for his publication.

Birchall wasn't sure if *SiD*'s popularity had any influence on Queensrÿche's adoption of the internet and technology in the information age, citing how forward-thinking the group was with its 1996 video game, *Queensrÿche's Promised Land*. But *SiD* certainly was certainly a driving force that united Queensrÿche fans during the internet's infancy.

"[F]or the first half of the 1990s, I was an online advocate, evangelist and 'community organizer' for Queensrÿche and their fans," Birchall said. "This was before the internet was a big commercial thing that everyone had access to, so in hindsight I feel a little like I was a John the Baptist voice crying out in the wilderness, 'prepare ye the way of the 'Rÿche!'"

Websites Take Hold

As Queensrÿche fans became more versed in website development in the mid-1990s, pages about Queensrÿche sprouted up all over the internet. Queries on early search engines such as Netscape, Lycos, or AltaVista would return dozens of sites devoted to speaking the word about the band's intelligent brand of hard rock and metal music.

Of note were sites such as Kevin Scurlock's "The Queensrÿche Campaign" and Sean Webb's "The Crossroad's Edge." There were pages devoted to Queensrÿche bootleg recordings (the "Queensrÿche Bootleg Guide" was one, spearheaded by Amy Lee, and later Johan Wall), collectibles and swag (Thomas Brogli's "Rycheitems") and countless tribute sites by fans that contained Queensrÿche's discography, tour history and more.

In fact, Scurlock, Webb and Birchall maintained an online Queensrÿche's Frequently Asked Questions (FAQ) page together through the late 1990s. As of this writing, the page is archived at http://personalpages.tds.net/~dreemland/tce/faq.html.

Put simply, the sheer volume of Queensrÿche content on the

Web likely contributed to some of the band's staying power during the grunge, post-grunge, and nu-metal eras of popular rock music.

"I think the thing that impressed me the most when I discovered the Queensrÿche online community was how vibrant and closely knit it was," said Sean Webb, one of the original editors of Queensrÿche.com and webmaster of "The Crossroad's Edge" fan site. "Not only was the fan community vibrant, but the band started to realize how useful it would be for outreach to its fans and to expand its audience. They were certainly ahead of their time in that regard."

One listen to "My Global Mind" from *Promised Land* was evidence that the members of Queensrÿche were dialed into the World Wide Web, and aware of their digital presence. Ultimately, Kevin Scurlock's site would become the band's official website. "The Queensrÿche Campaign" transitioned from one of Scurlock's personal URLs to "Queensrÿche.com" in November 1997. Webb became the site's editor. Eddie Richardson, and a host of other fans such as Natasha Weaver and Alan Birdsell helped contribute graphics and photos to the official site before and after its debut.

With Birchall's extensive history covering Queensrÿche on SiD, it was a surprise to some that "Shag" didn't become Queensrÿche's first official webmaster. But Birchall was quite happy doing his own thing. "I was very happy that Kevin took on running the official site, because I wanted SiD to stay unofficial and independent," Birchall recalled.

Discussion forums, where fans could chat regularly with one another was also a platform in full-swing by late-1997. Fan forums on Queensrÿche such as "The Void" and "Sanctuary" had been a haven for Rychers for years. Queensrÿche would launch its own official discussion forum on November 19, 1997, enabling the band members to interact with fans as they desired.

Having a place where fans could congregate in an official capacity also helped change the dynamic of Queensrÿche's fan club. As Martha Wilton stepped down from overseeing the operation, "Ziggy" (aka Susan Tate, Geoff's then-new wife) took over, and the band took advantage of technology to reorganize their fan club on a regional basis. Called "Empires," with official status granted by the band, these individual organizations popped up worldwide, many with websites helping to promote Queensrÿche.

With the title "official" hanging over it, however, the tenor of Queensrÿche's forum changed over time. As fans watched the back-and-forth drama of guitarist Chris Degarmo leaving, Kelly Gray replacing him, and ultimately DeGarmo's failed reunion with the band for *Tribe* in 2003, the official discussion forum began warning and banning fans for expressing negative commentary on Queensrÿche's music and decisions.

As a response to that, this writer created "The Breakdown Room" (BdR), an unofficial online discussion forum about Queensrÿche. Named after "Breakdown Room," the demo title of "Breakdown" from the band's 1999 album, *Q2k*, the forum was launched in December 2004. The Breakdown Room served as a place where freedom of opinion on Queensrÿche was welcomed.

"It felt like a home on the internet where we could gather and discuss heavy and progressive metal and it allowed us to explore Queensrÿche's albums and tours in depth with other passionate and loyal fans," said Steve Duvall, one of BdR's moderators. "Constructive criticism, which many bands preferred to keep off of their official forums, was encouraged and led to expansive discussions between users and helped build some long-standing friendships as well."

Establishing the tone of The Breakdown Room wasn't easy. The forum had a strict list of rules that governed member conduct. The idea was to create a place that held people accountable for their words, trying to encourage respectful critique, as opposed to the outright insults seen on various forums across the Web.

"I was a regular visitor to a site called 'Television Without Pity' at the time and loved how their strict rules kept mature discussion flowing and weeded out trolls and baiting," added Staci Heaton, BdR's lead moderator. "We wanted BdR to have the same kind of intelligent discourse for fans of the 'Thinking Man's Metal Band,' so I stole the rules and we modified them for our site. A few people hated us for it, but most of our posters loved the rules because they could have respectful discussion and debates without all the childish nonsense that plagued so many other fan sites."

The Breakdown Room wasn't for everyone, but it was undeniably successful. At its peak in 2012, the forum received thousands of unique visitors daily. Registrants included fans, record industry executives, well known musicians and members of Queensrÿche and their family members.

"I was astonished at how many members actively participated and how much traffic BdR generated right up until its closure," said John Schneiderwind, another of the forum's moderators. "I think that is a testament to BdR adhering to a model that worked to keep the board functioning and on-topic for so long."

Registrants of note included Michael Wilton, Todd La Torre, Wilton's then-wife, Kerrie-Lynn, and extended family members of Geoff Tate. Neil Kernon, the producer of *Rage for Order*, also had an account. The most active poster among those connected professionally or personally to Queensrÿche however, was the late Jason Slater, who jumped in the fire with candid remarks in many of the discussions. Slater served as producer, mixer, engineer and songwriter for the band on numerous albums, starting with *Operation: Mindcrime II* in 2006.

As he told this writer over the years, Slater came to The Breakdown Room in late-2004/early-2005 to "get an idea what real fans of Queensrÿche wanted from the band." He explained that he used the forum to try and help steer the direction of the songs he was writing with Mike Stone that would eventually become *Operation: Mindcrime II*.

"Having Jason Slater, someone associated with the band and the production of the music, added credibility to the community," said Gregory Twachtman, one of BdR's primary moderators. "The question of whether there was anybody listening within the organization to the many compliments and critiques that fans posted was a clear 'yes.'"

What attracted the most attention to The Breakdown Room was the Queensrÿche lawsuit in 2012. When Wilton, Eddie Jackson and Scott Rockenfield fired Geoff Tate, the resulting public legal documents associated with the lawsuit were downloaded by this writer from the website of King County Superior Court in Washington and posted publicly on The Breakdown Room.

The rationale was to finally give people clarity into the depths of dysfunction that Queensrÿche had been operating under for the past decade. The move shined an even bigger spotlight on the forum, as fans and the press logged on to view the latest documents and take part in discussions about them.

As most fans know, the lawsuit was settled in 2014. The Jackson-Rockenfield-Wilton version of Queensrÿche was given the band name, while Tate would have exclusive performance rights of the *Operation: Mindcrime* and *Operation: Mindcrime II* albums in their respective entireties.

Unsurprisingly, after two years of staggering web traffic, The Breakdown Room's popularity began to decline after the settlement. The rise of social media also contributed to the waning forum activity, as BdR's web-based platform became obsolete. The forum was archived and closed for good in December 2016 after 12 years. The main website where The Breakdown Room was hosted, AnybodyListening.net, remains active, and now serves as this writer's Queensrÿche-related blog and news site devoted to the band's original lineup.

Discussion about Queensrÿche continues both on the band's official forum (which was closed briefly, then re-established in 2013-2014) and throughout social media platforms on Queensrÿche's official accounts. The band—through their third-party social media coordinator—interacts with fans daily. In addition, some of the band members have their own individual pages on Facebook and Twitter, where they communicate directly with fans.

A Look Ahead

Dozens of independent fan communities about Queensrÿche continue today, primarily on Facebook where the remnants of the old fan club "Empires" still exist. But there's a sheen of familiarity to many of the online resources about Queensrÿche that are presently active, calling into question how online discussion of music will evolve in the years to come.

"When I look at Discord or Slack, I basically see IRC with a fresh coat of paint and a turbocharger," Birchall said. "When I look at Facebook or Reddit or anything with threaded discussions, I basically see Usenet with a fresh coat of paint and rocket-assisted takeoff."

Years ago, Geoff Tate wrote in "My Global Mind"—"I want no connection, just information, and I'm gone." But while simple data-gathering is still a vital part of the online world, fans are seeking a deeper relationship with the musicians who entertain them. And the technology is finally at a point where bands can deliver—if they choose to.

With bandwidth exploding worldwide and limits slowly becoming a non-issue, particularly during the COVID-19 pandemic of 2020-2021 which shut down touring, many bands have shifted to doing online performances and events. As of this writing, Queensrÿche has not yet taken part in that trend. Current Queensrÿche singer Todd La Torre (2012-present) explained in a 2021 interview with Aftershocks TV that the band had talked about doing a livestream event. But concerns about safety of the band and crew during the pandemic are what stopped it from happening. "It's a tough dilemma, because on the one hand, you wanna do everything you can do be as safe as you can," La Torre said. "On the other hand, you are human, and you can't live in a bubble forever. How do you balance those two things with some semblance of sanity and still be cautious? I don't know. So, it's weird."

Birchall, however, sees online connectivity between bands and fans continuing to evolve in the years to come. "If I can't go see the guys live, can I see them on a streaming concert?" Birchall asked rhetorically. "If I pay extra, instead of backstage meet-and-greet, is there a virtual meet-and-greet on Zoom or whatever? There are lots of possible ways forward."

CHAPTER 13:
BREAKDOWN

A t the close of 1997, Queensrÿche was left without a record label, management, and their main songwriter and one of the leaders of the band, Chris DeGarmo. They had only played 48 concert dates in support of *Hear in the Now Frontier*, when they normally did well over 100 for other albums. That included skipping Europe, Japan and the UK (due to lack of finances). EMI-America initially pushed the album with some promotion at the start, but once they went bankrupt that ended. DeGarmo had negotiated with Virgin, which absorbed their label, but ultimately, the record company did not sign the Seattle act. Things looked dire.

The remaining four members of Queensrÿche took time off for Christmas and New Years following their final shows in December 1997. Starting in 1998, they sat down and took a hard look at everything. It was speculated they might add a keyboard player to the band, or even just continue as a four-piece and change the arrangements to account for the loss of a second guitar. Tate even tested the waters outside of Queensrÿche by auditioning for Journey. He tried out and sang on demos for three songs with Neal Schon and Jonathan Cain – one of which, "Walking Away from the Edge", would end up on Journey's *Red 13* EP in a re-written form. Steve Augeri ended up landing the gig as they felt Tate wasn't the right fit vocally. Tate even admitted at the time that he couldn't see himself singing a song like "Lovin' Touchin' Squeezin'" for Journey every night. After that, Tate renewed his focus on Queensrÿche.

It was ultimately decided they would move forward as a band and find a replacement for Chris DeGarmo. The band made the official announcement on January 27, 1998, that DeGarmo had left the band and they were going to replace him and continue on. "As you could imagine, November 1997 was a very shaky and uncertain time for me," Michael Wilton explains. "For sixteen years I had been part of the team. When that changed, I was suddenly faced with the question of, 'What do I do now?' A lot of thought and emotions were flooding my mind. It was also hard to believe that the shows in South America would possibly be the last time anyone would see a Queensrÿche show. What followed those last shows were cordial good byes and then everyone headed back to their families for the holidays. In early January, Geoff called me and asked what I wanted to do. I told him that I loved playing guitar and I loved being part of Queensrÿche. I didn't want to go solo or join another band. So, the next step was the lineup. We thought about being a four piece, but that was uncomfortable for me. I have built my playing as a team member in the guitar department. So, it was up to me to now find and create the new dynamic guitar team duo. There began the search, I called a few people and so did Geoff. Everyone I called was busy building a solo career or guest spotting with other bands on tour."

They talked about a few possible candidates, but they decided to stick close to home with somebody they had known for a long time—Kelly Gray. They had already asked him to produce their next album, so it made sense to also see if he wanted to step into DeGarmo's shoes. "It was kind of ironic really," Gray says. "I was doing the Brother Cane record [*Wishpool,* released in 1998] and I came up to do some [recording] work for *Bob's Garage,* a small radio special Queensrÿche was doing [in June 1997]. We did "Silent Lucidity" and a few other songs that day, and the guys and I talked about me producing the next Queensrÿche record." The former Myth guitarist and main songwriter had gone through a number of bands post-Myth—Fade To Grey, Lyon House, and Dog Daze (with Kim Harris even managing the latter two)—but none managed to break out of the local club scene. Gray moved into the production world working at London Bridge studios in the 1990s, and had done very well for himself in that regard. He worked on albums by Candlebox, Dokken, Second Coming, Nevermore and others. "After that, Chris got a hold of me about helping me wire some stuff in his home studio," Gray adds. "I didn't know anything about what he was up to at the time, and then I never heard anything from Queensrÿche. Out of the blue, Geoff called me up one day, and told me Chris left. We started talking about guitarists ... and Geoff tells me he was thinking about me."

Adds Wilton: "One day, Geoff called and mentioned Kelly Gray. My first thought was, 'Yes!', but I answered, 'Isn't he into producing these days?'" Gray was still doing production and studio work, but he was also interested in joining up with his old friends. It seemed like a perfect fit. Scott and Eddie had known Kelly since high school, and Geoff had been in a band with him and was still friends with Gray as well. Kelly brought his playing and songwriting skills to the table, along with his experience in the studio. "I've known each of these guys before they even knew each other," Gray says. "There is a history to it. The only one I didn't know that long was Michael, but still, I knew him in The Mob days. I'm the historical element of Queensrÿche. Geoff and I did some good things back in the day with Myth."

"After Geoff and I talked about the dynamics of the group and whom we would be bringing in as part of our team, I decided to give Kelly a call," Wilton states. "It was now the 1st of February [1998]. When we finally hooked up on the phone, I realized that he was someone I wanted to hang around with. I was surprised by his humbleness. He had no big ego and was not even close to being a freak show. He just had a genuine hunger to do something new with a bunch of guys he has known for almost 20 years. Kelly and I spoke on the phone that day for a while and then he asked me to come over to his house and jam. What a concept! I had not done that in years."

Michael continues on: "I brought over a Marshall head and 2 x 12 Wizard cabinet and a Les Paul. I really did not know what to expect. I walked in with my gear into his home studio that he built there. The sound was great! He is really an amazing producer/engineer. We set up the cabinets, miked them through the Mackie mixing console and his first words were, 'So, what ideas do you have?' I was surprised. No elaborate presentation? No ADAT mix? No DAT tapes? No drum machines? So, I pulled out a riff that I had in my head and he immediately wrote a counterpart to it. We began going back-and-forth until we had the basic arrangement of, 'The Right Side.' [Later re-titled

"The Right Side of My Mind.'] I thought to myself, 'This is so easy, so cool, so back to the way I used to write.' Then we jammed until we had ear fatigue, and then Kelly spoke the magical words, 'Do you want to go get coffee?' I knew then that this guy knew me. Instant friendship. Later, we put some songs together on an ADAT and had Scott listen to them. He was pumped. So, Kelly built Scott a drum room [that Scott fell in love with], and put down some guide drum tracks. Eddie vibed. Geoff vibed. Success! The next step was to bring all of our recording gear over and build a full studio with a digital workstation. I believe it was the third week in February when we all jammed and recorded live, the parts for, 'Breakdown Room' [later called simply "Breakdown"], 'The Right Side,' and 'What Kind of Man.' [the latter name adjusted to "Wot Kinda Man" on the album.] We were all in agreement that there was an exciting chemistry happening between all of us. That weekend we all celebrated my birthday at a restaurant in Seattle and began planning for the future."

Things came together quickly and Queensrÿche continued to jam and write more music over the next few months with their new fifth member. Kelly's home studio served as the perfect place to develop and record demos of new material and they started that process by mid-March 1998. One person wasn't as thrilled about the arrangement and had concerns about how long the new union would last with Gray—Kelly's brother, Howard Dee Gray. He states: "I moved in with my brother about '96. He showed up at my house with a Porsche and said, 'Hey, want a ride?' It was after Candlebox had hit. Then he asked me if I wanted a place to live. It was Mike Ferguson [Lyon House and Dog Daze drummer] who actually suggested it as Kelly had this giant estate and he was never home. That way he would have somebody to watch it. I was just living with another friend at the time. So I said okay. I was living in the basement and there was this other room nobody was using so I built a studio in it. [Then] Queensrÿche came back into the picture. Chris DeGarmo had left the band and Kelly joined them. And I knew once Geoff started showing up things would get crazy again. I had been living there for a couple of years and dating my wife, Shannon. The Queensrÿche guys started showing up more and more and changing the studio all around. Eventually, Kelly moved me out and Queensrÿche in. And I'm like, 'Are you kidding me?' My bedroom became a vocal booth. They started recording stuff in there and it got too difficult to manage. So, I eventually moved out and moved in with my girlfriend."

Despite Kelly's brother's concern about the "craziness" that had often enveloped Myth in the past, his brother joining Queensrÿche seemed like a good thing and everybody in the band was happy with the way things were progressing. On May 16, 1998, local fans would get their first taste of the music Queensrÿche had been working up with Kelly, at a listening party at a fan club gathering called "Seattle '98" held at the Showbox Theater. This was a good gauge of fan response and four new songs were played—"When the Rain Comes", "One" [later titled "One Life"], "Breakdown Room" and "Right Side." Kelly Gray was in attendance, giving fans the first glimpse of the man who would step into DeGarmo's shoes. Up until then, Queensrÿche was coy about who they had selected to replace DeGarmo, posting photos from the studio on queensryche.com with Gray's face obstructed. Tons of guesses were bantered around, including former Fates Warning axeman Frank Aresti and local guitarist James Byrd (formerly of Fifth Angel). Eventually, it was announced that Gray had stepped into Chris' shoes and was not only playing on the album and co-writing material, but that he would be part of the band as well.

By the end of the year, they had enough material for an album recorded and were shopping for a new manager and record label. Everybody was feeling pretty good about their direction and results so far. "The injection of Kelly Gray into what we do has been nothing less than pleasurable," Rockenfield states. "I feel more relaxed and at peace in my life and creatively than I ever have. I think that the challenge of learning a new chemistry that comes with having a new member and from us redesigning our infrastructure has  made me look at things differently. I have had more fun making music with the guys and Kelly than I have had in years. We've been together for nine months as the new Queensrÿche and the tunes are flowing like a severed artery. The future holds beautiful things. The 'evolutionary train' was meant to stop at our depot. The beauty is in the chemistry."

Chris DeGarmo also popped back up in the public eye at this time as a member of Alice in Chains guitarist Jerry Cantrell's solo touring band in 1998 (in support of his solo album, *Boggy Depot*). Chris played 28 shows with them on through the summer and fall. They wrapped it up with local appearances at the DV8 club and the Showbox Theater on October 30 and 31, 1998. Included in their set were covers of the Pink Floyd songs "Brain Damage" and "Eclipse." Many Queensrÿche fans noticed that DeGarmo had covered over the "Tri-Ryche" tattoo on his arm. This certainly seemed to be a sign that his exodus from the band he co-founded was final. DeGarmo would continue his friendship with Cantrell and the other Alice in Chains members as the years went on. Following the tour in 1998, he also made a guest appearance on a song on Jerry's follow-up solo album, *Degradation Trip*, in 2002. DeGarmo also partnered with Alice in Chains bassist Mike Inez and drummer Sean Kinney to form Spys4Darwin, which also featured Sponge vocalist Vinnie Dombroski. The group created a six-song EP, *Microfish*, in 2001. The group made one live appearance at KNDD's Endfest on August 4, 2001, but by the next year, all the members moved on to other projects.

In early 1999, Seattle's KISW Radio hosted Queensrÿche and they played three songs on air - "Breakdown Room", "Liquid Sky" and "Sacred Ground." They also played a special "fan club" only concert in Seattle at NAF Studios (where bands such as Soundgarden often rehearsed), premiering some of the new songs that would end up on the new album, which would be called *Q2k*. This was Kelly's first live performance with the band—January 16, 1999. Queensrÿche's eleven-song set contained five new songs, including "One", "Breakdown Room", "Right Side", "Sacred Ground" and "Burning Man."

COLLECTOR CULTURE & FAN DEVOTION A KEY FACTOR IN QUEENSRŸCHE'S SUCCESS

By Brian J. Heaton and Brian L. Naron

Every successful band has a legion of dedicated fans behind them. But Queensrÿche fans hold a special place in the story of the group. In the pre-grunge era, there weren't many eyes on the Pacific Northwest for new musical talent. When Queensrÿche came to the attention of EMI Records, it was in large part due to the staggering record sales of the *EP*—an independent release that was gobbled up by local fans.

Once EMI noticed the *EP* had sold approximately 15,000 copies and signed Queensrÿche, it took a long time for the band to build a mainstream audience. The support of Queensrÿche's hardcore fans and collectors helped sustain the band during the lean years from the first *EP* through *Rage for Order*, before *Operation: Mindcrime* and *Empire* finally put Queensrÿche on the map and the rest of the world took serious notice.

A fan presence was established right at the very beginning thanks to the formation of Queensrÿche's fan club. Started by Kim and Diana Harris in spring 1983, the band's fan club has been a mainstay for decades, deftly shifting formats as technology improved and success enabled it to expand. In the beginning, a single 3.5 x 5 autographed band photo and a one-page welcome letter was the extent of the club. As 1983 went on, the slogan "Be on the Forefront" was used as a rallying cry encouraging fans to sign up.

In early 1984, the first fan club kit was created and sent to members, consisting of a numbered "Ryche Campaign" laminate, a numbered computer printout, an autographed 8 x 10 band photo and press kit housed in a black and gold mylar folder. Eventually, a newsletter was started, and fans would periodically receive a photocopied 8.5 x 11, multi-page, typewriter-written update on Queensrÿche. It contained the latest news and tour dates from the band and advertisements for swag. The latter would change over the years and include such items as t-shirts, Tri-Ryche pendants, key chains, and posters.

Metal Sushi (aka, Martha Wilton, Michael's mother) took over the fan club from Kim and Diana Harris in spring 1985. As Queensrÿche became more popular, so did the fan club. The newsletter expanded, shifting to a large format with multiple oversized black and white pages that could be folded and mailed out to fans. The content lengthened as well, containing exclusive photos of and interviews with the band, and more detailed information and merchandise.

As word about Queensrÿche spread, so did fan interaction. Queensrÿche certainly wasn't a secret. But from 1982-1987, if you were a fan, there was a sense of commonality and belonging that you shared, even with strangers. Queensrÿche played a more intelligent brand of hard rock and metal which united fans. Rychers would become pen pals, meet at gigs, and many became huge collectors of Queensrÿche memorabilia (we'll get to that shortly).

When Queensrÿche reached its commercial pinnacle in the early-1990s, many hardcore Rychers became just like the Deadheads, Phishheads, and Rush Rats before them. Large gatherings of Queensrÿche fans would travel from city to city, often for a week's worth of Queensrÿche shows, buying up t-shirts and merchandise in droves. At times, the band would play softball games with fans sponsored by local radio stations.

The sense of community and homegrown spirit of the band only encouraged collectors more. As technology grew more accessible, a dedicated legion of fans who would record bootlegs of Queensrÿche's live performances and gather online to trade them and discuss the band. (Queensrÿche even hosted a "taper's section" on its 1995 Road to the Promised Land tour for those wanting to capture their live shows.)

The togetherness and sense of pride fans had about Queensrÿche continued en force through the 1990s. In spring

1994, however, Metal Sushi stepped down from running the Queensrÿche fan club. The band briefly turned merchandise sales over to Chuck Anderson from South Carolina, before opting to run it themselves in 1997. Chuck was the creator and editor of the *Tri-Ryche Times*. The *Tri-Ryche Times* was a fan-created magazine that evolved from a simple newsletter to a slick publication featuring pages of color pictures, interviews, fan letters, merchandise for sale, and more.

After some experimenting with the fan club structure and leadership over a couple of years in the mid-1990s (with Tina Rose initially taking over Metal Sushi), the torch was ultimately passed to "Ziggy," (aka Susan Tate, Geoff's wife). Under her watch, *Eye on Queensrÿche*, a full color quarterly magazine, replaced the band's old newsletter and the fan club used the exploding popularity of the internet to form local subsidiaries called "Empires." These localized groups would put up collectible swag throughout their communities and organize official meet and greets among members. Many are still active today on social media.

"Ziggy" would revamp the fan club a few different times over the next 10-15 years, modifying it to provide members with reserved fan club tickets to Queensrÿche shows, backstage passes for before and after show meet and greets with the band, and at times, special access to soundchecks.

For many fans, however, seeing the band on the road wasn't enough. As Queensrÿche's popularity grew, the group's hometown of Seattle became a pilgrimage for many Rychers. In 1996, a semi-regular "Seattle" fan event would draw hundreds of the band's biggest supporters to the Emerald City.

Seattle '96

Seattle '96 took place on Friday, June 28, 1996, at the Best Western Orca Room in downtown Seattle, bringing together fans from all over the world to celebrate the music of Queensrÿche. Seattle '96 wasn't an official fan club event. But Anita Moor, who worked for the fan club, had an idea to bring fans together and started the process to organize the gathering.

Unfortunately, Anita couldn't attend herself, so needing "boots on the ground" in Seattle, Sharon Harkins Lundstrom stepped in to help organize the event. Sharon was dating and would eventually marry David Jackson, the brother of Queensrÿche bassist Eddie Jackson. Sharon and Anita enlisted Claudia Salgado and Helen Kopec (who was President of the Windy City Empire at that time) to help bring Seattle '96 together and the foursome began planning it in late-April 1996.

The plan was to have the Orca Room outfitted with TVs and VCRs to provide a Queensrÿche soundtrack for everyone in attendance. Sharon and Claudia would also provide food and decorate the room. But when it came to decorations, the team felt more was needed. They called Tim Shelton, a fan and collector of Queensrÿche memorabilia to help dress up the room. Tim then contacted Brian Naron (one of the writers of this article) to join him.

 Between the two of them, Shelton and Naron organized their extensive Queensrÿche collections for display and spare collectibles for sale, thus planting the seed for the Rÿchean Archÿves - Queensrÿche Memorabilia Gallery that would follow in the years to come. The initial display at Seattle '96 included rare posters, test pressings, tour shirts, and even some of the gold and platinum album awards honoring the band's milestone record sales.

At 6:00 p.m. on the day of the event, guests arrived, checked in, and picked up their name tags while rare and live videos of the band were playing. Attendees hailed from France, Japan, Germany, and all over the United States. People were getting acquainted with new and old friends as collectors were perusing

Shelton and Naron's wares. The room was full of laughter and smiles as Rychers enjoyed like-minded company. Shortly before 8:00 p.m., as the group was being updated about the official  fan club, Lundstrom walks up to Shelton and Naron and whispers "the band is here."

Precisely at 8:00 p.m., the party was suddenly interrupted by a loud familiar voice asking, "Is this a Shriners convention, or what?!" Geoff Tate entered the room, followed by the rest of Queensrÿche. The band mingled for two hours, signing autographs, posing for pictures, answering questions about the new album (which would be titled *Hear in the Now Frontier*). The guys were in great moods, all smiles and appreciative of everyone in the room. Scott Rockenfield was sleep deprived due to his daughter Navee Dae being born six days earlier and Geoff sang "Happy Birthday" to one of ladies in attendance who traveled all the way from Japan.

"As for the band showing up, I had told Ed, weeks before the event, that it would cool if the band could show up or do a video to say hello or something," said Lundstrom. "He pretty much ignored that, but Geoff Tate's sister Amy and his mom wanted more information. They in turn told Susan, Susan told Geoff, and suddenly the band was coming."

Prior to the band leaving the event, Chris was asked by Chuck Anderson about his thoughts and feelings on Seattle '96. Chris answered: "It was great! It was really nice to see everyone and get a chance to talk with the people that listen to what it is that we do and appreciate what we do. That's the point of us showing up there was to say a personal thank you."

Fans spent Saturday and Sunday visiting Seattle area landmarks including the Space Needle, Pike Place Market, Mt. Rainier, Snoqualmie Falls, and the Bite of Seattle food festival.

The Rychean festivities culminated with a farewell dinner at the Old Spaghetti Factory on Sunday evening. The dinner provided the Rychean horde had one last chance to commune with their newfound friends and enjoy one another's company.

Most of the event attendees signed an excellent drawing of the Tri-Ryche and Space Needle hovering over the band, with the Seattle '96 logo at the bottom. It was created by Laura DePuy, a comic book colorist and Queensrÿche fan. The framed art, commemorating the Seattle '96 event, was then presented to Sharon, for her hard work for putting on such a great event.

SCENES FROM SEATTLE '96

Seattle '98

There was no "Seattle '97" event, as Queensrÿche was out on the road supporting *Hear in the Now Frontier* across the United States. Sadly, original guitarist Chris DeGarmo had left the band, but Queensrÿche welcomed guitarist Kelly Gray into the group in early 1998. Gray, who was a bandmate of Geoff's in his pre-Queensrÿche band, Myth, had gone on to become a successful producer for the likes of Candlebox and Brother Cane, among others.

Gray was introduced to Queensrÿche fans at Seattle '98, held on May 16, 1998, at the Showbox Theater in Seattle. The event was well attended by hundreds and the affair featured an informal meet and greet with the band. Fans also got to hear some new songs Queensrÿche was working on that were being played over the sound system during the event. These tunes would eventually be featured on 1999's *Q2k*.

"Most of us had never met in person, but it felt like a big family reunion because of our connection through the music," recalled Seattle '98 attendee Staci Heaton. "I remember everyone being very excited to meet the man who would be replacing our hero Chris DeGarmo, and Kelly Gray was very gracious and humble despite all the attention. I can only recall snippets of what we heard that night, and what would go onto be *Q2k*, and that it was different. And to me that was okay. I considered every Queensrÿche album a new chapter anyway, so I was ready to follow along."

Having gotten some great feedback about his collectibles display during Seattle '96, Naron hosted the first official Rÿchean Archÿves event at his record store, Innergroove Music, in downtown Tacoma during the Seattle '98 weekend. Fan Kory Pohlman was the first to see the fabled Archÿves. "His store was packed with rare collectibles and records," Pohlman said. "He had one Queensrÿche *EP* on 206 records, unopened. So, I snatched that up. I was in heaven, he has so much cool stuff to look at, it was a lot to take in."

Seattle '99

Eight months later, on January 16, 1999, Queensrÿche held another event, dubbed "Seattle '99," at NAF Studios in Seattle. The event was an official fan club-only ticketed affair, as the band would perform exclusively for its members. The gig would also mark Queensrÿche's first performance without Chris DeGarmo.

Queensrÿche's team dressed the rehearsal space up nicely, using *Operation: Mindcrime*-era staging and chain link fencing to set a darker mood. As hundreds of Rychers crammed the space, the band played a blistering set of songs from *Operation: Mindcrime, Empire,* and *Promised Land,* fused with tunes from its forthcoming record, *Q2k.* New songs performed included "Breakdown Room" (later renamed "Breakdown"), "One" (later renamed "One Life"), "Right Side" (later renamed "The Right Side of My Mind"), "Sacred Ground," and "Burning Man."

The show served as a testing ground for the material Queensrÿche was working on and was met with resounding approval from the fans in attendance. The performance was stopped briefly as fans sang "Happy Birthday" to Geoff Tate, who had celebrated his 40th trip around the sun just two days earlier. Cake was provided for the band and fans. The event was a success (minus some grumbling as the beer ran out), as fans left the venue excited about the energy in the new songs (not to mention coming from the band) that they had witnessed.

The July 1999 issue of *Metal Edge* featured a letter from fan Kristi Nohelty that described the new Queensrÿche songs performed at Seattle '99 as "outstanding, very heavy."

"Kelly Gray had some blazing solos and the band was energized," Nohelty wrote. "Geoff Tate's voice was as fresh as ever—evidenced by 'Spreading the Disease' and 'The Needle Lies' from *Operation: Mindcrime.*"

Queensrÿche – Seattle '99

Photos by Kristi Garrison (Nohelty)

S2k1

Queensrÿche didn't have a "Seattle" event in 2000, as the band was touring heavily in support of *Q2k* throughout the year. But they made up for it in 2001, as the fan weekend brought in thousands of Rychers from all over the world for not one, but two Queensrÿche-related shows and various get-togethers. First up was Geoff Tate's debut solo performance on Friday, June 1, 2001, at the Catwalk, in Seattle.

Fans lined the streets to get in and were treated to a mixture of rarely played Queensrÿche songs and various cuts from Tate's forthcoming debut solo album. Geoff and his band opened with a version of Queensrÿche's rendition of "Gonna Get Close to You" by Lisa Dal Bello—with fans getting a kick out of Tate sporting a pair of fangs in his mouth while singing the tune.

The main event of the weekend would be a live performance from Queensrÿche the next night, on June 2, 2001, at the Showbox Theater. Queensrÿche would perform a career-spanning set that was recorded for an online stream that would be broadcasted later that summer. The band broke out classics such as "En Force," "No Sanctuary," and "Queen of the Reich," all of which hadn't been played live for almost a decade. Pamela Moore reprised her role as "Sister Mary", singing with Geoff Tate during "Suite Sister Mary."

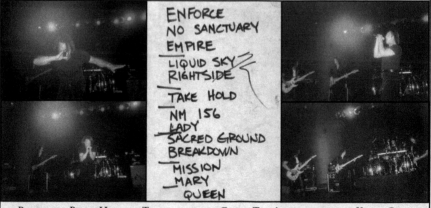

PHOTOS BY BRIAN HEATON. THE SETLIST WAS GEOFF TATE'S AND SIGNED BY KELLY GRAY.

Rychean Archyves 2001

Photos by Brian Heaton.

FROM THE COLLECTION OF BRIAN NARON

Welcome to the RŸCHEAN ARCHŸVES. Please feel free to look at all of the items within. Take the utmost care when handling these items and leave them as you found them. These treasures have been graciously donated for all to view and enjoy. Items with price tags are for sale, please see the curator to make a purchase. Thank you for visiting the ARCHŸVES, Take Hold.

Welcome to the
RŸCHEAN ARCHŸVES
You can leave now, but I think you'll stay...

HOURS

FRIDAY JUNE 1
NOON- 4:00PM

SATURDAY JUNE 2
11AM - 3 PM

SUNDAY JUNE 3
11AM - 3PM

Brian Naron, Curator

Revolution Colin,
Editor of the Rychean Archyves

...Thank you for stopping by!

But while the shows were the high-profile portions of the S2k1 weekend, it was the fans, not the band, that truly made the event an experience. For example, Carla Park created a beautiful commemorative poster with the Tri-Ryche and Space Needle. The image was also used on t-shirts and laminates for Queensrÿche's show. Local fans such as Nancy "Summer" Daly volunteered time to organize activities for those coming from out-of-town. Others organized a Queensrÿche jam fest at a local rehearsal studio. Dozens of the more musically inclined Rychers such as guitarists Thomas Morningstar and Jason Tomasulo, drummer (and later Queensrÿche roadie and tour manager) Scott "Fozzy" O'Hare and others showed up to play renditions of Queensrÿche songs.

Groups of friends reconnected in-person at various dinners and lunches throughout the Seattle area and took in the beauty of the Pacific Northwest—many sporting Queensrÿche-related shirts and doing their best to support the band. The Rÿchean Archÿves made another appearance as well, and to-date, the S2k1 display of Queensrÿche memorabilia was likely the largest in history.

Naron, Colin Connelly (president of the Commonwealth Empire in Virginia), Doug Wirachowsky, and Ken Edwards took over two conference rooms at the Holiday Inn Express near Seattle Center. They set up both rooms wall-to-wall, with a massive collection of Queensrÿche artifacts. The rooms were set up in a museum-like gallery format. Band memorabilia was displayed in chronological order which featured framed promotional posters, RIAA record awards for gold and platinum sales, a six-foot *Promised Land* Tri-Ryche CD display, rare fan club items, bumper stickers, LPs, CDs, tapes, and press materials. There was also a table with many items the fans could buy.

Fans perusing the curated Queensrÿche collections were also treated with music, as Naron and company played rare live and demo songs from pre-Queensrÿche bands such as Myth, and live Queensrÿche videos from the *Hear in the Now Frontier* tour in 1997, and *The Warning* tour in 1984-1985. In addition, the curators had a Q&A with artist Matt Bazemore, who created *The Warning* album cover.

The "Seattle" events would fizzle out in the years that followed, but Naron hosted the Rÿchean Archÿves two more times. During the weekend of October 5-6, 2004, for the Empire Summit Collectors Forum, Queensrÿche was playing a two-night stand at The Moore Theater in Seattle that was billed as an evening with Queensrÿche featuring two acts—the first a set of hits through the years, and the second a full production of *Operation: Mindcrime*.

As of this writing, the last Rÿchean Archÿves happened during the weekend of October 13-15, 2006, when the band filmed their performances for what was touted as, Rock, Revenge, Redemption - Queensrÿche *Operation: Mindcrime I-II*. Both albums were performed in their entirety. (A video release of these shows, *Mindcrime at the Moore,* would be issued in 2007.) The Archÿves were again displayed in a gallery style presentation, this time at the Holiday Inn Express in downtown Seattle on Dexter Avenue, and created an additional point of destination while fans were in town.

While Queensrÿche never again rose to the arena-level heights of bands such as KISS or Rush, Rychers continue to hold their own as a fan group. Queensrÿche's hometown performances continue to be a catalyst for fans to travel to Seattle and gather with one another.

For example, droves of supporters from all over the world, including Japan, descended on Seattle on June 26, 2013, for the band's 2013 self-titled album release show at The Crocodile—the first Queensrÿche record with Todd La Torre on vocals. People lined the streets trying to get into the venue and those who did snapped up rare silver-colored vinyl of the band's new LP. Fans even attended the Seattle Mariners baseball game the afternoon before the show to root on Queensrÿche throwing out the first pitch. (It didn't bounce.)

Time and technology have shifted the ways fans interact over 40-plus years, but the dedicated support of Queensrÿche by diehard Rychers has been and will always be, a key element of the band's identity.

Queensrÿche eventually signed on with Ray Danniels (owner of the SRO Group), who had managed Rush from their early days, and also handled Van Halen, Extreme and King's X. Danniels was able to get Queensrÿche signed with Atlantic Records in the U.S., and also with Anthem Records in Canada [which Danniels owned as well], on the strength of the new recordings and the band's name and reputation. It looked like everything was falling into place with a new record deal, a big manager, and a new member that fit in well and everybody liked. Despite this, there were already "chinks in the armor" from the start in many people's minds, with whether or not Danniels was a good fit for the manager opening, or a good manager at all. Danniels had gotten the Van Halen gig when their longtime manager, Ed Leffler, had passed away. Alex Van Halen was married to Ray's sister and suggested him for a replacement. Sammy Hagar reportedly did not like or trust Danniels and eventually was replaced by Extreme singer Gary Cherone. The lone album with Cherone in 1998, *III,* was the biggest flop of Van Halen's career and almost split them up as well.

Gray finished the Queensrÿche recordings and had his friend and co-worker at London Bridge, Jonathan Plum, mix the album at that studio. *Q2k* was released finally on September 14, 1999, and was initially promoted well by  Atlantic. They pushed the advance single "Breakdown," to radio stations with decent results (an alternate version of the demo with a different arrangement, toned down Tate "screaming" vocal, and shortened title). It hit in the Top 40 at #27 and the album at #46 on the Billboard charts. The record itself also charted at #21 in Germany, #65 on the Japanese charts and #60 on the Swedish charts. "The Right Side of My Mind" (re-titled slightly from the original demo), was the second single and an animated video was made for it by Queensrÿche lightman Rory Berger. It got some play on VH1 Classic in 2000. It had a cool trade-off guitar solo, and an epic sort of feel to it, but failed to make any impact with the listening public. "Falling Down" and "Beside You" were also released as promo singles, but neither charted nor got any radio play.

There were at least four songs leftover from the sessions that didn't get included on *Q2k*: "Discipline", "Monologue", "I Howl" and "Til There Was You." Kelly Gray elaborates: "The way the writing process

works, sometimes we don't get the vibe on to finish a song. Actually, 'Discipline' could probably get resurrected. It is a cool tune, it just wasn't done yet. It's a very 'Queensrÿche-ish' song. 'Monologue' is something that Eddie wrote. It's a little wacky. (Laughs). The vibe is a little too 'punkish' for Queensrÿche though." Tate included "Til There Was You" in his solo tour set in 2001, and it ended up being included on the 2006 reissue of *Q2k*, along with "Howl" (with both song titles modified slightly).

Q2k was also significant in that it was the first album that credited the songwriting to just "Queensrÿche" instead of individual band members. It was stated they did it as a way to unify the band with the lineup changes, but it also was rumored to be an appeasement for some unhappiness about songwriting royalties and disbursements. In reality, Gray shouldered a large amount of the songwriting burden in the music department stepping into DeGarmo's shoes. He wrote or co-wrote ten out of the eleven songs on the record, as well as three of the songs mentioned above not used on the intitial release of *Q2k*. Despite that, it was still very much more of a group effort with Wilton co-writing the music for three songs: "Falling Down", "Breakdown" and "The Right Side Of

My Mind", and writing all of the music for "When The Rain Comes." Rockenfield co-wrote three songs: "Sacred Ground", Liquid Sky" and "Burning Man." Jackson co-wrote "Breakdown", and solely wrote the unused, "Monologue." Tate wrote all of the lyrics on the album.

The "Electric Shockwaves" tour (coined from a line in the song "Liquid Sky") kicked off on October 27, 1999, in Boise, Idaho, at the Bank of America Center. Following that, they did two nights at the Hard Rock Hotel in Las Vegas. The return show to Seattle on November 1, at the Paramount Theatre, featured a lengthy 24-song setlist that was well-received by fans. Newcomers doubleDrive opened for Queensrÿche on the western half of the North American tour, and Caroline's Spine on the eastern half. This concluded on December 7, 1999, and then a break for the holidays. During this leg of the tour, Queensrÿche added a version of U2's "Bullet the Blue Sky" to the setlist. Adding cover tunes to the set was unusual for Queensrÿche following the *Rage for Order* tour (where they played their cover of Lisa Dal Bello's "Gonna Get Close to You"). Kelly Gray explains how it came to be: "We weren't talking about playing covers, and then Scott started playing 'Bullet the Blue Sky' one day at rehearsal, then I started playing, then Mike started, Ed started getting the bass groove on it, and then Geoff strolled out and started singing it, and it sounded great, and we decided to do it." Queensrÿche would drop "Bullet the Blue Sky" on the next leg in Europe, but would perform "Join Together" by The Who, instead.

The Tea Party (another Danniels-managed band) opened for Queensrÿche in Europe and the UK from January 13 - February 7, 2000. Following that, it was back to the U.S. to finish the second leg of the tour. Jesse James Dupree and Project 86 opened for them for most of the shows. They played a couple of nights at the House of Blues in Chicago on March 25 and 26 and then took a bit of time off again. They wrapped it up with dates throughout June 2000 at the Las Vegas and West Hollywood House of Blues, and the Warfield in San Francisco, the Sun Theater in

Anaheim, Celebrity Theater in Phoenix, and a couple other locations. Queensrÿche played mostly theaters and a few larger amphitheaters on the tour with a minimized set. Their final show on the tour was back in Seattle, as part of Microsoft billionaire Paul Allen's Experience Music Project museum opening on June 25, 2000.

Queensrÿche: June 25, 2000
Experience Music Project Museum Opening

Photos by Brian Woodwick

Despite doubling up on the tour dates, *Q2k* sold only 150,000 copies total—far short of the 500,000 needed for gold RIAA certification, and half the copies that *Hear in the Now Frontier* shifted. Many hardcore Queensrÿche fans didn't like the album and were critical of Kelly Gray. They felt his look, personality and his playing style didn't fit the band at all. His "wah-wah" infused sound, was a stark contrast to DeGarmo's clean, crisp and melodic style. Gray wasn't at all interested in replicating the former guitarist's solos, either. "Honestly, I don't remember solos all that well," Gray says, laughing. "I come from a little more blues-based background. I've never been a very static solo writer. I like writing melodies and that kind of stuff."

The complex vocal melodies that Chris was a big part of, both in working with Geoff Tate on, and also performing in the studio and live, were lacking on *Q2k* and in concert. This was something Queensrÿche was very much known for in the past. The thought-provoking lyrics on social commentary and other subjects that had garnered them the "thinking man's metal band" moniker, were gone, replaced by songs about personal relationships (a trend that would continue as time went on). The sound of the album was typical to Gray's other productions, and to what other bands were doing around the late `90s, which was muddy, plain and simple—i.e., "grungy" sounding. It wasn't bad at all, and some people like it and some people don't. "*Q2k* has a healing element on it," Gray elaborates. "Being a little looser on the songwriting helped the guys bridge the gap and move forward. It's not the greatest record, but it's a good, solid record. It gave the band some confidence that we were able to do it, as I am sure there is a bit of security lost in the ordeal of losing Chris. It was a good kick in the pants. When I signed on, I was full of energy and ready to go. Having me in the band, there was immediate gratification because we were able to record and produce it with no waiting. On *Q2k*, a lot of those tracks are directly from that spontaneous writing element. They were written and recorded at the same time. 'Breakdown' was actually a one-take from a rehearsal. The main portion of it is live."

Following the EMP show, Capitol/Virgin released the *Greatest Hits* album, as likely a contractual obligation (since they had declined to keep the band after absorbing EMI-America), but it was perfect timing regardless. It featured 14 tracks from the albums up through *Hear in the Now Frontier* (two major singles from each, basically, with the exception of one from *Hear in the Now Frontier* and three from Empire), as well as the bonus tracks "Chasing Blue Sky" and "Someone Else?" (full band version). If it had been released a few years earlier, it likely would have sold a lot better, but it still managed to hit #149 on the Billboard charts in the U.S. The tour with Iron Maiden in summer/fall 2000 was a bright spot around the *Greatest Hits* album during that time, as Queensrÿche was still a popular enough live band, and the dedicated heavy metal

audience was perfect for an all "hits" setlist. They served as direct support for Maiden, with Judas Priest singer Rob Halford's solo band, Halford, as opener. They kicked it off with a show on August 5, 2000, at Madison Square Garden in New York City that sold out within two hours of it

being announced. The Tacoma Dome show was on September 19, 2000, and was packed as well. They did 35 shows total together with the last one being a one-off in Mexico on January 19, 2001. Rumors were that there was a bit of angst between Queensrÿche and Dream Theater during this time. As the story goes, Queensrÿche and Dream Theater had made plans to tour together as co-headliners in 2000. As a result, Dream Theater turned down an offer from Iron Maiden to be direct support on the tour. Then Queensrÿche swooped in and took the direct support spot instead, backing out of any plans with Dream Theater. If there was any animosity around this it was resolved a few years later.

Queensrÿche took a break from playing concerts after that for the rest of the winter and the spring. During the five months off, it was decided that Ray Danniels was not working out as manager. Susan Tate suggested Lars Sorenson, who she had worked for as an assistant manager. Some members of the band were not as keen on getting rid of Danniels. "Immediately there was a strong resentment in the rest of the band about firing Ray Danniels," Michael Wilton stated in 2012. "It was not a unanimous decision, but it was the first of many 'my way or the highway' ultimatums from Geoff Tate." The band eventually agreed to give Lars a shot, and

Susan still assisted him and continued to run the Queensrÿche fan club as well. "I've known Lars for a long time," Kelly Gray said at the time. "He's worked with me on projects in the early days before Candlebox. For Queensrÿche, because it is a localized family business now, we wanted someone local. Lars is a good guy, and fits perfectly." They also decided to look for another record label, as the band felt Atlantic had not really gotten behind them with the support they needed.

During this period (2000 – 2001) various members worked on solo projects. Scott Rockenfield and Kelly Gray joined forces with Brother Cane singer Damon Johnson and bassist Roman Glick, to form Slave to the System

as a side project while Queensrÿche was on a break in 2000. Scott Heard, Kelly's old bandmate from Lyonhouse and Dog Daze, rounded out the lineup on second guitar and backing vocals and also contributed to songwriting for the album. They recorded and self-released a self-titled album in 2001, with Gray at the helm producing and engineering, and played two shows around it—one in Seattle and one in Tennessee (Johnson and Glick's home state). Spitfire Records later signed the band and reissued the CD with new artwork in February 2006. Slave to the System played 19 shows in the South, Midwest and West Coast in support of it. Johnson said they had a follow-up album done after that, but only three songs surfaced on the internet in 2008—"Zero," "Freak," and "Who Am I Today."

Geoff Tate started work on his first solo album during the spring of 2001. He hired all local musicians to help him create the record with bassist Chris Fox (Bitter End), guitarist and vocalist Jeff Carrell (Diamondback, Dr. Unknown), drummer Evan Schiller (Sadhappy), keyboardist Howard Chillcott, and second guitarist Scott Moughton (who would end up working with Tate much later on) rounding out the lineup. Ryan Hadlock engineered the album and recorded it at both Bear Creek Studios and Zulu Sound (both in Washington). It was eventually released on Sanctuary Records on June 25, 2002, and hit #22 on Billboard's Heatseeker's

chart. While Scott and Kelly's sideband was similar to Queensrÿche and Brother Cane's music, as you might expect, Tate's first solo album was quite different than his Queensrÿche output. There were a couple heavier songs on the disc, but most were much mellower dance-type music, pop, and dramatic mid-tempo tracks.

Michael Wilton also explored the side project world with his band, Soulbender. He formed it with his friends from the band Fallen Angel (which also included Travis Bracht from Peace and Silence and Second Coming), guitarist Dave Groves and drummer Wes Hallam, along with My Sister's Machine singer Nick Pollock. Bassist Martin Van Keith completed the lineup. Soulbender recorded 17 songs in 2001, and played their debut show opening for Geoff Tate's solo band, at the EMP, on June 22, 2002. Eventually, their self-titled debut album was released on Licking Lava Records in 2004. They toured a bit around it at that point, with Chuck Miller (Peace And Silence) replacing bassist Van Keith. People often describe the album as 'Tool meets Alice in Chains" and it definitely fit in the "Alternative Hard Rock/Metal" style.

On June 1, 2001, Geoff Tate performed his first-ever solo show at the Catwalk in Seattle. The next day, Queensrÿche played another fan club show (also in Seattle), this time dubbed "S2k1". They featured a special setlist that included rarely played tracks such as: "En Force" and "No Sanctuary" (from *The Warning*), and Pamela Moore also joined them onstage for "Suite Sister Mary." The show was filmed for an online broadcast later on, and Tate also announced they had signed with Sanctuary Records.

Following that, they played a couple of rock festivals in Utah and Wisconsin on July 19 and 20, 2001, respectively. They completed the *Greatest Hits* tour with two nights in Seattle at the Moore Theater, on July 27 and 28, for the recording of a live album. Local band Second Coming, a band Kelly had produced their second self-titled album for Capitol Records, opened for Queensrÿche for the shows. Gray recorded and engineered both nights. It was marketed to fans as completely different sets for each night. There were unfortunately some audio issues from the start. Some was useable and some was not, and a lot of it had to be corrected later on in the studio, and cut up a bit more from both nights. Additionally, only the first half of the show was different with the second half of them being the same, not what was initially promoted.

Live Evolution was released as a two-CD and single DVD set on September 5, 2001. It was split up into four "suites" with them being: *The EP/Warning/ Rage for Order; Operation: Mindcrime; Empire/ Promised Land; Hear in the Now Frontier/Q2k*. It was praised at the time for great picture quality on the DVD, but the video only included twenty of the thirty songs on the double CD set. There are a few audio issues on the disc, but overall, it came out fine and was well-received by the media and fans. It hit #143 on the Billboard 200 U.S. Charts and #20 on the Billboard Top Internet charts. It was eventually certified "Gold" by the RIAA in 2008.

Queensrÿche did a short tour around the release starting on November 1, 2001, back at the Celebrity Theatre in Phoenix, Arizona. They were scheduled to play a few dates in Japan just prior to that, but they canceled due to security concerns around the 9/11 terrorist attacks (this would unfortunately come back to haunt them a bit down the road and was a factor in making a certain record a few years later). They played just 20 dates around the U.S., concluding the jaunt in New York City at the Beacon Theater on November 21. It was reported that none of the band members were speaking to each other, and Tate, Wilton and Jackson left the stage in New York without a bow. It was Kelly Gray's final performance with Queensrÿche, and they were back to four again....

CHAPTER 14:
THE GREAT DIVIDE

K elly Gray was out of Queensrÿche by the start of 2002. There
was an official statement finally in May, and he was not going
to be part of the writing, playing or production for the next
album. Fans turned sour on Gray's style of playing, and he also had
trouble dealing with life on the road. Gray had always played mostly
local shows in Myth and his other bands, so likely this was an eye-
opening experience touring outside of the Pacific Northwest. Geoff
Tate would later reveal in the liner notes of the 2006 reissue of Q2k:
"We were in a brand new world, Kelly's world... Kelly lived hard and
fast and the people around him were the same. I have personally never
seen as many drugs and as much alcohol consumed as when Kelly
was in the band... The toll of indulgence was heavy. The band wasn't
speaking, the new manager was fired, we were looking for a new record
company, and three of our friends were dead. Road life is tough. It's not
for everyone, and some people can't pace themselves, and then they get
into trouble." As the members of Queensrÿche were no strangers to the
party scene of the 1980s (Metallica dubbed them "Krellryche" during
their tour together due to their fondness for the white powder), this
was saying something. It could likely have been that his bandmates had
matured and grown out of their younger, crazier days, and Gray had
not, contributing to some of the tension. Kelly continued to produce and
engineer albums for other bands
such as Nevermore, Red Halo,
Candlebox, and others after that.
Despite not being a member of
Queensrÿche anymore, he would
still continue to work with them

EXPERIENCE *MUSIC* PROJECT
GEOFF TATE CD RELEASE
SKY CHURCH
06/22/2002   DOORS OPEN AT   7:00 PM
Regular $20.00
NO REFUNDS

in that capacity in the studio as time went on, and with Tate on his solo projects.

Regardless of Gray's role as a member of Queensrÿche fizzling out, he was a major reason they kept going after DeGarmo leaving. It's entirely possible the band might have split up at that point shortening their legacy considerably. Unfortunately, it didn't hold it together for long. By 2002, there were numerous issues mounting within the band. At the time, specifically on June 30, 2002, Tate even commented on a radio interview on 100.7 WMMS in Cleveland that the members of Queensrÿche only communicated through managers and lawyers now.

Michael Wilton, Eddie Jackson and Scott Rockenfield started writing for the next record in the summer of 2002, and Geoff Tate joined them once his solo tour wrapped up to write lyrics. Tate had kept a journal on the road jotting down ideas and "taking the pulse" of society post-9/11 for use toward lyrics on the new album. Geoff also brought in some ideas on the music his solo band guitarist, Jeff Carrell, had come up with based on Tate's lyrics. Wilton especially felt this approach was wrong for Queensrÿche, which caused tension. "I believe this album should be hard and intense," Wilton said at the time. "What I have heard so far is not that. I have no desire to change Queensrÿche into an adult contemporary band. This should be a Queensrÿche album and not a Geoff Tate solo album." Wilton's inspirations at the time were from bands like Tool, that featured low tunings, heavy riffs, rhythmic drumming, progressive time signatures and arrangements, and aggressive, hypnotic vocals. Wilton had been incorporating the 'dropped-D' tunings in the last couple of albums, especially Q2k. "Low tunings make the guitar sound better," he said. "I think it fills the low midrange frequencies and really fills the mix. ESP has a 7-string that is cool. Having a low 'B' string really changes the playing spectrum."

Guitarist Mike Stone (Peter Criss Band, Eden, Jonas Hansson Band) was brought in by Lars Sorenson to help collaborate. "Ironically, when I was first contacted by the band, it was more of a songwriter than a guitar player," Mike Stone explains. "It was one of those things where their manager had known me for many years and was looking for someone who could sit down with the guys and maybe come up with some fresh ideas. He called me up and I said that would be awesome."

Out of the sessions, Stone contributed the song "Losing Myself" and helped with some parts on a couple other songs. Queensrÿche recorded at Robert Lang Studios in Shoreline, Washington, and also The Grove in Seattle. Scott Olson and Adam Kasper were the main engineers, and Sam Hofstedt assisted. Tom Hall also lent a hand with some of the recording. At some point in the fall, it is believed that Chris DeGarmo was contacted by one of the engineers working on the album, Olson or Kasper, to see if he would be willing to help with the album. DeGarmo was friends with both guys so it is highly likely it was one of them. The "theme" Tate had penciled out appealed to Chris, and he agreed to come help his old bandmates work on the album. His involvement definitely helped bring together the band, who were at odds with each other, and help bring the album to life. "I'd worked with the guys a little bit writing songs, and then I heard Chris DeGarmo was coming back. I thought that was great. I was busy working on my Transonics [side project] record anyway." Stone says.

DeGarmo had mostly focused on his piloting career during his time away from Queensrÿche, but had still stayed active to a small degree in the local music scene. As mentioned earlier, he had done a small late summer/fall tour with his friend (Alice In Chains guitarist/singer) Jerry Cantrell's solo band in 1998, and had also worked on in the band Spys4Darwin with Mike Inez, Sean Kinney and Vin Dombrowski. Additionally, Chris also appeared on Jerry Cantrell's second solo album in 2002, *Degradation Trip*, adding slide guitar to the song, "Anger Rising."

QUEENSRŸCHE TRIBE

Although the band itself made no official statement about a reunion with Chris DeGarmo, it appeared to fans and the public that a reunion was happening. It was hard to deny. Pictures were posted on the internet of him in the studio with the rest of the Queensrÿche guys, promotional photos with Chris and the band were taken and he was contributing to the sessions. He wrote the music to three songs: "Falling Behind," "The Art of Life" and "Doin' Fine." He also co-wrote

"Open" and "Desert Dance" with the other guys. Additionally, there was a fourth song DeGarmo wrote, "Justified," that some work was done on in those sessions, but it was not completed at the time and not used on *Tribe*. Chris did, however, pen that song entirely himself, including the lyrics. It was completed and mixed by Terry Date in 2007 and included on *Sign of the Times: The Best of Queensrÿche* in 2007. More on that later.

"The Art of Life" became a modern fan favorite for its epic feel. But the track's title dates back well into Tate's past. Back in the Myth days, Tate had written the lyrics to songs with titles that were re-used on Queensrÿche tracks. The titles of Myth demos such as "Take Hold of the Flame" and "Walk in the Shadows" became titles of Queensrÿche tunes—the songs were  completely different, but the titles were borrowed. "The Art of Life" was another example of this. While it is unknown whether the original track is Myth, the demo is clearly from sometime in the 1980s with Tate on vocals and Kelly Gray on guitar (the keyboards, however, sound a bit more modern than the preferred Hammond sound Randy Gane played in the earlier versions of Myth). Interestingly, however, on promotional copies of *Tribe*, the title of "The Art of Life" appears as "Under My Skin," or "U.M.S." When those promo CDs are played, the song is clearly Queensrÿche's "The Art of Life." Whether "Under My Skin" is a different song entirely that was subbed out for "The Art of Life", a misprint, or simply re-labeled later because Tate liked "The Art of Life" title better, is unknown.

A New Year's Eve 2002/2003 gig was booked in Anchorage, Alaska, that was supposed to include Chris DeGarmo, but he declined to do it and Mike Stone stepped in for him. "They had a New Year's gig in Alaska and Chris couldn't do it. I said sure. Then I had to learn all of the material in like five days," Mike Stone laughs. "Trial by fire, but I made it through, and then went back to mixing my Transonics album." It was also announced at that time that DeGarmo would likely join the band for their summer European dates in support of *Tribe*. He took part in a lengthy photo shoot for the album and it seemed to everybody at that time he was back in the band. Still, no official statement on him rejoining the band was made though. DeGarmo continued working with the band in the studio for the next month or two, but left before the sessions were completed.

If DeGarmo actually had any intentions to rejoin the band at that time, something happened during their time in the studio that made him change his mind about an actual reunion. Or at least contributed to that decision. Tate and DeGarmo were at odds about working on vocal arrangements together as they had in the past. Kelly Gray had taken a more "hands off" approach with Geoff, and let him work up his own vocal melodies and arrangements for *Q2k*, so Tate was likely used to doing it on his own now. This may have caused more tension between the two and helped contribute to DeGarmo's exit. "When Chris was in the band, he used to take part in a lot of Geoff Tate's vocal sessions, and they would work together on creating vocal harmony ideas," Eddie Jackson stated in 2012. "However, Geoff's demeanor [during the *Tribe* sessions] continued and when it was his turn to start recording, he rudely told Chris that he wasn't needed. Not a pleasant, 'Hey, thanks for coming back and recording with the band,' attitude. Chris DeGarmo, like a true gentleman, just kept his composure and simply got up and left." Tension between Tate and DeGarmo had been happening since at least the time in Big Log when they were working on *Promised Land*. Eddie Jackson was witness to an altercation between the two at Big Log and later revealed it: "While in the studio, I witnessed something that was a bit disturbing. I was sitting at a table reading some of the band's fan mail and started hearing yelling and cursing. As I turned my head towards the direction it was coming from, that's when I saw Geoff Tate slam through one of the studio doors while screaming at Chris DeGarmo from two feet away. 'Don't bring any more of your bullshit here. I don't need any more of your bullshit!' He was in such a rage I thought he was going to physically assault Chris. He continued to yell a couple more expletives and just walked away. Chris, like a true gentleman, just kept his composure and started walking towards the front door."

DeGarmo's departure before finishing *Tribe* caused some delays on completing the album in time for the scheduled June release. The album was pushed to July then. The five songs DeGarmo contributed music for were used on the album, but the sixth, "Justified," was left off due to being unfinished. Mike Stone was brought back in and he contributed one song, "Losing Myself," and a slide guitar solo on "Rhythm Of Hope" (which was likely intended for DeGarmo to do). One more song was worked up in the latter stages of the sessions,

but not used at that time, "Hostage." It was later reworked and included on Queensrÿche's next album.

To meet the deadlines, *Tribe* was likely pushed through and not fully completed. While on tour, Michael Wilton later added a solo for the song, "The Great Divide" that he had planned to include in the version on the album, and it was rumored that "Blood" was intended to have a second guitar part by DeGarmo that was never recorded. *Tribe* was sent to the label in time for the July release and Chris was digitally removed from the photos shot for it. Despite the fact that Chris had left during the sessions and did not contribute to all of the final album, Sanctuary marketed it as a new release featuring "the original lineup" with hype stickers on the CD wrapper, in ads and also included the intitial photos with DeGarmo in some (along with tour dates with Dream Theater). A bit misleading to fans, certainly.

Tribe was finally released on July 22, 2003, and had a pretty good public response intitally hitting #56 on the U.S Billboard charts, and #52 on the German charts. "Open" was released as the single and hit #38 on the singles charts. Just prior to the album drop, Queensrÿche played a handful of metal and rock festivals in Europe and the UK with Whitesnake, Motorhead, Saxon, Paul Dianno's Killers, Krokus, Budgie, Angra and others from June 4-8, 2003. At the Sweden Rock Festival, Kamelot also joined them on the bill featuring Casey Grillo on drums (who would figure into the Queensrÿche story much later on). "Saved" from *Hear in the Now Frontier* also made its live debut during this run of shows. Following that, they launched out on a co-headline tour of the U.S. and Canada with Dream Theater, and Fates Warning joining on many dates as the opener. They did 70 dates starting on June 23, 2003, in Texas. A highlight of the shows were members of Queensrÿche

and Dream Theater joining each other onstage for an encore, with usually a song from each band and a cover: "Take Hold of the Flame", or "Real World," Dream Theater's "Peruvian Skies," or "The Spirit Carries On", and Pink Floyd's "Comfortably Numb", or The Who's "Won't Get Fooled Again." Despite the positive fan response, tensions between the two bands were still simmering by then. "A co-headline [tour] with the band Dream Theater was another great concept, but due to a mud-slinging between Geoff Tate and the drummer, it ended up being an uncomfortable and trying time for us," Wilton explained.

Like tours of the past, the setlist included a good amount of new songs from their latest album. The title track, "Open", "Losing Myself," "Desert Dance," "The Great Divide" and "Rhythm of Hope" were included at various points with typically four or five included per show. Queensrÿche's headline shows would include a small acoustic section featuring some rarely performed live songs such as acoustic renditions of "Roads to Madness" (albeit an abridged version without the aggressive ending), and "My Global Mind." Some other rarities such as "Anybody Listening?" were also included in the shows. Mike Stone replaced DeGarmo in the touring lineup and at first seemed an odd fit, with his "punkish" haircut and image, but his guitar style and sound seemed to fit with Wilton's better than Gray's. He also had a great voice and helped with the backing vocals a lot. "Geoff and I had stayed in touch, and he called me and said they needed a guitar player for the tour—I've been with the band ever since," Mike Stone said at the time. Michael Wilton shouldered the load of having to help Stone learn the material quickly. "It was a year of hard touring with yet another new guitarist that I had to teach all of the material to in a short period of time," Wilton stated later on.

In the fall of 2003, Scott Rockenfield launched RockenWraps. It supplied customized drum wraps to many artists and companies—including ddrum and Bucketdrums. He said at the time that he wanted to design a drum kit that was unique and stood out in the crowd, as they usually came in just solid or sparkle colors or wood tones. For the initial launch he offered a signed copy of his first solo CD, *The X-Chapters*, to anybody who purchased a minimum set of three wraps through his website. Scott had released *The X-Chapters* the previous year on December 11, 2002, and it had garner positive response from fans and critics. He wrote all the music and played all of the instruments on the album. Some people described it in the vein of Jean-Michael Jarre, Kraftwork and Tangerine Dream, with some elements of Pink Floyd mixed in.

During the time Queensrÿche were out on tour, "Losing Myself" and "Rhythm Of Hope" were also released as singles, but failed to garner much attention. After the intial push by Sanctuary Records, the label support waned and the record failed to sell very well. Unfortunately, shades of EMI-America appeared again as Sanctuary was also on its way to folding. The record sold a disappointing 75,000 copies as of 2007. The record was also issued on DVD-Audio format, enabling fans to get a higher quality audio experience. Overall, *Tribe* likely only received one pressing and then once those were gone, fans couldn't find it. Some were probably disappointed to find out prior to the tour that Chris DeGarmo was not in the lineup and had only contributed to the album. Either way, it continued the downward trend for a band that a decade before had been on top.

(Author Note: Pirated copies of *Tribe* have been around for years with a cover of "Dust in the Wind" by Kansas included. It is unknown who the band is performing that track, but it is not Queensrÿche.)

CHAPTER 15:
MINDCRIME REVISITED

T he concert DVD, *The Art of Live,* was the last gasp with Sanctuary Records and released on April 20, 2004. Some delays with the CD due to audio issues caused it to come out later on in June. Queensrÿche had invested in recording and filming equipment prior to the 2003 tour, and utilized it to document many of the *Tribe* shows. It had been announced that a live DVD and CD would be released, with the video in full color and the album in 5.1 stereo audio. Unfortunately, the stage lights over-powered the cameras and it washed out all the color into a sepia tone. The audio for the CD also isn't mixed very well and had some vocal mistakes by Tate that probably should have been fixed in the studio. Susan Tate is credited as the producer of the DVD and Eddie Jackson is credited as supervising the audio for the CD. Eric Janko (Soulbender, Sunny Day Real Estate, Criminal Nation) recorded the shows and mixed the album at Triad Studios. Likely it was done to save costs on production, but the results

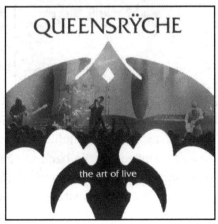

unfortunately weren't great. Many fans felt it was one of their worst releases in the catalog and it sold poorly. The track listing of the DVD/CD was nearly identical. The DVD featured songs from Queensrÿche's 2003 headline shows along with some behind the scenes and interview footage, The CD featured mostly the same songs, but "Anybody Listening?", which was on the CD, was cut off the

DVD in favor of adding two covers performed jointly by Queensrÿche and Dream Theater—"Comfortably Numb" by Pink Floyd and "Won't Get Fooled Again" by The Who.

Queensrÿche did a short tour around the release from March 13-April 25, 2004, with Symphony X as support for some of the dates (on the East Coast and in the Midwest), and Snake River Conspiracy (SRC) for the West Coast shows (in California and Las Vegas) from April 28-May 5. The latter band featured Jason Slater on bass, and he was also SRC's main songwriter and producer. Slater had also worked on albums for the bands Earshot, Enemy, Slaves On Dope, Twisted Method, and others, and was starting to make a name for himself at the controls. The Queensrÿche guys became friends with Slater, and he would become an important part of their creative team before long. Slater was a big fan of the band, particularly the older heavy metal material, but was also into newer crossover music that was being called "Nu Metal" that was liked by Wilton and the other Queensrÿche members.

After the band completed the *Art of Live* tour with dates in the UK, and some festivals in Europe [including the Arrow Rock Festival featuring: Heart, Yes, Steve Vai, Saga, Joe Satriani, Symphony X and others], they took some time off and then looked to continue playing concerts for a few more months, as well as started to think about recording their next album. Queensrÿche also decided they would should revist doing a full production of *Operation: Mindcrime* on the road again. This was surprising to many fans, as the band had said after the *Building Empires* tour ended in 1992 they wouldn't perform the album in its entirety again. A lot had changed for the band during the last twelve years, with a series of unsucessful albums, waning attendance for shows, and they had lost another record label with Sanctuary being absorbed by their parent company, Universal (who only kept the reissue part of their catalog).

To warm up for the next tour, they played a small, acoustic concert on September 23, 2004, at Graceland (formerly the Off Ramp) in Seattle with Jerry Cantrell's band opening. After that, they kicked off 49 dates with two shows at the Moore Theater on October 5-6, 2004. This first leg lasted through October 29, and then they took the holidays off, resuming on January 19, 2005, for a number of shows through February 19 for the last of the "Evening with Queensrÿche" performances. The tour was a big success and it helped pay off some of the band's debt and rebuild the Queensrÿche brand name. They sold out large theaters and casinos across the United States, and many people went to see the whole album performed again live, or for some the first time. Sometime during that first leg of the tour cycle in the fall of 2004, the band decided they would do another concept album and discussions led to a sequel of *Operation: Mindcrime*. A lot of the impetus behind this was likely additionally fueled by the continuing growth of the internet, both with the official Queensrÿche website, and other related fan sites (where fans continued to gather and discuss their favorite albums, shows, etc.).

During this tour cycle, Queensrÿche treated fans to a surprise. At

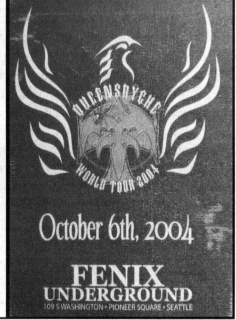

the end of the show, over the PA system, they played "Hostage," one of the leftover songs from *Tribe* that was completed after the album was sent to the record label. The song was used as a "preview" of sorts for Queensrÿche's next album. This initial version of the song, which would ultimately be adjusted and re-recorded on *Operation: Mindcrime II* in 2006, did not include the courtroom effects, and featured a ripping guitar solo (instead of the slower, harmonized version that appears on the album) by Wilton that got the crowed excited for Queensrÿche potentially moving in a more aggressive direction.

In early 2005, Susan Tate assumed control of the band management. Geoff and Susan convinced the other band members that Lars Sorenson wasn't working out and she should move up into the manager spot. "In 2005 things got worse," Michael Wilton stated in 2012. "Geoff Tate came to the band and wanted to kick Lars Sorensen out and have his wife manage the band. There was huge resistance from the rest of us, but Geoff said unless we hired Susan, he would no longer work with us. Reluctantly we agreed to this, feeling we had no other choice if we wanted to remain as a band, but we refused to sign a binding contract with her."

One of the first things she did in her new position was help the band with a marketing campaign toward the *Operation: Mindcrime* sequel. The idea was to build up suspense and attention for it, and also re-write history to and say that it was "always planned." In all previous interviews with the band, when asked about a sequel to the original record, the party line was always "there will be no sequel" and that *Operation: Mindcrime* was a complete story. So, a bit of revisionist history was done so they could move forward with the project. Based on the plan, they were signed to a three-album deal with Rhino Records/ Entertainment, a division of Warner Brothers. "The idea came about [for a *Mindcrime* sequel] because I had been toying with the idea of writing a screenplay for the album," Geoff Tate said at the time. "When I got started, I noticed there were a lot of holes in the story and questions to be answered. So, as I began writing and filling in the blanks, I realized there was room for a sequel."

Rumor has it, however, that finances were the driving point behind doing a sequel to *Operation: Mindcrime*. Queensrÿche had signed contracts to perform in Japan in the fall of 2001. But when the 9/11 terrorist attacks happened, the band canceled their appearances. Allegedly, the group had received money in advance and never returned it, leading to legal issues between them and the promoter. By capitalizing on *Mindcrime*, and the lucrative tour guarantees performing the original album and doing a sequel would bring, it would help inflate the band's coffers and help settle whatever legal entanglements that arose from the canceled 2001 Japan dates.

Starting on May 30, 2005, Queensrÿche launched out on a tour with Judas Priest as direct support for 32 dates in the U.S., ending on August 12 (dubbed simply the "Summer Tour"). During that leg, they played a very "metal" set of older songs including: "The Whisper", "Surgical Strike" and "En Force," as well as a medley of the four EP songs. They also debuted a new song, "I'm American" and announced it as a song from the forthcoming *Operation: Mindcrime II* album. All throughout the winter, spring and summer that year, they  were working on the *Mindcrime* sequel with new producer Jason Slater. "We were writing and recording on the road, coming back to the studio and then stopping again to go back on the road, so the record was a little more difficult because of that," Jason Slater explains. "It was just about as unorthodox a recording as you could make. The experience was cool though and I wouldn't change anything about it in hindsight." When the band was off the road, writing continued at the Tate's house as Slater and Mike Stone were staying with them. Geoff and Susan's basement became a makeshift studio for writing and recording demos. According to Slater, Geoff Tate would come up with an outline and then need a song for a particular scene, based off of a certain emotion. Then Slater and Stone would try and come up with the songs to match those. Once the music was written, Tate would work on lyrics.

"This time, everyone's roles were different because there was no Chris DeGarmo," Slater continues. "[He was] the guy who came up with the seeds for the majority of the music and played a producer role in the band, as well as being a guitar player. Somebody had to come in and pick up those jobs... and this time out it was me and Stoney."

Sessions were set up for Michael Wilton to contribute to the writing and recording, but his contributions to the album were limited with a slightly reworked version of "Hostage" from the *Tribe* sessions, (sound effects added in and less aggressive vocals from Tate), and the primary guitar riff in both "Murderer?" and "The Hands." Tate and Jason Slater said that Wilton showed up and didn't really contribute anything much, but Wilton later claimed otherwise. "During the initial writing phase, I would show up to bring my input to the creative process only to find that the producer, the new guitar player (who were both staying at the Tate's at the time), and Geoff Tate had been up late the night before, or early that morning, and written the songs without me," Wilton says. "I was then told my ideas were not needed as the songs were now done. I could, however, "bring my own style" during the recording, after learning to play what they wrote for me. In frustration, I gave up on the writing process knowing that I would at least get to make changes in the studio, to bring in the Queensrÿche sound we were known for." Unfortunately, that didn't happen as Wilton said he was shut out of some of most of the studio recording at the Tate's house and down at Slater's studio, The Annex, in California.

Eddie Jackson co-wrote three of the songs on the album, the aforementioned "Hostage", "Freiheit Ouvertüre," and "Circles," and also contributed bass parts to a number of other songs as well. Slater, who was a bassist, also played bass on several songs on the record. The rest of the songs were written by Slater, Mike Stone and Geoff Tate. Mike Stone elaborates: "A lot of [Operation: Mindcrime II] was created in Geoff Tate's basement. Jason Slater is an awesome producer, engineer and songwriter. He brought up a lot of his cool gear from his studio in the Bay Area. Geoff would explain his concepts and ideas and we'd just start making music. Both Jay [Slater] and I were staying at the Tate's so obviously we had a big part in it. What else were we going to do? (Laughs)" Scott Rockenfield did not contribute to the songwriting, or if he did, nothing was used that rose to the level of a credit or co-credit for him. Additionally, Rockenfield said he recorded all of his drums at home for the album, but Slater said he felt the playing wasn't as intricate as needed and the drums were removed and re-programmed by Slater. Matt Lucich also recorded a lot of the drum tracks used on the album.

Whether it was due in part to growing tensions between certain band members, Tate's strong vision and direction for the sequel, the changing styles and tastes of the original members, or all of the above, Operation: Mindcrime II became the first album with significant contributions in the studio by outside members. In other words, a "studio creation." Not the first time an album was done by a producer who brought in a number of outside musicians and writers (see KISS, Heart, etc.), but the first time Queensrÿche had done that. Slater worked very hard on making it sound like a "Queensrÿche" record, most specifically the original 1988 *Operation: Mindcrime* album. Ironically, this meant using himself and other non-members to help create this. Slater felt that Geoff Tate was really the commonality between their previous albums. "The common thread between Queensrÿche records is Geoff," Jason states. "Listen to the band's albums as instrumentals back to back, if you didn't know [better], you'd think it was a different band, because they change stylistically so much from album to album."

Mike Stone had only previously contributed the one track to *Tribe* ("Losing Myself"), and played on a couple of others, but this time he played on pretty much everything and co-wrote a lot of the material with Slater—including contributing "One Foot In Hell." "That song started off as this blues rock thing and there was some tension within the band about it being used," Slater recalls. "So we had to turn it into something the band would be proud of and want to play. It's hard as a songwriter to go back and rewrite your work to make it fit the confines of the record. Stone did that, and it really impressed me." Mike Stone speaks on his expanded role on the record: "*Operation: Mindcrime II* was the first full album I did with the band, top to bottom, front to back. It was definitely an exciting process."

Jason Slater's studio engineer, Mitch Doran, also contributed guitar parts, drums and programming for the album. Doran wrote and recorded the solo in "Murderer?" The late Ashif Hakik (the composer behind a number of PlayStation video game classics like *Sly Cooper and the Thievius Raccoonus* and *Crash Nitro Cart*) did the orchestral arrangements for the album and contributed keyboards and some additional guitar work. Sadly, Hakik passed away in April 2021. Pamela Moore was back to reprise her role as "Sister Mary" and sang on a number of tracks, including the duet on the closer "All the Promises." "Pam is a great singer," Slater states. "She's an amazing person. Totally dig her." "This time around I was able to sing more and help out on vocals," Moore explains. "The latter part of the year we really concentrated on bringing to life the *Mindcrime* show. Since I do have a theater background it was very enjoyable to pull that out again." Geoff's stepdaughter, Miranda, sang background vocals on "The Hands." A special guest was also brought in to play Dr. X. Both Rob Halford and Ronnie James Dio were the choices, and Dio agreed to do it. "Ronnie has an incredible delivery and his voice is just pure evil," Slater says. "Halford would have done a good job, but it would have been different. No one else could have come in and pulled it off as cool as [Dio] did." Dio sings the duet on "The Chase", but was not used elsewhere on the album. "I think him [Dio] singing any more parts would have been gimmicky and would have taken away from the story," Jason maintains.

Slater added, however, that Dio was so efficient with recording "The Chase," that they wrapped up the session in just a couple of takes. Tate had left the studio, so for fun, Dio laid down vocals on a number of other *Operation: Mindcrime II* tracks. These recordings were kept by Slater and never released.

Operation: Mindcrime II is done more in the style of a Broadway-style rock opera, in contrast to the original *Operation: Mindcrime,* which is more of a heavy metal concept album. Each song is basically a chapter in the story, or scene. It tells of Nikki being released from prison at the start, after being locked up for eighteen years. He vows revenge against Dr. X, who has become rich and powerful during that time. Throughout the tale, he struggles with his own conscience, and the voice of Sister Mary, killed in the first one, haunts him. Motifs from the first album from various songs were used in certain places on *Mindcrime II* to help capture the spirit and sound of the original.

When they finally got to the point of mixing the album, they were pushing the deadline and scrambled to get it done in time. Slater, Doran, and assistant Chris Wolfe pulled a number of all-nighters to get the album finished, but unbeknownst to the group, the deadline had been pushed back a full month. In hindsight, Jason Slater wished they would have been told that by manager Susan Tate, so they had more time to listen to the tracks and reflect on them before mixing it. "The time constraints during mixing was a total drag," Slater admitted. "We were heartbroken because we could have spent a lot of time on those mixes." The album was mastered by John Greenham.

On February 18, 2005, Chris DeGarmo came out to join his friends from Alice In Chains – Jerry Cantrell,

Mike Inez and Sean Kinney – onstage for a special benefit for relief for the Tsunami victims in Asia the previous year. They were additionally joined by Ann and Nancy Wilson of Heart, Maynard James Keenan (Tool, Perfect Circle), Pat Lachman (Damageplan, Halford, Gargoyle), Wes Scantlin (Puddle of Mudd), Sir-Mix-A-Lot and the Supersuckers. Krist Novoselic of Nirvana was the host of the show. It was sponsored by the K-Rock radio station (96.5 FM) and they raised more than $100,000 for the relief effort. DeGarmo played specifically with Alice in Chains, serving as second guitar during the band's electric set, and according to fans in attedance, lead guitarist during its acoustic set.

Operation: Mindcrime II was released on April 4, 2006, by Rhino. Videos were made for "I'm American," and "The Hands," which tied into the concept and helped to promote the release and hype the story. Anticipation for the sequel by fans pushed it and it sold well out of the gate. It sold 44,000 copies in its first week and hit #14 on the U.S. Billboard charts, and in the Top 30 in various parts of Europe and Japan. Critics were mostly all positive in their reviews and many called the album "a return-to-form for Queensrÿche." Due in part to keeping the costs very low on recording (with using Tate's house and Slater's studio), the album was an immediate financial success for both the band and the label. Rhino was able to recoup the advance they gave Queensrÿche in the first month of the record's release. Following that, the revenue from sales went directly to the band and songwriters. Wilton stated in 2012 that the album sold 150,000 copies by that point. It didn't go Gold, but it was a step in the right direction as far as renewed interest in the band and financially it helped the band immensely at that time.

Queensrÿche went out on the road in support of Operation: Mindcrime II in the summer of 2006, starting with the famous Monsters of Rock festival in England on June 3. Alice Cooper, Deep Purple, Journey, Ted Nugent and others rounded out the bill. Queensrÿche played a number of other festivals and shows throughout Europe, the UK, Australia, etc. on through July 17, 2006 (15 total). Due to the time they were allowed, their setlist just consisted of a number of tracks from both Mindcrime

Photos by Michael Lindgren

albums and a couple from *Empire*. Following that leg, they kicked off their North America tour with two nights at the House of Blues in Lake Buena Vista, Florida, with complete performances of both albums. Production-wise, and length-wise, this was the biggest tour that Queensrÿche had done in almost a decade. Some of the old staging was brought out of storage and used to create a new setup (including parts of Rockenfield's drum riser from the *Rage for Order* tour). There were sets for the courtroom scene, Sister Mary's suicide scene, and various other sets throughout the show. Pamela Moore also joined them on tour in the U.S. for the shows. The Seattle vocalist wasn't aware just how violent and graphic the depiction of Sister Mary's death scene would be in the live performance, with Mary committing suicide by shooting herself in her head. "I didn't realize it was so bloody," Moore says. "At the time [the show] was being rehearsed, I was on my honeymoon and wasn't able to return until a day before the tour started." The additional "actors" were various members of the Queensrÿche crew and friends (including Scott "Fozzy" O'Hare, Rory Berger, Lars Sorensen and Christian Sorensen), as well as fans that were selected to be part of the "jury". In select cities (including Seattle), Michael Igor Delassandra – who was a former composer for the Vatican – directed the orchestra and also played some piano in the set. Queensrÿche played 69 more shows total on this jaunt, wrapping it up with two nights at the House of Blues in Anaheim, California, on December 1 and 2. This leg also included three nights in Seattle at the Moore Theater from October 13-15, 2006. The shows were recorded and would be released the following year as a special CD/DVD package titled *Mindcrime at the Moore* to commemorate the tour.

Just after their tour had ended, it was announced that Geoff Tate and Mike Stone had raised a significant amount of money for VH1's Save The Music fundraiser. The two Queensrÿche members were motorcycle

Queensrÿche

PO BOX 5000 PMB 168 DUVALL WA 98019 WWW.QUEENSRYCHE.COM

enthusiasts and had done a special ride with fans throughout various cities in the U.S. "We did this thing with VH1 where Eric (Buell) donated a couple one-off, custom, Ulysees motorcycles – a Geoff [Tate] model and a [Mike] Stone model – that were just gorgeous," Mike Stone explains. "In between cities on that whole tour, Geoff and I would ride to dealerships and do a thing, and then go do shows. People could sign up and do the ride with us, and the money went to the VH1 Save The Music fund. In the end, we ended up raising over $80,000."

Queensrÿche ended the year on a high note with their most successful run in quite a while. They paid off their debts and had a resurgence in popularity. But the cracks in the armor were worse and tension and resentments continued within the band. With bringing in outside writers and players for the first time, it highlighted the disfunction. When *Operation: Mindcrime II* was released, it was only credited to the five Queensrÿche members and producer Jason Slater. Songwriting credits were not featured on the album, nor were session musicians listed out— only guests such as Moore and Dio. So, the public was not aware initially of the true credits, but this would later all come out....

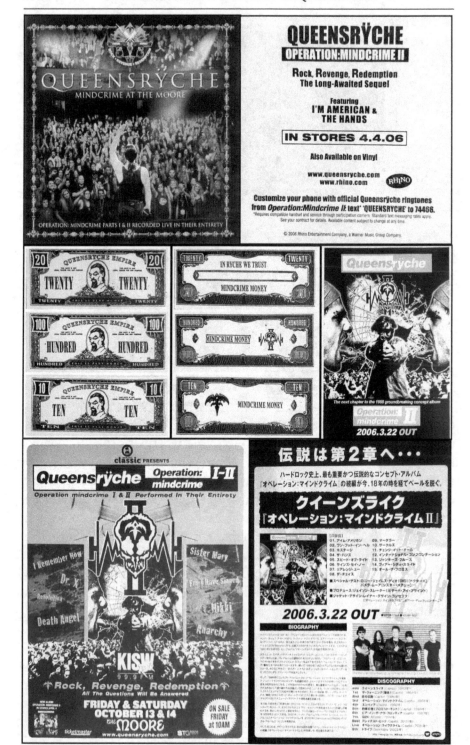

CHAPTER 16:
SIGN OF THE TIMES

Queensrÿche took some time off for the holidays in December 2006. Moving into 2007, Sony/BMG licensed some of the material from their 2001 album, *Live Evolution,* for their *Extended Versions* series. This was released on February 27, 2007 and featured a picture of the current lineup with Mike Stone, despite the fact Kelly Gray played on the recordings. Around this time in February, March, and May, they played a handful of casino dates in Michigan, Arizona, New Mexico and California (including the Key Club with Tesla and Jani Lane of Warrant). They included a couple of songs from *Operation: Mindcrime II* ("I'm American" and "The Hands"), as well as tracks from *Tribe, Q2k* and older albums. Following those, they flew over to Japan to play four concerts with the complete *Operation: Mindcrime* and *Operation: Mindcrime II* sets

from May 31 – June 5 (presumably they had mended fences with the promoters over there from the post-9/11 cancelations in 2001).

On July 3, 2007, Rhino released the *Mindcrime at the Moore* DVD/CD set. It features the complete performances of both albums over the three nights at the Moore Theatre in Seattle the previous year, along with the encores of "Walk in the Shadows" and "Jet City Woman." The DVD includes the bonus cut of Ronnie James Dio performing "The Chase" with Queensrÿche in Los Angeles. The other special features include a tour documentary and a "Queensrÿche Rock N' Ride" featurette. A Blu-ray edition of the video was subsequently released a few months later on October 18. It did very well and was certified Gold by the RIAA on March 21, 2008. This was the best-selling release from Queensrÿche since *Promised Land*. Originally, the cover of *Mindcrime at the Moore* consisted of a photo of the crowd at The Moore in black and white, with the band name, Tri-Ryche, and a cross in the center, with some additional artistic flair present in the corners. At some point before it was released, however, that cover was scrapped in favor of a photo of just Geoff Tate with his hand up waving to the crowd.

According to Jason Slater, there was a mishap with the recording on night one, requiring him to fly up to Seattle from the Bay Area to make sure the last two nights were recorded properly. The audio was cleaned up significantly, and some of the performance needed to be overdubbed later. Slater called the overdubs "routine". He handled the fixes and would subsequently mix the audio on the project.

Following the release of *Mindcrime at the Moore*, Queensrÿche kicked off a number of summer concerts with a show in San Antonio, Texas, on July 14, 2007, at the Sunken Gardens Theater. This was notable due to the recently reformed Florida hard rock band, Axe, joining them on the bill. Having played with them on that first tour with Quiet Riot in the summer of 1983, it was a reunion of sorts between the remaining original members of both bands (only two in Axe by that point – guitarist/vocalist Bobby Barth and keyboardist Edgar Riley Jr.). Next up was the well-known Rocklahoma festival in Prior, Oklahoma. Queensrÿche played the final night, Sunday the 15th, along with Twisted Sister, Great White, L.A. Guns, Britny Fox, Jackyl, Steelheart and others. On July 21, they played a special acoustic set at the Looney Tunes record store on Long Island, New York, and did a signing afterwards. It was an exclusive event with limited seating and only people who got a special wristband from ordering *Mindcrime at the Moore* from them could get in. It was stated at the time by the press that the show was to be filmed for a possible use in the future, but nothing has surfaced to this point. After that, they flew to California to do a special live performance for *Rockline* on August 1. The radio broadcast was popular with fans and bootlegged extensively. Kelly Gray was also present, assisting the band and host Bob Coburn.

Then it was back home to Seattle to pack for some festivals and shows over in Europe starting on August 14, 2007, in the Netherlands.

They played a handful of dates there, including the Metal Heart festival in Norway, on August 16, with fellow Seattle metalers Nevermore, Udo Dirkschneider of Accept, Blind Guardian, Testament, Dimmu Borgir, Circus Maximus and others. Following those dates, they flew back home to prepare for a big tour in the U.S. on through the fall with a couple icons.

Capitol/EMI released *Sign of the Times: The Best of Queensrÿche*, on August 28, 2007—a greatest hits compilation. It was produced by Mike Ragogna and David K. Tedds (who also worked on the Queensrÿche CD reissues in the early 2000s) and was mastered by Evren Goknar at Capitol's in-house mastering studios. Hugh Syme again provided artwork throughout the booklet and package. It was released in a special deluxe double CD edition, a single CD edition and

in digital download format. The gatefold double set includes various singles from the first EP in 1983, on up through *Operation: Mindcrime II* on the first disc (also featuring "Real World" from the *Last Action Hero* soundtrack that was a big hit). The second disc features three unreleased Myth demos from the 1981/1982 period with Geoff Tate on vocals. These three songs have titles he later used for songs on *The Warning*, and *Rage for Order*, albeit with different lyrics and music. It also includes three demos from *The Warning* sessions: "Waiting for the Kill", "No Sanctuary" and "Prophecy." The rest of the disc is filled out by various b-sides and non-LP tracks from EPs, singles and soundtracks. The final track is a completed version of Chris DeGarmo's unfinished song from the *Tribe* sessions, "Justified." It would signify DeGarmo's last work with Queensrÿche to date, with him completing his guitar parts and Tate adding the vocals. Terry Date (Metal Church, Pantera, White Zombie, Fifth Angel, Slayer, etc.) did the additional mixing on it. Liner notes for the compilation were written by former

Metal Edge Editor-in-Chief Paul Gargano (a friend of the Tates), with some additional notes on the Myth tracks, etc., written by Tate. The iTunes digital version swaps out the songs on the first disc, "Until There Was You" and "All the Promises", for "Empire" and "You."

It was rumored at the time that DeGarmo had once again reached out to his former bandmates to collaborate and rejoin Queensrÿche. As the story goes, DeGarmo's focus was to capitalize on the success *Operation: Mindcrime II* had enjoyed by making a great follow-up album with the original lineup. DeGarmo allegedly wanted the band to work together (as opposed to how *Mindcrime II* was created) to write the record and invest time and money into the recording. Not everyone in the band was supportive of the idea, however, and DeGarmo's overtures were rebuffed.

On September 5, 2007, Queensrÿche kicked off a tour with twenty dates opening for Heaven and Hell (the Dio-fronted version of Black Sabbath), and Alice Cooper, at the Memorial Arena in Binghamton, New York. They were back in big arenas and stadiums once again, and the tour was a big success. Following these U.S. performances, they jumped over to England to play a concert with Thin Lizzy supporting them on November 22. Another high point around this time was Geoff Tate was invited to sing the National Anthem at the Seattle Seahawks and New Orleans Saints game on October 12, in Seattle.

Queensrÿche capped off the year with one last full-length release on November 13, 2007—*Take Cover*. The album was a collection of cover songs the band recorded throughout the year. It was reported that the concept came from Michael Wilton and Mike Stone, who would play riffs during soundchecks as a fun game and see who could guess the songs. Queensrÿche's webmaster at the time, Kevin Scurlock, is credited on the release as being the one who

time, Kevin Scurlock, is credited on the release as being the one who suggested the cover songs album specifically. The idea was each member of Queensrÿche would choose two songs that were important to them, favorites, etc. Wilton chose Pink Floyd's "Welcome to the Machine" and Queen's "Innuendo." Mike Stone chose Black Sabbath's "Neon Knights" and the Andrew Lloyd Webber/Tim Rice-penned "Heaven on Their Minds" from *Jesus Christ Superstar*. Scott Rockenfield chose the Police's "Synchronicity II" and Peter Gabriel's "Red Rain." For some reason Eddie Jackson only picked one song, "For the Love of Money" (originally done by the soul group The O'Jays). Geoff Tate ended up picking three songs with a cover of Buffalo Springfield's "For What It's Worth"; Crosby, Stills, Nash & Young's "Almost Cut My Hair," and an opera, "Odissea." The album is rounded out by a live cover of U2's, "Bullet the Blue Sky," that was recorded live with Kelly Gray on the Electric Shockwaves tour in support of *Q2k*. Each member contributed quotes for their picks on why they chose them and so on. Jason Slater again produced the album, with help from Wilton, Stone and Kenny Nemes. Slater also did the arrangements for the studio recordings. His assistant, Leopoldo (Leo) Larsen, played some additional guitar in the studio on the record. "Leo played some guitar on it, and a bunch on *American Soldier* as well. He is a great guitar player," Slater stated.

"Welcome to the Machine" was released as a single just prior to the album hitting stores, and received a bit of airplay, and the record did reasonably well out of the gate. It sold around 5,500 copies the first week and cracked the Billboard 200 charts at #173. Fan and critical reception was mostly positive, with some complaints regarding the vocals (which Tate reportedly did at home in one or two takes). Some fans noted the lack of material by the band's earlier influences, Judas Priest and Iron Maiden, and Slater commented that Tate and the rest of the band didn't want to cover songs by bands they considered their peers.

They took time off for the holidays with their families and made an appearance on the compilation album, *Monster Ballads: Xmas*, released by Razor & Tie Records. The CD featured '80s hard rock favorites Cinderella, Dokken, Lita Ford, L.A. Guns, Skid Row, Twisted Sister, Warrant, and others. Queensrÿche's contribution was another cover, "White Christmas."

Queensrÿche toured in support of the *Take Cover* release starting on January 22, 2008, in Aspen, Colorado. They played four covers from the latest release ("Red Rain", "Welcome to the Machine", "Neon Knights"

and "Synchronicity II"), along with a variety of songs from their previous albums. The tour was also billed as an opportunity for fans to see Queensrÿche perform rarities. "The Killing Words" made an appearance in the setlist, as did cuts such as "Someone Else?", "Anybody Listening?", "Another Rainy Night (Without You)" and others. They played various theaters, casinos, etc. throughout the United States (including some return dates at various House of Blues venues) on through March 1, with a return stop to the Paramount Theatre in Seattle during the Northwest leg. After that they played on through New Mexico and on into Mexico itself starting on March 14 and ending on April 26.

The American tour was notable for the *Take Cover* singing contest. Fans could add their lead vocal to one of the tracks on *Take Cover* and submit it to the band for a chance to appear on-stage and sing with them. The choices were "Welcome to the Machine," "Neon Knights" and "Synchronicity II," and all were available as instrumental downloads. Multiple finalists were chosen for each show (likely by manager Susan Tate) and those finalists would come to the venue early and perform in front of fans (to the backing track) before Queensrÿche took the stage. The audience (via a decibel reader) determined the winner, who was brought back later that night to perform the song with Queensrÿche on-stage. The contest was divided into three tour segments consisting of 10 dates each. Each "segment winner" would be chosen by the band, and those three "semi-finalists" were flown to Seattle for a sing-off prior to Queensrÿche's

performance. The overall winner would sing that night with the band, but also make a guest appearance on Queensrÿche's next album. Vincent (Vince) Solano, from New Jersey, won the competition, and performed "Neon Knights" during with the band in Seattle, and as we'll get to later, appeared on "A Dead Man's Words" from *American Soldier*.

Next was a jaunt down to South America for dates in Brazil, Argentina and Chile. Then it was over to Europe to play shows and festivals in Spain, Portugal, Italy and Switzerland (including: The Electric Weekend with Metallica, Machine Head, At the Gates and others; and The Rocksound Festival with Europe, Opeth, Avantasia [who Geoff Tate later worked with as a guest contributor] and others). Following that, Queensrÿche played a number of dates in the UK, and a few more dates in Europe, before heading back home to continue in North America. A couple more standouts during that time was the Bang Your Head festival in Germany with: Judas Priest, Saxon, Iced Earth, Lizzy Borden, Agent Steel and many others on June 27, 2008; and Seattle's longstanding Pain In the Grass festival on August 23, at the White River Amphitheater, in Auburn, WA, with Sevendust, Shinedown, Seether, Drowning Pool, Jet Black Stare, and the Slater-produced band Earshot (the festival was relocated from Seattle Center). They wrapped up the year with three more dates in October in Missouri and Texas. All told, Queensrÿche played 80 dates during 2008, illustrating that the band made its money as a live act now. This was something other bands were also discovering was happening more and more in recent years with increased digital sales and reduced compact disc revenues.

Despite renewed interest in the band and recent releases being reasonably successful, the divide between the members of Queensrÿche continued. Signs of continued tensions between Tate and Wilton especially showed with Tate recording his vocals for *Take Cover* at home, rather than working with Wilton, Stone, Slater and the others in the studio. Many people felt Geoff and his wife Susan called the shots and it was the Tate's band now. The democracy had long departed when DeGarmo left, if not before that....

CHAPTER 17:
MIDDLE OF HELL

During the second part of their touring cycle in 2008, Queensrÿche and a group consisting of Jason Slater and Kelly Gray commenced writing and recording for their next album. They spent about nine months writing and recording *American Soldier*, starting around the late spring of that year. They dropped an official press statement in October that it was slated for an early 2009 release. Mike Stone was not part of the making of the record this time, both in playing and writing. Although he and the band didn't make any announcement until February 2009, Stone was already out by the end of the touring cycle in October 2008. Stories differ on why, with the band and Stone both publicly saying he stepped down due to wanting to pursue his side projects. "I'd been with the band for seven years," Stone explained in early 2009. "Through that time, I would still write and record all sorts of other music. Opportunities would come up, but quite frankly when you're touring nine months out of the year, you can't do them. We got to a place where we wrapped up touring in 2008, and were between album cycles, and if there was a time to step out, that was it. Nobody was left hanging and now I'm digging full-speed into my band Speed-X."

Michael Wilton later revealed (in his court declaration in 2012) that Stone was let go by the Tates in 2008, without consulting the other Queensrÿche members first. Wilton stated he received a call from Stone, letting him know he was being fired. Michael said he had no knowledge of this, or that "the band" was considering letting Stone go. Wilton called Geoff and Susan Tate and requested a band meeting. They were then told that Stone was being replaced by Miranda Tate's new boyfriend, Parker Lundgren. He said that the Tate's said that Stone was making too many "grand demands" and that hiring Parker was cheaper. Wilton also stated that he had never heard Parker play, nor was he or the rest of the band included in this big decision.

Parker Lundgren was born in Port Townsend, Washington, on December 28, 1986. Music was pretty present in his house growing up and he started playing acoustic guitar as a kid. He switched to jazz guitar a while later and by high school, was in three or four bands (including his school jazz and rock band). Django Reinhardt was a big influence, but he also liked Chris DeGarmo's playing a lot and learned some Queensrÿche songs at that time. He played in the punk bands The Nihilists and Seattle's Sledgeback (after moving there post high school). In 2008, he joined Tate's solo band and he also became friends with some of the Queensrÿche members. With his knowledge of some of their material, he was able to slide right into the slot.

The idea for *American Soldier* stemmed from Geoff Tate's father sharing combat stories with his son. The elder Tate served in the Korean War, and Geoff was born on a military base, but his father never talked much about his experiences until 2006. Tate recorded the conversations with his father and his wife, Susan, convinced him to use the story as a template for a song. Later it would be expanded into the idea of a whole album. Geoff interviewed other military people while the band was on tour to flesh out the theme. The other Queensrÿche members bought into the idea and work began on the record in 2008. It is a sort of a loose concept album (unlike the *Mindcrime* records that had a specific storyline and characters) and each song illustrates a part of a soldier's life. It goes from boot camp, to combat, to returning home from war and dealing with the aftermath of trauma and PTSD. Excerpts of the interviews Geoff did were incorporated into the songs to help flesh out the songs and tie the theme together. Additionally, a couple of years before the work on *American Soldier* began in earnest, around 2006, Geoff Tate and Jim Matheos of Fates Warning started working on a handful of songs for a Tate solo project. While the album between the two never panned out, three of the tracks that were demoed by Tate, "30,000ft" (which ultimately became "At 30,000 ft"), "Forgive a Killer" (later called "The Killer"), and "Middle of Hell" had Tate's lyrics and melodies used for Queensrÿche tracks on *American Soldier*. Matheos took the music and turned it into various songs for his Arch/Matheos and OSI projects.

Jason Slater was again tapped to produce, and he jumped in and started writing music for the new Queensrÿche album. He worked on songs while the band was on the road and traveled up to Seattle a number of times that summer and fall to write with Tate and record. "There's a lot of stuff on this record that goes back to my Snake River Conspiracy days," Jason Slater explains. "'Unafraid' was one of those unused recordings and the original demo got copied. I gave Tate that old demo with I don't know how many songs on it. The process has always been he'll decide what he wants to do, and then convince the band to record them. That's always been the way. If Geoff's not feeling it, it's not getting done." Slater is credited for the music on eight of the songs on *American Soldier*, although he claimed that he wrote a ninth song too, "Man Down!", that he says is incorrectly credited to Kelly Gray. Gray wrote the music to "Hundred Mile Stare" and also contributed music in the form of two more songs he had written with Scott Rockenfield and Damon Johnson while they were doing the Slave to the System project/band ("Middle Of Hell" and "Home Again"). These are the only two songs Rockenfield is credited for on the album and Wilton and Jackson did not contribute any songs (the first time that Wilton didn't have any credits on a QR album). However, all three Queensrÿche musicians played on all the album's songs, and Wilton wrote and performed the guitar solos. This helped to give *American Soldier* a lot of the Queensrÿche style and sound.

Kelly Gray was also on board to help produce and engineer the new album. Despite his exit from Queensrÿche a few years earlier, he was still friends with the band members and had the experience at the controls. He was available to help and lived close to the Tates. With Slater traveling there and back from California, that meant the work could continue without interruption. Recording was done at some of the members' homes, and Tate again recorded his vocals at his house. Scott recorded his drums at London Bridge Studios in Seattle and some additional recording was also done there. Vincent Solano, the winner of the *Take Cover* singing contest about a year prior, guested on the song, "A Dead Man's Words", doing lead vocal trade-offs with Tate and also singing backup. Gray and Damon Johnson are credited as guests with guitar on the Slave to the System tracks, and Randy Gane contributed some keyboards on the record. Tate's daughter, Emily, contributed vocals on the duet "Home Again", Jason Ames (Saunders),

Susan Tate's ex-husband, sang backup on two songs ("Sliver" and "If I Were King"), and former military member and friend of the band, A.J. Fratto, guested on "Sliver" as well.

The album was ultimately credited as being co-produced by Jason Slater, Kelly Gray, Susan Tate and Kenny Nemes. It was intended to be a co-production by Slater and Gray, but due to the proximity of Gray to the Tates on the eastside of Seattle, Kelly ended up doing most of the recording and initial mixing. Slater did some remixing on the album after receiving initial mixes from the band. Dialogue was added toward the end of the process using bits of the various interviews Tate had conducted with veterans. "I wasn't involved with the dialogue," Jason Slater says. "I was entirely out of the picture by the time it was added. I just tried to make the songs flow into each other. Here's the order, here's the songs and here's how they all work together." It's possible that other members of the band might have been more comfortable with Gray, considering what had transpired with the session musicians on *Operation: Mindcrime II*. Ultimately, this caused some tension between the two producers. Regardless, this was more of an overall band effort for Queensrÿche in general. "I think part of what makes this record decent was the tension between Kelly and I at the time," Slater adds. "We were both fighting for, like, the best of what we could do. I think the combination of us two is why the record came out better sonically. Kelly did a rad job."

American Soldier was released on March 31, 2009, on Rhino/Atco Records. The first single was "If I Were King," and a video was made for it and dropped around the time of the announcement of Mike Stone leaving the band in February. Rhino posted a press release which included Hugh Syme's advance cover art for the album which included an American flag on the ground. It caused some controversy, being viewed as disrespectful to the United States and the U.S. Armed Forces, most notably by members of the Queensrÿche fan site and discussion forum, The Breakdown Room. The cover was quickly changed before the album's drop in March. It hit #25 on the Billboard charts in the U.S., #39 on the Japanese charts,

#65 on the German charts, #71 on the Swiss charts and #100 on the Dutch album charts. It would sell reasonably well overall with just over 40,000 copies sold in the first week of release, but slid off the charts after a couple of weeks (unlike *Operation: Mindcrime II* which stuck it out for about six weeks on the charts in 2006). Quite a number of songs on the album were embraced by fans and those who were veterans seemed to appreciate the support and focus on them. Some felt that it was missing that sense of patriotism and pride many soldiers felt in serving their

country, and the songs were somewhat one-sided with the negative stories/situations they told within. Coupled with the initial "flag on the ground" artwork, it could be interpreted as a bit of an anti-government/ military theme. In addition to "If I Were King," "Home Again" was also given the video treatment, splicing fan-submitted military pictures with black and white footage of the band (and Emily Tate) performing the song. "Man Down!" was also released as a promotional CD single.

Parker Lundgren was brought in during late-2008/early-2009 and rehearsed with the band until he knew the material for the concerts. Many fans initially decried the choice of Lundgren due to him being Geoff Tate's son-in-law at the time. Parker took it in stride and even had humorous guitar pics made up at the time that said, "Dude, I am totally nailing Geoff Tate's daughter..." further fueling fan criticism of the Tates' nepotism. Despite the criticism, Lundgren had played in Tate's solo band and made a concentrated effort to learn and play the guitar parts as close to the album versions as possible, which quickly helped endear him to fans who didn't like the deviations his predecessors had done. Queensrÿche kicked off their tour in support of *American Soldier* with two nights at the Snoqualmie Casino in Washington (just over the hills on the eastside), on April 16-17, 2009. This was the first time they played there, and it would end up being a regular stop on future tours. Following that, it was down to Portland, Oregon, for a show at the just under 1,000 person-capacity Roseland Theater. (This was where they were originally slated to open for Ronnie James Dio way back in October 1983, but they canceled, and Portland's Wild Dogs opened for the man instead.)

While Queensrÿche was immersed in the *American Soldier* tour, they also continued to get overtures about *Operation: Mindcrime*. On June 12, 2009, Playbill.com ran an article on Tony-award-winning *Rent* star Adam Pascal, who was developing a Broadway-style musical adaptation of *Operation: Mindrime* with Queensrÿche's blessing. Pascal stated that he was a big fan of the band, and singer Geoff Tate especially, and felt he "wouldn't be where he was today" nor be the style of singer and performer he was without that influence. Pascal planned to play the part of Nikki himself, and that the musical would include new songs and connective material by Queensrÿche, along with the music and storyline from the original album. Unfortunately, nothing has ever come of this project, which likely was shelved when future events occured within the Queensrÿche camp.

The setlist for Queensrÿche's headline trek supporting *American Soldier* was notable. The band played three suites of music, each of which featured songs from three different albums—*American Soldier*, *Rage for Order*, and *Empire*. Instead of just playing the most popular songs from each, Queensrÿche rotated many of the songs featured in the suites. As a result, rarities such as "London," "One and Only," "Hand on Heart" "Surgical Strike" and other rarely played tunes made appearances at various dates. Queensrÿche continued down the west coast playing gigs in California, then on to Nevada, Arizona, Colorado and the rest of the United States. Then they traveled to Europe for a number of festivals and shows during the summer. A couple of highlights was the Hellfest 2009 in France (with Amon Amarth, Dragonforce, Dream Theater, Europe, Manowar,

Mastodon, Napalm Death, Stratovarius, Suicidal Tendencies and many others), and Gods of Metal in Italy (with Lita Ford, Heaven & Hell, Motley Crue, Tesla, Voivod and others). Additionally, they

EVENT CODE	SECTION/AISLE	ROW/BOX	SEAT	ADMISSION
PF0920	SEC11	1 11		METAL

$ 30.00 ENTER GATE 8   30.00
$ 7.05 INC. FAIR ADMISSION....
SECTION/AISLE
  SEC11   COLUMBIA BANK PRESENTS
VI 106X   PUYALLUP FAIR CONCERTS
ROW   SEAT
  1 11   QUEENSRYCHE
ZWS0818   W/ SPECIAL GUEST TESLA
G 3JUN0   9/20/10 7:30PM RAIN/SHINE

played shows over in Japan again and some down in Australia. The band also stopped at military installations for meet and greets and performances throughout the U.S. Queensrÿche would also eventually get clearance to travel overseas to Afghanistan to perform multiple shows for U.S. Armed Forces personnel. All told, Queensrÿche played a little over 100 shows in 2009.

Closing out the year, Lita Ford, and her then-husband Jim Gillette (ex-Nitro) would join Queensrÿche on a number of their fall dates back in the U.S. In an odd setup, Ford joined them onstage mid-set to perform a section of her songs with Queensrÿche (three songs from her latest album, *Wicked Wonderland*, along with a duet with Tate on "Close My Eyes Forever"), and then Queensrÿche finished up the last part of their set. *Wicked Wonderland* was Lita's first album in 15 years and featured many songs with strong sexual overtones. A number of people speculated this was an influence on what Tate had planned next for Queensrÿche's stage shows....

CHAPTER 18:
AT THE EDGE

Queensrÿche kicked off 2010 in February with two nights at the Snoqualmie Casino in Washington. This was the first of the adults-only "Cabaret" shows they had announced they would do that year. It was to be a show in that style with strip-tease dancers, aerialists and other erotic/exotic acts. As they had continued to tour heavily the last few years, they had made repeated appearances to the same towns and venues and eventually oversaturated the markets. It was a survival move that Susan Tate had driven as record sales continued to wane. In the past, a band could make a record and tour in support of it for a couple of years and survive off the album sales and tour revenue. As album sales continued to decline for bands overall in the 2000s, more and more they depended on touring and merchandise sales to live off of (an unfortunate trend that has continued for many mid-level name bands). Anything that helped draw attention to the band, helped get people out to shows and help drive back up guarantees and bookings seemed to be on the table. *Operation: Mindcrime II* and the subsequent shows featuring performances of both albums helped boost the Queensrÿche's popularity and pocketbooks, and the concept of *American Soldier* helped a bit too, but by the new decade they needed something new. A "gimmick" to grab some attention and generate interest.

Both Susan Tate and Misty Rockenfield had been strippers when they were younger, and took part in the show, as did Susan's daughter, Miranda. The idea was presented to the band to have the stage show based around songs from their catalog that fit the "theme." Scott was down for the idea and was happy to be able to spend time with his

wife on that tour, as was Geoff, but other members were not so thrilled about the idea. "The Queensrÿche Cabaret tour... I was totally not involved in that decision," Michael Wilton stated a short while later. "In fact, I was the only member who stood up for not doing this degrading show. I knew that this would definitely tarnish what was left of the Queensrÿche 'brand.' I was of the mind that Queensrÿche was a class act and would never stoop to such a degrading situation with women on stage, especially the band's own wives and daughters! However, as a majority vote was made to continue with this tour, I felt I had no other option but to continue as a team player, thinking of my bandmates, sucking it up and then giving my best to fans. And again, Geoff Tate threw a temper tantrum and would not sing requested fan favorites. I came home from this tour disgusted." Wilton initially wore a hood and sunglasses for a few of the shows to "just try and hide and just play the songs."

Queensrÿche mixed the Cabaret dates throughout the spring and summer with a "Greatest Hits" show for some dates at fairs, casinos, festivals (including the Bang Your Head Festival in Germany with Fates Warning, Hades, Nevermore, Twisted Sister and others), etc., that were intended for all-ages (versus the "adults only" Cabaret shows). The salacious concerts lasted for all of 25 shows and was eventually put to bed on October 30, 2010. One positive from the failed experiment was fans were very happy about the inclusion of

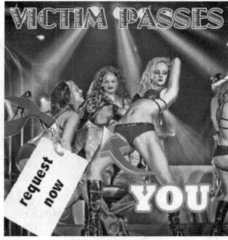

songs either rarely, or never played live, such as: "Dis-con-nec-ted", "Lady Jane", "Promised Land" and "The Art of Life." However, most fans and critics crucified the band for the Cabaret show. Publicly, the band had historically been against the idea of objectifying women, so the cabaret performances went against that completely. Some people felt the idea could have done better if they had put more money into it hiring professionals, instead of family and friends, which made it seem cheap and suffered in their view.

In fall 2009/winter 2010, Queensrÿche started writing for their next album, which would be called *Dedicated to Chaos*. Initially, it was supposed to be a band-written album as the three founding musicians weren't happy that they were limited on their contributions for the last two studio releases. Sometime just prior to the work starting on it, Wilton called a meeting of the band to discuss looking at the possibility of new management. ""At this time, I was really worried about the future of Queensrÿche," Michael explains. "As this band had made major changes in its career, I felt it was time for another change. I began approaching and talking with different managements to gather different possible scenarios for the band. I asked for copies of the financials and began to do some budget reports. I called a meeting to share my thoughts and brought my figures to show the data. I presented a new management company to the guys as an option to think about only. I was open for discussion, but what I got from Geoff Tate was a personal, slanderous attack of emails saying I had no right to question his role and how I lied about the numbers to prove my point, numbers that were taken directly from statements from our accountant and were not lies, nor were they manipulated in any way."

Wilton continues: "I thought this was a democracy, but I guess not. The other band members did not want to rock the boat, and I was literally being asked to leave the band by the lead singer. After talking this over with Eddie Jackson, who was shocked I was being asked to leave the band and asked me not to quit, and with my family, I agreed to stay with the band. After we, the band, agreed that changes would be made on how the business was being run, and also with the writing process on the next album. I had worked too long and too hard to walk away without giving it one more chance."

Once it was resolved, the work started on the new album, but it didn't quite go as planned as Tate "flipped the script" before long. Wilton elaborates further: "We started the next recording [for *Dedicated to Chaos*] and it was to be called a 'rant session of manic music.' It was to be a band effort with everyone contributing and we would write as a band again. Everyone went to town and convened at Scott's studio and dropped all of the ideas into his computer. The process of piecing together was going good and a few demos were surfacing. Then all of a sudden, without notice, the project was canned and it was back to Geoff calling the shots with outside writers again. The direction was supposed to be more like *Empire*, but what transpired was more unorganized confusion. No one was sure who was producing the album. Again, it was Jason Slater and Kelly Gray trying to figure out who was doing what. I was consumed by Jason's tunes to make them heavier like he instructed me to do. I recorded with Jason at Scott's house, and then Jason disappeared! The album went in a different direction taking the emphasis off my guitars, and my songs were not used." Michael later said something very similar in his interview with *Guitar World* when asked about his contributions. His guitar work is featured on a couple of songs, but that is about it.

Scott Rockenfield and Eddie Jackson were much more present on the album, with a number of songwriting co-credits and their drum and bass work very prominent in the rhythmically driven vibe and sound. Scott was quoted at the time likening it to a classic progressive album of theirs. "It's huge rock but with a great dance vibe to it, real modern dance," Rockenfield said at the time. "It's kind of like *Rage* through a time tunnel, bringing it into the now. There are a lot of electronic elements to it. It's a big rock thing that is going to have a lot of color to it—it's good and really intense." Parker Lundgren made his first appearance on the album with some rhythm guitar, and Kelly Gray also played some guitar on the album. Randy Gane guested on keyboards, as did Jason Ames (Saunders) and Miranda Tate on backing vocals. Besides the recording done at Rockenfield's home studio, some was also done locally at London Bridge Studios and El Dorado Studios in Burbank, California. Kelly Gray did the mixing of the album. The album was mastered by Eddie Schreyer.

Michael Wilton also took the opportunity in the summer to announce a new solo project, "Wratchet Head." It featured Michael and Jesse Paul on guitars, Rane Stone on vocals, Adam Clark on drums and Steve Jackson on bass. An album was slated to be released in October 2010 on Rat Pak Records (Metal Church's current label) and nine song titles were dropped ("Coming for You", Doomsday", "Your Confession", "All For You", "Only Human", "Broken", "Black And Cold" and

"Defy"). The single, "Coming for You", was released in October in the form of a CD single, and for purchase via various digital services. The band opened for Hellyeah and Hail the Villain on December 3, 2010, at the Sodo Showbox as part of KISW's "Holiday Hangover Le-Ball-Ski." Two more songs were dropped by Rat Pak on their website and Soundcloud pages, in 2012 and 2013, but as of this writing, the album has yet to be released. In 2019, Wilton said in an interview that he started Wratchet Head, and has a hard drive full of songs recorded, but hadn't had the time to finish it yet.

It was also announced on August 27, 2010, on the Queensrÿche website, that they had signed a new record deal with Roadrunner Records, on their side label Loud & Proud. The new album was slated for a spring 2011 release and they were on target for that. In advance of the release, both Tate and Rockenfield did interviews to promote it and tried to sell it on it being very rhythm driven and experimental. "Get Started" was dropped as a single in May 2011 on iTunes and also as a promotional CD single to radio stations. On the back of the sleeve it listed tour dates with Judas Priest that summer in the UK and the drop date for the album. It got some minor radio play but failed to chart. *Dedicated to Chaos* was released in the U.S. on June 28, 2011 (one week earlier in Japan) and landed at the #70 spot on the Billboard charts. It sold 20,000 copies in the first week or two and then slipped right off the chart. Reviews were mostly unfavorable, with the exception of a couple that loved the album as daring. Fans mostly disliked it with many saying it was the worst album Queensrÿche had ever done. It was released in a regular version, and also a special deluxe edition with four bonus tracks (one co-credited to Rockenfield, Gane and Tate, and the other three by Gray, Gane and Tate). Slater ended up with only three production credits on the album, with Gray having done most of the engineering, production and

mixing in Seattle. Around the time it was released, Wilton was quoted as sarcastically saying, "I hope you like my guitar parts on the new album," and Jackson just vaguely apologized to fans on his Twitter page. Parker Lundgren also said in an interview then, that when the record came out, there were songs on it he had never heard before.

About six months before *Dedicated to Chaos* was released, Michael Wilton helped ring in the new year with a special appearance at the Seattle Seahawks game on January 8, 2011. Joining him onstage for a medley of hard rock and metal hits (including Ozzy Osbourne's "Crazy Train", Led Zeppelin's "Kashmir", and Rush's "Spirit of Radio") was Alice in Chains bassist Mike Inez, Heart drummer Ben Smith and his old friend, Chris DeGarmo. The "group" was flanked by the Blue Thunder Drum Corps and The Army of Guitars. This was the first time the original Queensrÿche guitar duo had performed on stage together since 1997 and the crowd loved it. DeGarmo even played one of his iconic multi-Tri-Ryche guitars, in what some people interpreted as a "tip of the cap" to Queensrÿche fans.

Queensrÿche mostly focused on their band's 30th anniversary during the subsequent tour in 2011, so only a couple of songs were played from *Dedicated to Chaos* at that time (the single, "Get Started", the Beatles-inspired "Around the World," and occasionally the progressive track, "At the Edge"). They kicked it off with a couple of dates in the Midwest on May 15, 2011, and then headed over to be part of the Sweden Rock Festival in June with: Judas Priest, Joan

Jett, Accept, Saxon, The Cult, The Damned, Gwar, Saxon and many others. Other highlights were the High Voltage festival in London, in July, with: Judas Priest, Thin Lizzy, Slash, Michael Monroe, Caravan, Neil Morse and others; and a return to the Pain in the Grass festival at the White River Amphitheatre in August with: Duff McKagan's Loaded, Korn, Five Finger Death Punch, Chevelle, etc. Besides that, it was a return to many of the casinos, theaters and House of Blues venues from previous tours. All told, they played 79 shows on through December 2011 (the last stop being an appearance at the Emerald Queen in Tacoma on the 17th) before taking a break for the holidays again.

Heading into 2012, in what was the 30th anniversary of Queensrÿche recording their first EP, and changing their name from The Mob, the tension building in the band would finally come to a head. The proverbial "shit" would hit the fan a few months into the new year and it would take

a bit before the band could scrape it off their shoes....

CHAPTER 19:
FALLOUT

The truth shall set you free....

January of 2012 started off with a chance meeting. Michael Wilton was attending the National Association of Music Merchants (NAMM) show in Los Angeles, California. There he received his first signature series acoustic guitar from ESP. He was invited to a private dinner party hosted by the Seymour Duncan company, and met Todd La Torre at that event. La Torre was the singer for the Florida power/ prog metal band, Crimson Glory. He introduced himself to Wilton, mistakenly thinking Michael was Testament guitarist Eric Peterson. Once he quickly realized his mistake, they hit it off and Wilton asked Todd if he would be interested in working with him on some music for commercials, videogame and soundtrack projects. Wilton sent him four demos and was hoping to get the recordings back with vocals in a month or so. Todd sent back the first demo with lyrics and melody lines in three days. One of the songwriting collaborations, a song called "Don't Look Back," would find its way onto a Queensrÿche album later on....

La Torre is a bit younger than Wilton and the other Queensrÿche members. He was born on February 19, 1974, to Jeannie and William La Torre, a prominent chiropractor. He was raised with his sister, Kristina, in St. Petersburg, Florida. Music was prevelant in the La Torre household as he was growing up. His mother took him to jazz concerts of David Sanborn, Spyro Gyra, Lee Ritenour, George Benson, and others, while he was introduced to the likes of Elton John, Billy Joel and Steely Dan through his father's record collection. Todd got his first drumset at the age of seven, and by age ten, his mother gave him a classical guitar and he started taking lessons. His father purchased Todd a professional drumset at age 13, and he joined the Seminole High School band. He also started playing drums with various local rock bands, and even played guitar and sang for two concerts. Todd recorded his own songs at home, playing all the instruments and doing the vocals as well. He was introduced to Queensrÿche's *Operation: Mindcrime* when he was 14, through his sister's boyfriend. Prior to that his favorite bands were Heart and Fleetwood Mac, but after being exposed to *Mindcrime*, he got heavily into hard rock and heavy metal with bands such as, Iron Maiden and Testament. He also discovered *Rage for Order*, and *The Warning*, with the latter becoming his favorite Queensrÿche album. Ultimately, Queensrÿche became one of his favorite bands.

As time went on, La Torre attended a trade school and trained toward a career. He owned La Torre's Upholstery & Custom in Largo, Florida, for 17 years, while he played drums in bands on nights and weekends. "Music was always my passion," La Torre says, "But I didn't want to be a starving musician sleeping on a friend's couch." By 2009, Todd was considering starting up his own Iron Maiden tribute band. Matt LaPorte, a friend and longtime guitar teacher at Seminole Music and Sound, helped Todd get to the next level by encouraging him to do original material. He gave La Torre a piece of music to write to, and LaPorte was impressed by the results. He gave it to singer Jon Oliva (Savatage, Trans-Siberian Orchestra), while he was a member of Jon's solo band, Pain. Oliva said Todd would be perfect for Crimson Glory, a well-regarded power/prog metal band from the '80s, from Sarasota. Crimson Glory guitarist Jon Drenning was impressed with Todd and asked him to join himself and some other musicians for a performance at a memorial service for former Crimson Glory singer, Midnight. La Torre fit right in and before long he was making his debut at the ProgPower X on September 12, 2009 (as a special guest vocalist). It was formally announced in May 2010 that Todd replaced Crimson Glory's previous front man, Wade Black (Leatherwolf, Seven Witches), as the band's new lead vocalist. Following that, Crimson Glory played the Pathfinder Metal Fest in Marietta, Georgia, on October 30, 2010. The band started work on writing and recording a new album, and dropped a demo of one song, "Garden of Shadows," online in 2011. They also did a European tour that year to celebrate the 25th anniversary of their first album. Despite that momentum, as time went on, Crimson Glory stalled on completing their new album.

Todd was excited for the opportunity to work with Michael Wilton, after meeting him in early 2012. He had no illusions for anything past that, as Queensrÿche still had Tate as their vocalist, and he was still with Crimson Glory at the time, but that would soon change....

Somewhere around that time, in early 2012, Geoff Tate made a New Year's resolution to record and release a second solo album and tour in support of it. He quickly started working on it in January, writing with Kelly Gray and Randy Gane again. Greg Gilmore was tapped to play drums and Miranda Tate and Jason Ames (Saunders) provided some backing vocals. Miranda's then-boyfriend, Chris Zukas (who was also a guitar tech and webmaster for Queensrÿche) played bass. Lyle Ronglien, a local musician from the '80s club band Aurora (who had also recorded an album at London Bridge in 1989), co-wrote two tracks on the record. Tate landed a deal for it with Inside Out Records, a division of Century Media. *Kings & Thieves* was slated for a fall 2012 release. It took about six months to complete starting in January and ending in July. During that time, things came to a head in Queensrÿche...

As Michael Wilton had relayed in the public court documents filed in 2012, the three founding members (himself, Scott and Eddie) took to discussing the possibility of a management change toward the end of 2011, and that discussion continued into the new year. They felt that Susan Tate had her husband's interests as her priority, instead of Queensrÿche's. Coupled with that, things were coming to light of mismanagement of the band's finances by the Tates (including expenses and charges ran through the Queensrÿche accounts without permission for a new band Susan was managing, The Voodoos, for work visas, touring costs, etc.). "Thus, in 2012 the animosity truly began," Wilton said. "There was no communication from our manager, Susan Tate, with the rest of the band. No performances were getting booked and non-Geoff Tate posts on the wesbite were taken off. When some shows were finally booked, one was on an agreed black out day. We were left to fend for ourselves. Geoff was touring with his solo band and that was the main focus for management." People working with the band also noticed these issues and offered advice and opinions. "Kelly Gray had taken notice of the band's decline in record sales and direction and commented several times that, 'Susan Tate as band manager has run out of gas, and you should consider seeking new management,'" Eddie Jackson related.

Things were starting to look dire for the band financially as the year was continuing on. Over-saturation of the market in the previous years had hurt the band and the continued change in musical direction also contributed to lack of interest. Without many gigs, expenses were pilling up and something needed to change. Rockenfield felt that they could save money immediately by hiring a merchandising company, instead of having it in-house with family running it. "In February 2012, the band held a meeting at our offices in Duvall regarding some ideas and offers of merchandising," Rockenfield stated. "Geoff Tate became upset and stormed out of the room to get Susan Tate, who eventually blamed one of our other employees for our merchandising problems." Eddie Jackson adds: "We had a discussion about the current fan club situation, because it was costing the band so much money monthly. Since we weren't performing many shows in 2012, we weren't going to generate a lot of revenue. Basically, more money was going out than was coming in. The idea of hiring an online company to do this was much more cost effective. Geoff refused to go along with the idea because his wife and daughter were on the payroll. Needless to say, after eliminating the rental office lease agreement, employee payroll, utility expenses and accounting fees, the band's accountant, Neil Sussman, was also in agreement of the amount of money the band would save on a yearly basis by switching to an online merchandising company."

Some other ugly things were coming to light during that time that were revealing how much their lead singer and manager were focused on themselves and his career. This book's co-writer, Brian Heaton, founder of AnybodyListening.net/The Breakdown Room, was good friends with Jason Slater, who called Heaton in late 2011/early 2012 and dropped a bombshell about Tate. Slater told Heaton that Tate was planning to do a 25th anniversary tour of *Operation: Mindcrime* with Queensrÿche in 2013, and following that, he would leave the band. Slater explained to Heaton that Tate had negotiated selling the rights to *Operation: Mindcrime* to a third party out from under the nose of the band, and the windfall from that would enable Tate to walk away from Queensrÿche, and help set up his career as a solo artist.

"Michael Wilton and his family were also friends of ours, my wife and I, and I was put in a weird position," Heaton said. "Do I break one friend's trust to help out another whose livelihood was going to suffer, or do I keep my mouth shut and see how it all played out? Either way, somebody was going to get hurt. So, I made the choice to give Michael a call and let him know what Slater said. He said he appreciated it, and then all of a sudden things started changing in the band."

It wasn't long before Scott Rockenfield got an email on the *Operation: Mindcrime* "rights" deal. "During this time, Scott got an email congratulating on the deal that was made to have *Operation: Mindcrime* made into a movie," Wilton stated. "He contacted Eddie and I to see if we knew anything about it, but we were as just as shocked as he was! We had no knowledge this was being done, nor had we any time to look into the deal, or even see how we would fit into the project. Chris DeGarmo was not notified, nor was he aware of this agreement either, and he was one of the principal songwriters and contributors to the story outline. A check had been sent to our attorney to be held in escrow, and at this time we sent a notice that this was to be held, and no cash distribution was to be made until this was looked into and we were all in agreement. Moreover, when I inquired if these funds were to be distributed to the band, I was informed they were Geoff Tate's alone. As *Operation: Mindcrime* belonged to the entire band I was astounded."

This was the final straw for the other three members of Queensrÿche. In March 2012, a meeting was called to make some changes. "Scott sent out a meeting request via email to all of us asking for a board/shareholder meeting," continued Wilton. "Timing was of the essence as finances were tight at this point. Geoff was out on his solo tour and there was not much time [that] we were all in the same city. Scott listed the topics that would be discussed in the email. Out of the four of us, three agreed to the date and time. Geoff replied back he was not available until the next day. That didn't work for everybody else and we stayed with the original time and date requested. Many times in the past, others have had to rearrange their schedule to make meetings that a majority had agreed upon. We felt this time was no different and that Tate would be there. The band meeting went on as planned, with myself, Scott, and Eddie in attendance. Geoff was not there." During this meeting, motions were made and passed to move the fan club and merchandising operations to Tinman, who they were already using to manufacture their products. Employees were let go, including Miranda and Susan Tate, from the fan club and the house rental and day-to-day expenses were to be stopped as Tinman took over. The topic of management was also discussed, with a motion made and majority vote to replace Susan as manager and consider other interested firms. The meeting was recorded and transcripts of the meeting's minutes were sent to Geoff and Susan Tate and Neil Sussman. The following day, they flew out to Brazil for a concert.

"On the day of our show in Brazil, Geoff demanded a meeting before the show," Wilton commented. "We agreed to meet before sound check, and we all agreed it was best to record the meeting. Tate asked why we fired Susan as manager and what it was we wanted. We stated that we were no longer interested in her as management and we wanted different representation. He asked if we had anyone in mind and we told him we were in talks with AGPS [Management], but that nothing was agreed to. He then asked about our thoughts regarding him selling the rights to *Operation: Mindcrime*. He said, 'You have frozen my money.' We stated that we felt it was done behind our backs, and as we were part of the creation of *Mindcrime*, it was an intellectual property issue and needed to be reviewed by an attorney. Geoff stated that he had nothing more to say, got up and walked towards the door, and then said, 'Have a nice show.'"

Michael and the others did not see Tate until the show was about to start, as he elected to stay in the hotel bar and arrive later. As they were setting up their individual stations, Geoff knocked over Scott's drums, and proceeded to spit in Wilton's face and scream obscenities, as well as punch him in the face. When Rockenfield stepped in to try and break it up, Tate swung at Wilton again, who ducked, and hit Scott instead. He told Geoff to back off, but he swung again and eventually was restrained by their tour manager, Scott "Fozzy" O'Hare. Once things settled down and everybody got cleaned up, the band elected to continue on with the performance. Tate delayed the show by about 20 minutes, and then during the performance, Tate repeatedly spit at Rockenfield and tossed water at Wilton's guitar amps and equipment. Once the show was over, Tate was separated from the other band members and eventually sent on a separate flight home. The promoter was shocked and disgusted at Tate's display and thanked the other members for remaining professional and going on with the show. Tate showed no remorse and told them to keep away from him or he would go after Eddie Jackson next.

The three founding members of Queensrÿche decided to honor their last two show contracts in May for the M3 festival and Rocklahoma. "I was actually at the last show they did with Geoff Tate, the M3 Festival in Baltimore," booking agent Sullivan Bigg, of Biggtime Entertainment, shares. "We could tell something weird was going down. Eddie, Whip and Parker were all standing way back and were like statues. Becasue Geoff had done that threat, 'If you come close, I'm going to kick your ass.' And so he leaves during that long outro during, 'Eyes of A Stranger.' The Merriweather Post Pavillion has this big long walkway, and then this driveway up the hill, and Geoff's already halfway up the hill and gone. And the band was still on stage playing. I saw him walking up the road and I'm going, 'Wait a minute, something's weird here.' It sounded great, but they were on autopilot."

After that, they would decide if they could continue on with Geoff Tate as their frontman. Tate continued his acoustic solo tour, which lasted around 30 dates starting with a handful in January 2012, then some in April, and on through May and June (around the Queensrÿche festival dates). He also still continued work on his second solo album, and was on schedule for the slated fall release. Just prior to the May 12, 2012, festival in Maryland (the M3, also featuring classic `80s hair metal icons Dokken, Great White, Quiet Riot, Skid Row, Warrant and others.), Tate sent more threats through their tour manager that Wilton, Rockenfield, and Jackson, needed to stay away from him and his taped area on stage or else he would attack them again. They didn't move on stage knowing it was being filmed and that he might be provoked again. Flights were booked separately, hotels were separate and Tate did not come to the soundcheck. He also acted inapproprately by grinding on the cameraman and caused problems with filming. For the Memorial Day weekend in Oklahoma, Queensrÿche was the closing act for the huge Rocklahoma fest and Tate continued his unprofessional behavior shouting to the crowd "you really suck!" He also continued threats toward his bandmates and stayed in a separate hotel and had a separate flight once again. The media and fans blasted the negative outbursts and behavior across the internet, and Queensrÿche's brand name and reputation were going right into the toilet.

During the down time for Michael, Scott, and Eddie in May (between the two festivals), Wilton proposed a side band to play some gigs with La Torre as the singer. They christened it initially as "Rising W.E.S.T." which stood for "Whip, Eddie, Scott, and Todd." It was not known at the time if Parker Lundgren would be joining them. Once he did, the band referred to the name as "Rising West," which conveniently mirrored a line of lyrics in "Before the Storm" from *The Warning*—"The gathering winds the armies watch are rising from the west."

"That was when Geoff Tate was doing his solo shows and it pretty much shelved the band," Todd La Torre explains. "The other [Queensrÿche] guys wanted to do something, and make some money, so we formed a side project called 'Rising West.' We did just two shows and they were sold out at the Hard Rock in Seattle. It was an amazing response to that. And then of course shit hit the fan with them and Tate, and he was fired. I just kind of made a lateral move/transition. The rest is history." The back-to-back nights at the Hard Rock in Seattle occurred on June 8-9, 2012, and were both sold out. The band rehearsed for four straight days prior to the shows. The result was an epic throwback to Queensrÿche's metal years that left this book's authors amazed. La Torre effortlessly hit some of the amazing high notes Tate had been cutting for years. The performances set the stage for an incredible revival for Wilton, Jackson, and Rockenfield.

Rising West performed identical 75-minute setlists both nights, featuring many older songs they had not played in many years, as well as in the original tunings (which were often tuned down a half step to enable Geoff Tate to hit the notes in a lower register, as his voice and range had declined over the years). The band also tipped its cap to Eddie, Michael and Scott's beginnings with a popular cover from Iron Maiden. Here's the complete setlist:

1. Queen of the Reich
2. Speak
3. Walk in the Shadows
4. En Force
5. Child of Fire
6. The Whisper
7. Warning
8. The Needle Lies
9. Take Hold of the Flame
10. Prophecy
11. My Empty Room
12. Eyes Of A Stranger

Encore:

13. Wrathchild (Iron Maiden cover)
14. Roads to Madness

Both sold out concerts were a complete success and potential new management was in the house as well and were blown away. The band underestimated the demand for merchandise and quickly sold out all of the t-shirts. They resorted to even signing and selling Scott's drumheads on the second night to have something for the fans. Word of the show spread quickly through video footage posted online. Super fan Doug Wirachowsky was invited to hang out with the band on the rooftop of the venue after the second show. "There was intense enthusiasm from the small group of us fans hanging out with the band members while they celebrated their triumphant weekend."

Things moved quickly after that. Post-Rocklahoma festival, the three other members of Queensrÿche had already decided that they could no longer work with Tate. They were already only communicating with Tate by their respective attorneys, so he was informed of their majority vote to move on without him via counsel on June 6, 2012. Geoff Tate responded through his attorney stating he would not quit, nor would he accept their offer of settlement or to sell them his 25 percent share in the Queensrÿche corporation. He filed a lawsuit for wrongful termination on June 29, 2012, and the other three Queensrÿche members countersued in response. A gig that was scheduled for June 11, 2012, in Utah (opening for the Scorpions) was canceled due to letting Tate go. They offered to perform instead as "Rising West", but the promoter declined as it wasn't Queensrÿche. "We were then told by the promoter that it was either all four original members of Queensrÿche or nothing," Wilton stated. "It was not until the day before the Salt Lake City show that we heard that Susan Tate had worked a deal with the promoter to have Geoff Tate perform his solo acoustic set."

At this point, after the Hard Rock shows in early June, the three founding members decided to continue on as Queensrÿche with Parker Lundgren on second guitar, and Todd La Torre on lead vocals. Parker got along well with the other band members and was well-liked. His relationship with the Tates' daughter, Miranda, had long ago ended after lasting only six months and he had moved on. And La Torre proved he could step right into Geoff's shoes as frontman. Michael and Todd had also saw they could write music together as well. "What happened after this [the Rising West shows] was an explosion of excitement from not only the fans, but the media as well," Wilton said at the time. "We were happy this was so well received, but we didn't expect the high level of excitement that came with this. We were doing this for us and the fans, and for the first time in years we felt a rejuvenation of happiness playing together as a band. The shows were sold out in a week and a half and it was great playing these songs again and having the fans so happy! The next day we received offers from management companies and promoters askingus to bring the show to their cities. After these shows, we were now being called the 'New Queensrÿche' by the fans and media."

Glen Parrish of AGPS Management approached them after attending the Rising West show on June 9. He was well-regarded down in the

L.A. music scene, having managed many artists such as: Stevie Nicks, the Fabulous Thunderbirds, Steel Panther and others over the years. Parrish was very impressed and told AGPS that "I have something very hot here and we should grab these guys before someone else does." Wilton confirms, "In mid-June, Scott, Eddie and I flew to Los Angeles and met with Frontline/AGPS Management. They are the largest and most powerful music management company in the industry. We have agreed to have them manage us and help us assemble new booking agents, publicists and the like. We have put together a top-notch team and announced the new lineup through the industry leading Billboard. com to enormous reception. Within a week, we booked three shows [totaling] over $72,000 in revenue for the new Queensrÿche, with many more shows on the horizon. And, this is only the beginning with major bookings throughout the fall, the recording of a new album and a major push in 2013, all of which are in the works." After negotiations with "at least three or four record labels," Parrish chose to sign Queensrÿche with Century Media.

"I was handling Lynch Mob, who did a lot with Rat Pak Records out of New Hampshire," Sullivan Bigg says. "He also does John Corabi (Motley Crue, The Scream). I knew Joe O'Brien, the Rat Pak guy because I was working with those guys. He loved it because I could book a lot of dates for those guys and push their records. Michael Wilton was doing his solo record with them, Soulbender, and I think Michael had told the head of the label what was going on [with Queensrÿche]. And he told Wilton that he knew the guy for them. His name is Sullivan Bigg and he handles Great White, Warrant, Lynch Mob, and others. That's how it started."

Bigg continues: "Joe from Rat Pak hooked me up with Michael Wilton and we chatted. They had just signed with [new] management – Paul Geary – the right hand to Irving Azoff, and [Geary] was the [former] drummer of Extreme. He had become quite the formidable manager by then. I mean, he broke Godsmack and was their manager for years. But he signed [Queensrÿche], in partnership with another manager, Glen Parrish. He handled Fabulous Thunderbirds and Steel Panther for a while."

Rising West made its debut as "Queensrÿche" at the Halfway Jam in Minnesota on July 28, 2012. They played close to two hours and performed 19 songs, which was the longest set to-date they have done with La Torre. "I was at the very first gig without Geoff [as Queensrÿche]," Sullivan Bigg shares. "It was called the Halfway Jam in Minnesota. I booked it. And Todd was so fucking nervous. Pacing around and smoking. It was a gig that was on the books with Geoff. The promoter heard about what happened, and called me and said, 'I'm going to send a formal notice of cancelation to their former agent, and then I'm going to book it with you.'" Although they didn't officially announce a new album was being worked on until November, the rest of the summer was spent writing music and working on demos, around dealing with the lawsuit filings and responses. This time, everybody in the band contributed to the songs.

The transition from Tate to La Torre wasn't a completely smooth one on the road, however. Queensrÿche's two-hour performance at the Halfway Jam in 2012 exposed the singer's relative "greenness" as a touring vocalist. Bootleg recordings of the gig reveal La Torre struggling to a degree on many songs later in the set. Other shows later that year were shortened due to La Torre's cold and sinus issues. Queensrÿche's celebrated return to the New York-New Jersey-Connecticut tri-state area got off to a rocky start. The band had to cut its set short on March 8, 2012, at the Bergen Performing Arts Center in Englewood, N.J., due to La Torre picking up a cold. While he recovered and pushed through for the next two dates in Pennsylvania and Long Island, respectively (with the Patchogue, Long Island, N.Y., show being a dazzling performance that had the crowd chanting for more), he had more sinus issues as the tour moved further south that spring.

It bears mentioning that La Torre always considered himself a drummer who could sing, not the other way around. He flaunted at the time of joining Queensrÿche that unlike Tate, he was not a professionally trained vocalist. Although La Torre could hit the iconic Tate notes in the original key, and would get sinus surgery a few years later to help alleviate some of the issues he was facing, it became clear that Queensrÿche's new frontman would need time to develop as a singer. To-date, nine years after La Torre joined the band, most of Queensrÿche's headline performances now top out at 80-85 minutes, a far cry from the 105-115-minute shows they were putting on with Tate through early 2012, not to mention the 2-2.5 hour gigs from the 1990s.

They played a handful of additional shows as Queensrÿche just prior to heading into the studio in October through November with appearances at the Rock the Bay Festival, and the South Texas Rock Festival (both with Accept, Dokken and Michael Schenker), a couple of casino appearances locally in the Seattle area at Chinook Winds and Snoqualmie (which would be recorded and three songs from it included on the deluxe edition of the self-titled album), and a return to the West Hollywood House of Blues. All were very well-received and continued to fuel momentum for the new lineup. This kicked off the tour they called "Return to History" that continued on into the next year and for another 60 shows around the new album release. The band would focus the setlist on the EP through *Empire*, with an emphasis on material from *The Warning*, including the title track. In November, they announced they were recording a new album as "Queensrÿche" and it was slated for a 2013 release.

During this time, Geoff Tate also continued his acoustic solo tour under his own name, and then announced on September 2, 2012, he would call his band "Queensrÿche" for his post-solo tour stuff. A judge denied Tate's initial motion to stop his former bandmates from using the band name, and ruled that while the case was being decided both bands could continue using the name. "I don't see any reason that Mr. Tate can't have the benefit, if he gets other members, of whatever name he uses of using the brand," Superior Court Judge Carol A. Schapira said during the July 13 court hearing. "I think [doing that would be] inherently confusing, although I'm sure the market can get these things sorted out," she added. Which of course, it did cause much confusion for promoters not sure who they booked, and fans expecting to see the normal band, and so on, when Geoff Tate's Queensrÿche arrived. His "all-star" band at the time consisted of Kelly Gray (who quit working as a soundman on the Queensrÿche crew post-Tate firing) on guitar, Randy Gane on keyboards, Rudy Sarzo (Ozzy, Quiet Riot, Whitesnake) on bass, Glen Drover (Megadeth, King Diamond) on guitar and Bobby Blotzer of Ratt on drums. Drover stepped down in November 2012, before ever playing a show in Tate's band, and was replaced by Rudy Sarzo's brother, Robert (Hurricane, Snow). Geoff's second solo album, *Kings & Thieves*, was released on November 6, 2012 to mixed reviews and low sales. It sold only 1,800 copies in the first week and failed to chart. Undaunted, Tate continued on touring to clubs and theaters around the U.S. on through 2013. He played a number of tracks from his solo album along with Queensrÿche songs. He also quickly went back into the studio to record a new album to capitalize on the judge's ruling....

SNOQUALMIE 2012

PHOTOS BY BRIAN WOODWICK

CHAPTER 20:
F.U.

Geoff Tate reached out to a number of friends to contribute to his new album, which would ultimately be called *Frequency Unknown*. This was to be released under the Queensrÿche name while it was being decided who would ultimately own the brand. He first tapped Jason Slater to produce the record and it was recorded down in Sunnyvale, California, at A & D Studios. Slater wrote the majority of the music on the album, along with contributions from Randy Gane ("The Weight of the World", a song he wrote the bulk of based on a recent heart attack he survived on December 26, 2012), Chris Cox, composer/musician Martin Irigoyen (Vernian Process, Profundo Delle Tenebre), and Lukas Rossi (*Rock Star: Supernova* TV show). Tate had met Rossi previously during a Shiprocked cruise the previous year. The two hit it off and wrote two songs together after a couple of drinks.

According to the credits, the core group of musicians to play on the

CRAIG LOCICERO   JASON SLATER   DAVE MENIKETTI   SIMON WRIGHT
RUDY SARZO
BRAD GILLIS   KELLY GRAY   ROBERT SARZO   RANDY GANE
GEOFF TATE

album were: Craig Locicero (Dress the Dead, Forbidden) on rhythm guitar; Jason Slater on bass and keyboards; Randy Gane on keyboards; Paul Bostoph (Forbidden, Slayer) on drums; Martin Irigoyen on guitar, bass and drums; and Evan Batista (Animal Party, Stunt Monkey) on drums. Tate's additional touring band members—Kelly Gray, Rudy Sarzo, Robert Sarzo, and Simon Wright—also contributed to various songs. Many special guests contributed guitar solos on the record including: K.K. Downing (ex-Judas Priest), Brad Gillis (Night Ranger, ex-Ozzy Osbourne), John Levin (Dokken), Dave Meniketti (Y&T), Chris Poland (ex-Megadeth), Ty Tabor (King's X) and others. Tate's daughters, Emily and Miranda, added backing vocals. Locicero's heavy riffing, and Bostoph's drumming, especially added a more "metal" feel to the album, not present in Tate's previous solo albums.

Locicero's involvement was significantly more than just rhythm guitar, however. "It wasn't approached to me about rhythm guitar and I didn't just play rhythm guitar by any stretch of imagination," Locicero said. "My name is on there as rhythm guitarist, but I played basically everything on that record, minus the actual solo breaks." Expanding on his role, Locicero explained that he played all the acoustic guitars, rhythm tracks, what he described as the "thematic parts" on the album, harmonized sections, and any overdubs that were needed. He also played a significant, but uncredited role in songwriting, estimating that he re-wrote approximately 85 percent of the material.

Four bonus tracks were included on the album, re-recordings of classic Queensrÿche songs, along with the 10 original tracks. Tate said his original plan was to do reinterpretations of the songs as opposed to straight re-recordings, but Cleopatra Records (the parent label for Deadline Music that would release *Frequency Unknown*) wouldn't let him. The album was recorded in a whirlwind six weeks from January 2013 to February 2013. It was quickly mixed by Slater and sent to Maor Appelbaum to be mastered. An official announcement on the album's forthcoming release was made on March 4, 2013, hours after the Todd La Torre-led Queensrÿche announced their forthcoming album's release date. Part of the rush on getting Tate's Queensrÿche album out was to beat the La Torre-fronted version to the punch, but Tate also revealed the limited budget of only $1,000 to do the album was a factor in the speed.

"I always felt like if they would have cooled their jets and waited two months, let us demo and record everything with a solid drummer and a real band, those songs would have turned out really good," Locicero said. "Most of it would have been great." Locicero added that the whole process was "fast and chaotic," and more like sitting down and coming up with demo tracks as opposed to an actual album. "From the moment I got there it was all about 'we've got to get this done before the other Queensrÿche gets their album out,'" Locicero said. He added that he had two- to two-and-a-half weeks to re-write the songs and record guitars and had no time to take anything home and come back to it with fresh ears. It was all done spontaneously.

The title, *Frequency Unknown*, notably includes the euphemism of "F.U." ("Fuck You"), a common curse phrase used in America especially. A press release at that time stated that "F.U. might be perceived as a fitting tribute and salutation" and later clarified: "Coincidental abbreviation? Unlikely." The abbreviation "F.U." is further emphasized on the album artwork with a fist appearing to punch through glass and rings on the fingers depicting the letters "F" and "U" and the Tri-Ryche icon in between those. It was viewed as an obvious jab at his former bandmates and a sign to the public that Tate wasn't going down without a fight.

Locicero said he found out about the album cover when he was in the studio, as Geoff came in one day and showed it to Jason Slater and Craig on his phone. The guitarist recalled his initial internal reaction was to laugh, but instead he kept quiet. He said that Jason questioned Geoff about the image, asking if Geoff really wanted an album cover that says "F.U." to the fans, to which Geoff replied that it wasn't directed to the fans, but to everyone else. "If there's any regret I have, it's not speaking up and saying, 'you should probably not do that,'" Locicero said. "But I don't think he would have listened to me either way."

Frequency Unknown was released on April 23, 2013, on Cleopatra Records' sub label, Deadline Music. The single released from it was "Cold," and it was dropped in advance on April 3. The album was available as a digital download, CD, limited edition vinyl, and surprisingly on cassette (more recently audio tapes have made a small comeback in popularity, but at that time, they were still obscure). *Frequency Unknown* sold decently at first, moving just over 5,500 copies in the first week and hitting #82 on the Billboard 200 charts in the U.S. (Physical editions of the album were not released in the UK until June 3, and even then, just the CD. The digital version was immediately available on April 23, however.)

Immediately, there were complaints about the poor sound (especially on the vocals) and *Frequency Unknown* was slammed by most critics and fans. Following the negative responses in many blogs and forums, Cleopatra Records hosted a contest to let fans rip on/rant about how much they hated the album and submit it to Geoff Tate, who responded back to the submissions in his own video on YouTube (alternating between raising his eyebrows and laughing at the replies). The label also brought in producer and musician Billy Sherwood (Yes, World Trade) to remix the album due to "sonic issues." Eventually, the remixed version would surface in 2014 on a special deluxe edition including both versions.

"I just know that Jason got an incredibly bad rap on the entire thing," said Locicero, referring to producer/songwriter Jason Slater. "Once you try to fit a 10-pound bag of shit into a one-pound bag, someone is going to suffer. And it was going to be blamed on him. And it really should be pointed right at the top—to whoever handles Geoff's career and Cleopatra Records for their incessant need to get this thing done by a certain date. Jason would have done a great job of being able to mix it if they weren't rushed. And I think Geoff would have done better on his vocals. I know I would have had more complimentary, secondary guitar parts and third guitar parts to add to the thing. Everything would have been better had they just not tried to rush out with their shoelaces tied."

Many fans were disappointed to find out after buying the album that it was not really Queensrÿche at all, and basically just a Tate solo album, despite the album cover's indication. Locicero, himself a fan of Queensrÿche's earlier catalog, felt the same way. "They wanted a heavier album. They wanted my right hand, and that's what they got," Locicero said. While in the studio working on the record, he was convinced that Tate would eventually re-christen the album as a solo project. "It just never struck me as 'Queensrÿche,'" he said.

After the initial rush and sales, the album quickly slid off the charts. Despite that, some people liked several of the songs on the album, and they were much heavier than anything on Tate's two preceding solo records. The issue to the majority of the fanbase, however, was the contrived nature of the album. *Frequency Unknown* features very modern metal with tons of guitar solos and chunky riffs, which was exactly the opposite of what Tate's musical tastes were gravitating to leading up to the record's creation.

Locicero lists "Everything," "Fallen" and "The Weight of the World" as his favorites from the album. "I felt like 'Fallen' was the most 'Queensrÿche-ish' where I could make it sound a little more like Queensrÿche," he said. "There was a structure there I could work with, that I could lend that Queensrÿche vibe to it." Locicero continues: "I feel like *Frequency Unknown* is an album that had a lot of good intentions that got distorted and fragmented along the way. I feel like it's an album that could have been something pretty damned good—it just fell short because of the lack of time constraints associated with it."

Seemingly undaunted by the negative response to *Frequency Unknown*, Geoff Tate was back out on the road to perform Queensrÿche's *Operation: Mindcrime* in its entirety for the album's 25th anniversary. Tate started the tour on April 3, 2013, at Studio 7 in Seattle, and played all throughout the U.S. and Canada, capping off the tour back in Seattle at the Moore Theatre on June 29 (a total of 45 dates). Despite having both the new "Queensrÿche" album, and a solo album out within the last six-to-eight months, his setlist consisted of the complete *Operation: Mindcrime*, four songs from *Empire*, and various other

Queensrÿche songs. "Cold" would make an appearance in the set once *Frequency Unknown* was released.

Queensrÿche fans were often confused due to the ads for the billings (Usually billed as: "Queensrÿche featuring their vocalist Geoff Tate" and in smaller print at the bottom "featuring members of AC/DC, Ozzy, Quiet Riot, Whitesnake, etc."), and the Queensrÿche Tri-Ryche logo on the backdrop. People who weren't aware of the split went to Tate's shows, saw it wasn't really Queensrÿche, and went online posting about it and so on. Adding to the confusion was the fact that the "other" Queensrÿche was continually in the spotlight with interviews around their forthcoming album, and were also playing various concerts during that year.

The battle between the two bands continued during 2013, with nothing yet being decided between the two parties or in the courtroom. Fans became more and more divided into two camps, ones who supported the La Torre-fronted Queensrÿche, and the other for Geoff Tate's version of the band. The legal statements from each person in both parties were posted online at The Breakdown Room by this book's co-author, Brian Heaton, and those documents were dissected and discussed. For some it was a bit more of a look behind the "curtain" of the band's private business than they wanted. "As the guy who unleashed the legal documents into the mainstream, I was of two minds on the topic," Heaton recalls. "On one hand, I felt like I was doing a public service to the fan base by showing people the depths of Queensrÿche's dysfunction. On the other hand, I felt bad, because I remembered what it was like to find out the truth about my favorite band, and how it changed my perception of them."

While The Breakdown Room was the first online forum to shine a spotlight on the legal statements, the documents were of public record for anybody to see, much like a marriage license or bankruptcy filing. They were available to be downloaded for a fee from the court website. And as the judge had said, the court of public opinion would ultimately decide who had more claim to the name: The band that included three of the four original founding members; or the reluctant singer who finally joined the band permanently only after it looked like the group was destined for success with an established management team, a well received (and selling) independent EP and attention from major labels....

CHAPTER 21:
REDEMPTION

The recording of the new, self-titled *Queensrÿche* album started in December 2012. James "Jimbo" Barton was brought back to co-produce and co-engineer the album, and it was recorded at a few different locations—London Bridge, Uberbeatz, Reel Music Studios, Klaus Badelt Studios, Watershed Studios, and Rockenfield's home studio. An old friend even stopped by to hang out and ended up being drafted into helping out. "I knew they were tracking over at London Bridge a couple of years ago with Jimbo Barton," Tom Hall shares. "So, I said, 'Can I come by one day when you're recording and hang out?' I went over and hung out, and Jimbo goes, 'Man, we got to get you involved on this one. Do you want to cut the bass tracks with Eddie?' And I'm like, 'Sure, I'll do that.' So, I did a bunch of comping of parts." Recording went smoothly over the next few months. "The first record I did with the band, all of those songs were already written and demoed," La Torre explains. "There wasn't really much writing done (in the studio). The only writing that happened while we were recording was a vocal chorus for the song 'Spore.' But it was basically done."

This was the first time in a long time a Queensrÿche album was truly a "band" effort. Everybody contributed with the songwriting and creation. Rockenfield co-wrote seven tracks and solely wrote the instrumental intro ("X2"), Wilton co-wrote six songs, Jackson co-wrote three songs, La Torre wrote the lyrics for seven songs and co-wrote music for a couple as well, contributing some melodies and guitar and drum parts. Even Parker joined in with bringing in the demo for "Where Dreams Go to Die." Wilton helped him arrange and shape it into a finished piece and La Torre contributed lyrics. "I wrote a song and two guitar solos [on the self-titled *Queensrÿche* album]," Parker Lundgren stated at the time. "'Where Dreams Go to Die' and 'Don't Look Back.' Michael wrote the rest." It truly was a collaboration this time, and the chemistry was also there. Scott composed the orchestral arrangements and Andrew Raiher helped with some of those and also guested on violin. Their old friend Pamela Moore joined them to contribute guest vocals to the song "A World Without" on the album as well.

Barton's return most certainly signaled an attempt to return to the sound of the classic Queensrÿche albums from the late '80s, and early '90s. "James Barton is a legendary engineer," La Torre says. "He did *Operation: Mindcrime* and he engineered *Empire*, which is one of the greatest recorded albums of all time, in my opinion." One of the first things Barton asked Wilton was if he still had the amplifiers that they had used on *Mindcrime*. Thus, the Marshall JCM800's used for that were brought out of storage and put to work. Although it was a bit split up, as far as where some of the music was recorded at the various locations, it was still a joint vision of how it would all come together as a finished product. The advent of home studios with everybody having equipment at home helped cut costs overall. Rockenfield's home studio was again utilized, along with a new member's home studio. "I recorded all the vocals for the 2013 album at my house," La Torre said, who resides in Florida. "I have a home studio and recorded it all myself." The orchestral parts were recorded down in Santa Monica, California, at Klaus Badelt Studio.

In February 2013, La Torre announced he was leaving Crimson Glory due to the band's inactivity. He said it was not his initial intention to leave Crimson Glory when he started working with Wilton and the rest of Queensrÿche, but as things had progressed, he felt like this was the right situation for him. Nobody had put any pressure on him to choose, and the members of Queensrÿche were fine with Todd being in both bands, but ultimately, he did just that. In March 2013, Queensrÿche made the official announcement on the album's projected release date (which as mentioned previously, Tate's camp jumped on and made their album drop announcement a few hours later on the same day). A snippet of the song "Fallout" was posted on February 23, to give fans a taste of what to expect on the new album (some earlier demos had also been previously leaked in late 2012), followed by the full song posted in March. Another song title, "Vindication", was also revealed at that time.

Work on the new album was completed in April, and Tom Baker mastered the record at Precision Mastering in Hollywood. Craig Howell of Cheeba Productions contributed the design and artwork for the record, and local photographer Mike Savoia (now KISW's official photo man), took the band photos. Once the mixing was finalized at the end of April, the band members noted the length of the record was only 35 minutes and 3 seconds long, quite a bit shorter than most current releases. Wilton commented later that it reminded him of a Van Halen album in that regard. They had originally thought it would just be a five-song EP, but Century Media asked if they could expand it to a full album. As far as the  look of the record itself, it was a strong statement from the band as to who the true Queensrÿche was. "The band felt the title and cover were just staring us right in the face," Wilton explained at the time. "It's the iconic symbol of the band and what better way to signal the rebirth of Queensrÿche with a bold statement like that."

Queensrÿche was officially released on June 24 in Europe, on June 25 in the U.S. and Canada, and on August 21, 2013 in Japan (on Avalon Records including the exclusive live bonus track, a live version of "Eyes of a Stranger") to great response. Before it was even released, anticipation was high, and Wilton commented publicly that it had sold out in the pre-order stage in May and was already on the second printing. It sold 13,659 copies in its first week and hit #23 on the Billboard charts in the U.S. The album also impacted the newer Amazon charts where it hit #2, on the Hard Rock and Metal list, and it additionally hit #6 on the iTunes Top Rock Albums chart. It also charted well in Europe, hitting #44 in Switzerland and #47 in Germany. The first single, "Redemption", received significant radio play and a video was made. Overall, the responses were extremely positive with critics and fans. Although it wasn't intended to be a thematically linked album,

it was later stated as both the "rebirth" mentioned by Wilton, and a "rising up" by other band members, and described as, "going through turmoil and coming out on the other side of it in the light." It is a pretty obvious reflection of what they were going through at the time with the "divorce" from Tate. The word "revolution" is used in the lyrics in three of the songs, "Where Dreams Go to Die", "Don't Look Back" and "Fallout" which also links them together. The sequencing of the songs on the album was very important to the band as well, with wanting it to be a "dynamic journey" for listeners. A special limited-edition version of the album was also released with three bonus live tracks ("Queen of the Reich", "Prophecy" and "En Force") from their December 2012 Snoqualmie show with La Torre. A patch, sticker, guitar pick and button pack were also included in the box.

One of the major complaints from some fans was they felt the album was mixed a bit too "hot", which is more typical of metal albums in recent years (others commented they didn't notice any issues, nor did it bother them at all). Baker mastered it at a high compressed dynamic range around 4-5 dB (decibels), using limiting to push it to peak levels, which tends to cause some distortion when listeners crank the volume. Despite that criticism from some, many people felt it was the best album Queensrÿche had done since *Promised Land,* and a return to form for the band.

In that same month, an interesting solo project of Scott Rockenfield's was released. *Growing Apart* was an album by the recently reactivated early '90s Italian band, Headless, featuring guitarists Dario Parente and Walter Cianiusi. The founding members tapped former Yngwie Malmsteen front man Goran Edman, along with Rockenfield, and it was announced in October 2012 that the forthcoming album was in the works and that they were signed to Lion Records in April. The album was well-received and led to a follow up featuring

Jim Matheos of Fates Warning as special guest. Scott didn't tour with Headless in support of the album, as he was busy with his own recently revamped band blowing up.

Throughout 2013, Queensrÿche continued to play various dates for their "Return to History" tour, with a couple appearances in January, and fifteen more during March and on through half of April (ending with an appearance at the Prog Power festival on Sunday the 14th – along with Helloween, Gamma Ray, Circus Maximus and others). This was part of the reason they had a bit of a tight schedule around the recording of the new album, with much of it finished up around those six weeks of concert dates. They even had to postpone a European leg of the tour in the second half of April, to make sure they could finish the album within the time period Barton had available per his busy schedule, as well as the timelines the record label needed to complete things by. Those dates were later picked back up in October and November that year.

Just prior to the album's drop in June, Queensrÿche had a private pre-release party on May 1, 2013, at the Viper Room in West Hollywood. The complete album was played over the PA system, and the band performed the song, "Redemption" for the first time live, along with songs from their first five albums. It should be noted that "Redemption" was played live only a handful of times by Queensrÿche. As written, the song can be challenging to sing, as it gives very little time for a singer to breathe. The band would eventually drop "Redemption" from its live shows to concentrate on other new songs instead. Following the Viper Room party, Queensrÿche performed at the Rock Hard festival in Germany

on May 28, which included the first public performances of that aforementioned song, along with "Fallout." Three more dates followed in Mexico, Texas and Wyoming in early June, premiering songs from the new album, along with classic hits. Just after the album's drop, Queensrÿche held an album release concert on June 26, at the Crocodile Café in Seattle, to a sold-out crowd. Before the show, Queensrÿche collectively threw out the first pitch at the Seattle Mariners game. La Torre, sitting in the stands with his bandmates and a couple of friends of the band, revealed he had a bad headache, but it wasn't apparent at the show. Once the singer warmed up, he was in fine form, particularly when the gig's special guest took the stage. Pamela Moore joined Queensrÿche to reprise her role as "Sister Mary" in the band's epic "Suite Sister Mary" from *Operation: Mindcrime*. The performance was notable, as it was the first time Moore would sing the song with someone other than Geoff Tate. She and La Torre delivered that night, performing the song in the original key, receiving a raucous ovation from the crowd. As the summer and fall continued, Queensrÿche was out on the road for 33 more dates, wrapping it up at the Events Center in Reno, Nevada, on December 13, 2013. The shows were successful, and the album continued to sell well on through the year. As of 2015, the record had sold just over 40,000 copies in the U.S. and 80,000 copies worldwide.

A special promotional video was also created around the band's self-titled 2013 album, *Queensrÿche. Ad Lucem* clocks in as an 11-minute, 24-second mini-movie. It wraps a storyline around four songs from the album: "Spore", "Midnight Lullaby", "A World Without", and "X2". It was premiered on YouTube.com in November of 2013.

Ad Lucem

Directed by Daniel Andres Gomez Bagby

Executive Producer - Marco De Molina

Written by Christian Moldes and Daniel Andres Gomez Bagby

Director of photography - Kris Carrillo

Line producer - Jennifer L. James

Editor - Zac Surprenant

Color grading - Nick Novotny

Sound mix and sound design - James "Jimbo" Barton

Production designer - Keseh Morgan

Costume designer - Carolina Sapina

Special FX makeup - Melissa Jimenez

Hair and makeup - JoAnn Salgado

Created by Viva Entertainment Co.

Filmed on location at Central City Stages in Los Angeles, California in 2013.

Copyright 2013 Melodisc Ltd., under license to Century Media Records Ltd.

Cast:

Charlie - Geoffrey Kennedy

Brian - Brian Krause

Chief of Police - R.J. Adams

Detective - Miguel Borunda

Cathy (Nurse/Wife) - Cathy Barron

Thug #1 - Todd La Torre

Thug #2 - Erik Aude

Doctor/Obstetrician - Fredrik Scheike

Priest - Rudy Marquez

Maid of Honor - Jessica Prieto

Dead Girl - Gabriela Garcia

Receptionist - Laura Santa Cruz

Paramedic - Eddie Jackson

Doctor #1 - Scott Rockenfield

Doctor #2 - Michael Wilton

Patient - Parker Lundgren

Nurse #1 - Regina Saldivar

Man in Police Station at desk - Christian Moldes

Daughter in photo - Giovanna DeCarlo

Funeral Mourners - Eddie Jackson, Parker Lundgren, Scott Rockenfield, Michael Wilton, Todd La Torre, Jennifer James, Rafael Salinas, Marni Harris, Sarah Creager, R.J. Adams, Brian Krause, etc.

The story of *Ad Lucem* focuses on a young rookie cop named Charlie. At the beginning of the movie, he receives a phone call for his first case. He walks away from his desk and the camera zooms in on a photograph of him standing next to his older brother Brian, who is also a "plainclothes" police officer. The song "Spore" begins playing then when Charlie joins his brother and another cop. They enter a house where they find a dead girl, and then arrest two criminals returning to the scene of the crime with a bag full of money. Todd La Torre plays one of the two men and says, "You're making a big..." before he's cut off. Brian helps himself to some of the cash, and the other criminal lunges at him, but Charlie holds Brian back and the uniformed officer subdues the thug. Back at the station, the chief of police is seen looking through the hidden window as the second criminal is telling a detective to ask "his uniformed" about what Brian did during the bust, as "he saw everything." The chief summons Brian and Charlie to his office, after he discusses the situation with another officer (likely an internal affairs agent), who says the chief should get the younger brother to roll over on his older brother, to which the chief responds that Brian will be fired if that happens. The police chief then calls both men into his office, questions both officers and asks Brian to come clean with him, but he keeps quiet. The chief then looks to Brian's brother, Charlie, who denies it at first, but when the chief threatens to take action against him as well and picks up the phone, he caves. Charlie tells the chief what Brian did and where he hid the money. Brian is forced to hand over his badge and gun and is suspended pending disciplinary actions. Brian has a meltdown in the police station's parking garage and assaults Charlie. Then makes a quick getaway in a pickup truck driven by one of the criminals from the bust (La Torre). While he is getting patched up and recuperating at the hospital, Charlie falls for a beautiful nurse named Cathy. They start dating and later get married. It cuts into the song, "Midnight Lullaby," as Cathy dies during childbirth, leaving Charlie to raise their new child alone (Queensrÿche fans paying attention will note the voice on the loudspeaker saying, "Dr. Davis, telephone please" - a nod to *Operation: Mindcrime*).

The film then rolls into, "A World Without," as grief-stricken Charlie stands with a number of other mourners (the rest of Queensrÿche, the police chief, family and friends, etc.) at Cathy's funeral. The priest starts the eulogy, and then it shifts into him and the rest of the mourners laughing and pointing at Charlie, except for La Torre's character, who looks at Charlie with a serious face, as Charlie clutches his child wrapped in a blanket. His brother, Brian, is also shown laughing and pointing, but it is revealed to just be happening inside Charlie's head, which coincides with the song lyric, "what is real and what is fantasy", as memories play through his head of his time with Cathy. The song continues playing as Charlie is then seen sitting beside a crib and drinking heavily while a baby is crying. He sees a vision of Cathy picking up their child from the crib, and also of the look on Brian's face when he told on him. Charlie pulls out a gun from a drawer next to his bed and points it at his own head, but he stops as the ghost or a vision of Cathy assures him that she is there by his side. Fast forward to four years later, and Charlie is seen at his desk at work and smiling down at a picture that his daughter drew for him. As he gets up to walk away, the camera does a closeup on a photo on his desk of his daughter, and the same type of yellow flower in a vase that he first gave Cathy in the hospital. As Charlie enters the parking garage, his brother waiting for him by his car. Brian holds his hand out nervously and mouths "I'm sorry" to Charlie who hugs him, and the two are able to reconcile. The song "X2" then plays during the end credits.

When asked about the concept of the songs and video, Todd La Torre said this: "The overall theme of the song 'Spore' is one that deals with personal demons, relationship struggles, career pressures, personal/ professional morals and ethical dilemmas. These are issues we all face on some level and the video touches upon them all. 'Midnight Lullaby/A World Without' deals with the loss of a mother during childbirth, leaving a father as a single parent and struggling to move forward through the turmoil. 'X2,' though it opens up our album, provides for a nice outro to it all. The end result is a roller coaster of emotion in an effort to find a healthy resolve. Given our history, we feel that this multifaceted conceptual video, along with a great cast of actors to suit, will really resonate with our fans." (Century Media website - November 25, 2013)

During the first few years of La Torre's tenure in Queensrÿche, many fans marveled at Todd's range and ability to hit the high notes and sing the band's song in the original key they were written in, not to mention his stage presence and confidence in the live setting. It's easier to make somebody look good in the studio, but in a concert setting, you can't really hide it. As previously mentioned, while Todd had his struggles at times on the road, when he was on, La Torre was truly "hitting it out of the park" every night. Due to the strong new material, bringing back the older material from the first EP through *Empire*, and his powerful vocals and the band's renewed enthusiasm, La Torre and the members of this version of "Queensrÿche" continued to win people over along the way. "I am not a formally trained vocalist," Todd stated at the time. "I do have some touring experience with my former band and I'm well aware of the challenges and demands that my singing style presents. I have recently sought out two well-known vocal coaches as I am always interested in improving all aspects of my singing."

Sullivan Bigg also confirms that La Torre was quickly winning Queensrÿche fans over the more they played live: "I landed Queensrÿche with a brand-new singer. It was very difficult. Every band goes through a period, when changing out a member, where it dips. An adjustment period. Eventually it goes right back up about a year or so later. I went through the same thing when I first started booking Great White without Jack Russell. So, the thing happened with Queensrÿche and Geoff Tate. Yeah, he was the mighty 'Geoff Tate', but it was no different. It will be weird for a minute, and people will be like, 'Whoah.' But if he was good, and we all know that Todd's amazing, it would dip and then come right back up. And it did."

Bigg continues: "Todd made it a lot easier, because he's so damn good. I would see it at shows. People with their arms crossed, just daring him to compare himself to Geoff Tate. And they would come out and open with, "Queen of the Reich," which Geoff had refused to do for, like, twenty years. And from that opening scream (by La Torre), people were like, 'Okay.'"

Before long, the court case would finally be decided/settled for good and everybody would move on....

PHOTOS BY BRIAN WOODWICK

Chapter 22:
The Aftermath

T he lawsuits between Geoff Tate and his former band were eventually settled on April 17, 2014, with a statement by both sides made on April 28. It said that both parties had come to an agreement that the La Torre-fronted band would retain the rights to use the "Queensrÿche" name and brand exclusively for recording and touring purposes, while Tate would retain the rights to perform *Operation: Mindcrime I* and *Operation: Mindcrime II* live in their respective entireties in "unique performances." Tate was also to be paid out his 25 percent share of the Queensrÿche corporation in payments by the other three principal members (Wilton, Jackson and Rockenfield). It was filed as a settlement but not dismissed intitially to ensure the enforcement of the agreement through the court. Wilton made an official statement also on his Facebook page on the settlement on May 5, showing that Queensrÿche "is" himself, Scott, Eddie, Todd and Parker. It was finally done. Tate was also quoted at the time during interviews that he was glad they had finally settled it and was happy to move on, despite still feeling "betrayed" by his former bandmates. Sullivan Bigg comments: "At one point the band did call me and say, 'What if we did this?' And I'm not divulging anything that isn't public record. But it came down to a math equation: was one guy going to buy out the other three, or vice versa. And then of course what is the value of the band name and how do you put a price on it? They came to a settlement agreement and worked it all out eventually."

Bigg continues: "But at one point they said, 'What if Geoff did come up with the money to buy us all out and we decided to just move forward as Rising West?' And I said, 'You'd starve to death. I hope you get good money, because that would probably be the last decent paycheck you would get.' I don't mean any disrespect to Mr. Tate, but I'm going to say this: I think his biggest mistake was taking the payout and leaving the name. He's playing clubs and he can't even sell out 300 seaters from what I can see. When Queensrÿche goes to Vegas, I have them in a 1,200-seat room. When Geoff goes there he plays that little rock club for 300 people. They went through a lot to pay him [Geoff] off. But they did. I'm not going to go into specifics, but they're making just as much money, or in some cases more, then when Geoff was in the band. In many cases. But at the time, while the lawsuit was going on still, it was very difficult. There were literally two Queensrÿches. There was a lot of bad blood going back and forth and a lot of animosity. Promoters were like, 'I'm not touching this with the lawsuit, and this confusion going on.' It damages the brand, it's a mess and no one wins."

Queensrÿche continued on their "Return to History" tour on throughout 2014. They kicked it off with a show at Snoqualmie Casino, in Washington, on January 3, with Pamela Moore's solo band opening. She joined them onstage for a duet on the song, "A World Without", reprising her role on the song from Queensrÿche's latest self-titled album. Following that, it was back down to the House of Blues in Anaheim, California, later that month. Then a break for a few weeks, and then back on the road

in March. They played a couple dates on through the Midwest, then two nights on a cruise ship out of Florida as part of the Cruise to the Edge festival (along with prog rockers Yes, Marillion, Steve Hackett, PFM, Presto Ballet, Saga and others.). Moore joined them again on the cruise with her band playing sets, and she joined Queensrÿche again on stage for the "A World Without" duet. Then a few concerts on up the east coast and back to the M3 festival for a return appearance at the end of April. Again, it was another "who's who" `80s "hair metal" lineup featuring Autograph, Keel, Kix, L.A. Guns, Night Ranger, Slaughter, Stryper, Tesla, Winger and many others. Their old friend Lita Ford rounded out the bill. More dates on through May and then another appearance at the famous Sweden Rock festival in June (with Alice Cooper, Alter Bridge, Blaze Bayley, Dark Angel, Paul DiAnno, Jake E. Lee's Red Dragon Cartel, Magnum, Tesla, Rob Zombie and others). They were back to the U.S. for the rest of their summer gigs and played more festivals, casinos, and theaters.

Queensrÿche took September off and then back on the road in October for a few more gigs on through the U.S., with a popover across the Atlantic to Wales in November for the Hard Rock Hell festival. There they were joined by Blue Oyster Cult, Diamond Head, Girlschool, Krokus, Vardis, Y & T and many others. By then, Queensrÿche had dropped a couple of the songs they had been playing from their new album over the last couple of years and just included the "X2" intro with "Where Dreams Go To Die." The rest of the 90-minute set consisted of songs from their first EP on through *Empire*. They wrapped up their 2014 tour year with another appearance back at Snoqualmie with Pamela Moore again opening (although she didn't join them onstage for any duets this time). Only 37 dates total, but their focus was toward a new album planned to come out the following year.

On November 7, 2014, Queensrÿche opened up a special campaign drive through PledgeMusic for fans to pre-order their next album. They used the motto "Building the Empire", resurrecting and slightly modifying the name from successful early `90s "Building Empires" tour, with the idea you could help the band rebuild their career. Along with being able to pre-purchase the new CD or LP, additional rewards were offered of signed materials, musical instruments and other equipment, a phone call or golf outing with the band, and even a chance to invest $50,000 into Queensrÿche Holdings, LLC. Recording of the album was slated to start around the first of December and last on through the end of February 2015, with the album expected to be ready by late spring/early summer 2015.

Geoff Tate also continued on touring through a good part of 2014. Once the lawsuits were settled, he played five shows over three nights in May, at the Triple Door in Seattle, with a special "Rock and Vaudville" show. Tate and his band covered rock and roll songs from the `50s through the present day (featuring covers of Bill Haley, Elvis, Jerry Lee

Lewis, The Beatles, Jimi Hendrix, Rolling Stones, Prince and others). He and his co-creator/writer, Jason Ames (as mentioned previously, Susan Tate's ex-husband), again incorporated some of the "Cabaret"- type vibe with go-go and burlesque dancers, circus performers and so on. He announced the shows prior to that with an appearance on a local morning show called *New Day Northwest* (on King5 TV), where he performed a cover of the Kinks tune "Lola" in a wig, with go-go dancers (again featuring his daughters). Tate proved again how wide the gap was between him and his former bandmates as far as direction, but gathered quite a bit of publicity around this "stunt", even if most of it was negative. Nevertheless, it served to keep Tate in the spotlight a bit, and he also announced that his next solo offering would definitely be a "concept" album and he was excited to move forward with his musical career. Following that stint in Seattle, he played 29 more dates on through the end of August 2014 under the name "Geoff Tate's Queensrÿche". Per the settlement between Tate and his former bandmates, he was allowed to use the "Queensrÿche" name to fulfill the last of the shows contracted prior to the agreement reached in April. After that, he could no longer use the band's name....

Queensrÿche started recording their new album, which was eventually titled *Condition Hüman*, a couple months later than planned, in February 2015. This time, they went with producer/engineer/mixer Chris "Zeuss" Harris, who had worked on albums by Agnostic Front, Crowbar, Earth Crisis, Hatebreed, Muncipal Waste, Shadows Fall, Rob Zombie and many others. Zeuss had completed an album the previous year for another local band, Sanctuary, for Century Media that garned a lot of attention on their reunited effort. "Zeuss is a lot of fun to work with," La Torre said. "We talk a lot on the phone about life and things. So, it's super comfortable for me to record with him. And he's a musician too. He can grab a guitar and express his ideas, which makes the process easier. The whole process, with working with Jimbo (Barton) and Zeuss, was pretty different. But I have nothing bad to say about either one, they're both great. I had a lot of fun working with both of them." *Condition Hüman* was again a truly collaborative effort by all five Queensrÿche members. Michael Wilton co-wrote eight songs this time: "Arrow of Time", "Guardian", "Hellfire", "Toxic Remedy", "Selfish Lives", "Hourglass", "Just Us" and the title track. Scott Rockenfield contributed to six: "Guardian", "Toxic Remedy", "Selfish Lives", "Bulletproof", "Hourglass" and "All There Was." Eddie Jackson co-wrote three songs - "Arrow of Time", "Bulletproof" and the title track – and he was the sole composer of "Eye 9." Parker Lundgren also co-wrote three songs: "Bulletproof", "All There Was" and the title track. Todd La Torre wrote all the lyrics, and some musical parts, for ten songs: "Arrow of Time", "Guardian", "Hellfire", "Toxic Remedy", "Selfish Lives", "Bulletproof", "Hourglass", "Just Us", "All There Was" and the title track. And all five co-wrote the interlude piece, "The Aftermath." Additionally, there were three other tracks that were only available exclusively on the special deluxe edition of the album: "Espiritu Muerto" (Wilton, Jackson), "46° North" (Jackson), and "Mercury Rising" (Rockenfield, La Torre).

Recording was done again mainly at Uberbeatz Studios in Lynnwood, Washington, and some again at Scott's Rockenfield Music Studios at his home in Redmond, Washington. Additional recording was also done at Wilton's home-based Watershed Studios. Jesse Smith assisted Zeuss on engineering, and programming for the album was done by Rockenfield, La Torre and Zeuss. A lot of material was written by the time they started laying down tracks, so the recording process went fairly quickly again. "When Zeuss came into *Condition Hüman*, some of the stuff was written, but some stuff needed changes," La Torre explains. Around the end of March/early April, they were done and Zeuss proceeded to mix the album in May. It was also mastered by Zeuss at Planet Z, his own studio in Hadley, Massachusetts.

The audio clip for "Arrow of Time" was shared with Pledge Campaign supporters first on July 17, 2015, and then to the general public on July 20, both to a very good response. A short while later, on August 3, Queensrÿche revealed the *Condition Hüman* album cover and

track listing to fans. Joe Helm (J. Helm Photography) handled the artwork based on a concept and direction by La Torre. Helm and La Torre are extremely close friends, so the singer brought Helm into the fold for the project. A video for the song, "Guardian", was posted exclusively on the Billboard.com website on September 4. A second single, "Hellfire", was made available for streaming and purchase on YouTube.com and iTunes later that month. *Condition Hüman* was eventually released on October 2, 2015 and debuted on the Billboard Top Rock Albums chart at #5, selling 14,000 copies in its first week. It continued to sell well over the following weeks staying in the Top-40, but slid down a bit to rest at #27 eventually. It also charted well in European countries (hitting in the Top 50 in many) and in the UK (#77). The album was well received by fans and reviewers. Many in both camps cited it as Queensrÿche's best album "in decades."

During the summer of 2015, former member Chris DeGarmo appeared back in the spotlight to a degree, as an EP was released by "The Rue", a songwriting duo he and his daughter, Rylie, had formed a couple of years earlier. Recorded in Chris' home basement studio, the songs have an "alternative", dreamy pop sort of style and are driven by Rylie's vocals, backed by her dad on guitar and piano. The duo played a couple of low-key local

gigs around that time and promoted the release (via their website) in an interview on Billboard.com. They would later pop up as an unannounced opener for Alice in Chains, in Seattle, at the WaMu Theater, on September 20, 2019. Chris also took part in an ESPN Sportsnation Q & A chat in October 2015, as part of Jerry Cantrell's Fantasy Football League. Each musician put up a valuable piece of memorabilia to be auctioned off for the charity of their choice. Fans asked questions and DeGarmo responded in kind. He discussed how some of the classic songs he wrote for Queensrÿche came together, expressed (in response to a question if he felt an obligation to perform music) that he only ever felt an obligation to himself to write and play music, and that he would "never say never" about a possible Queensrÿche reunion, and he was still on good terms with everyone, but it was unlikely.

In the weeks leading up to, and after the eventual release of Queensrÿche's *Condition Hüman* in October, the band toured with the Scorpions. From early September, through the end of October, they played around 20 dates as direct support at various arenas and coliseums, mixed with a few smaller solo club dates on their own during and after their jaunt with the German hard rock/melodic metal kings. They wrapped up 2015 with a concert on New Year's Eve at the Nugget Resort Casino in Nevada. Following that date, Queensrÿche took a handful of days off before heading back out on the road in support of *Condition Hüman* in 2016.

Geoff Tate also kept busy during that time. After he wrapped up his last concerts under the "Geoff Tate of Queensrÿche" moniker, he announced in September 2014 that he was calling his band Operation: Mindcrime and they were starting work on the first of three linked concept albums. Writing and recording started for the first record, *The Key*, later that year and continued through 2015. It was a conceptual piece that focused on virtual currencies, internet banking and stock trading, with a storyline that continued through the three records. Tate elaborates: "I always wanted to do it for me. I started doing this because I like writing music. It's something I like to do. I'm always thinking about my next record. I always wanted to tell a story in three acts, like you would in a book, or a film. So I said, why not do that musically? When I hit upon this idea, it seemed lengthy enough, and complex enough to warrant three albums." His initial plans were to record and release each album every six months. "Geoff just started to go gung-ho on writing and recording on keyboards," Randy Gane explains. "He always played, he just never had it set up like now where he could just go in and record when he wanted to. He's going gangbusters."

The Key was co-produced by Kelly Gray and Tate, and again featured Gray on guitars and backing vocals, and Gane on keyboards. Local guitarist Scott Moughton, who had played with Tate on his 2002 solo album and tour (before eventually being found guilty of identity theft and other legal entanglements) was also back in the lineup, along with John Moyer (Disturbed) on bass, and Simon Wright (AC/DC, Dio), Brian Tichy (Fight, Whitesnake, Ozzy Osbourne), and Scott Mercado (Candlebox, Realms) all contributing drums. Gane continues: "Each one of those guys brings something different to the table. Simon is just a powerhouse. Brian is all about the groove. He just has that thing that's so sexy. Scott is more of a finesse guy. He just has that lighter tough. So you have that talent. For touring, I'm pretty sure it's going to be Simon. He's kind of 'the drummer.' And when he's got some other obligation we try and get Brian or Scott usually. John Moyer played most of the bass tracks I believe. Oh and Kelly and Scott also did some bass tracks. Kelly did all or most of the guitar work, I believe, and Scott, Geoff and I did the keyboards."

David Ellefson (Megadeth, Temple of Brutality, Metal Allegiance) also guested on the album playing bass on, and co-writing the track, "Re-Inventing The Future." Mark Daly, vocalist of the band the Voodoos (which Susan Tate had managed and brought over from Ireland), guested on the song, "Life or Death", as well, and Moughton also sang lead vocals on "Kicking in the Door." The main bulk of the songwriting was done by Tate, Gray, Gane and Moughton. The majority of the album was recorded at Kelly's main stomping grounds, London Bridge Studio, in Seattle, as well as at Tate and Gane's home studios. "We did drum tracks there [at London Bridge]," says Gane. "But pretty much everything else is done by the person who did your last album. Everybody kind of does things at home now. I have a little studio at home. Geoff has a much larger studio at home. Kelly kind of moves around for his. That's the way things are done nowadays with technology."

The Key was completed around late spring/early summer, 2015 and had five singles dropped in advance of the album's release on September 18, 2005 ("Re-Inventing The Future" on July 28, "Burn" and "The Fall" on August 19, "The Stranger" on September 1 and "Hearing Voices" on September 9). It was released on Frontiers Music Srl, a label out of Italy formed in the '90s. Frontiers is known for having many artists on its roster from the 1980s, such as: Asia, Jack Blades, House of Lords, Glen Hughes, Journey, Jack Russell's Great White, Lynch Mob, Stryper, Styx, Tesla, Vixen and many others. Tate had struck a worldwide deal with them in October 2014 for all three albums. Geoff Tate and Operation: Mindcrime went back out on the road in support of *The Key* starting on November 13, 2015 and played 24 shows on through December 19, concluding as part of the Knock Out festival in Germany with Blind Guardian, D.A.D., Rage and others. His touring lineup consisted of Gray, Gane, Moughton, the Sarzo brothers and Simon Wright. For dates where Wright couldn't make it, Mercado filled in on drums. They took a month off for the holidays, and then they were back out on the road starting in early February 2016, for another 45 concerts on through mid-April. Tate's setlists mostly consisted of Queensrÿche songs with a couple rotating tracks from *The Key* added in ("Re-Inventing The Future", "The Stranger", "Burn" and "The Fall"), and "The Weight of the World" from his version of Queensrÿche's only album, *Frequency Unknown*. The Operation: Mindcrime band also included some Queensrÿche songs that dug deeper into the catalog that had not been played in many years (to many fans delight), such as: "Neue Regel", "spOOL", "One More Time", "The Thin Line", "Tribe", "The Hands", etc. After those dates, it was back into the studio to complete the next record.

On September 16, 2016, Tate released the second of the Operation: Mindcrime albums, *Resurrection*, that continued the storyline started on *The Key*. It was again produced, engineered and mixed by Kelly Gray at London Bridge Studio and also Desmodromix in Seattle. The musicians that played on the album were Gray, Randy Gane, Scott Moughton, Simon Wright, Brian Tichy and Scott Mercado. The single from it was a duet with Tim "Ripper" Owens (Judas Priest, Iced Earth) and Blaze Bayley (Iron Maiden, Wolfsbane) called "Taking on the World." A video was made for it as well and got some decent rotation and attention. David Ellefson and Steve Conley were also co-writers on the track.

Geoff Tate additionally made an appearance on the seventh Avantasia album, *Ghostlights*, along with Dee Snider (Twisted Sister), Michael Kiske (Helloween), Bob Catley (Magnum), Robert Mason (Lynch Mob) and Jorn Lande (Ark, Masterplan). It was released on January 29, 2016, and did quite well around the world hitting #2 on the German charts, #6 in Canada, and even breaking the Billboard 200 charts in the U.S. at #101.

Queensrÿche continued touring in support of *Condition Hüman* through 2016, with a little over 100 more dates throughout the United States, Canada, the UK, Europe, Japan and Australia. Their setlist typically consisted of three or four songs (out of five total) from the new album in rotation ("Arrow of Time", "Guardian", "Bulletproof", "Hellfire" and "Eye 9"), along with classic songs from the EP through *Empire*. "Damaged", from

Promised Land, also was also featured in the set regularly. To the surprise of many fans, they skipped over the self-titled 2013 album completely, just focusing on the current release and older material, a pattern they continued as time went on. Todd also continued to tackle older songs that the band hadn't played in a while with Tate, such as "The Mission", "Best I Can", "The Killing Words", etc. Some highlights of that tour were: Two days on the Monsters Of Rock Cruise in February where they played Wednesday and Thursday nights with Doro, Extreme, Faster Pussycat, Helix, Michael Monroe, Uli Roth, Tesla, Steve Vai, Winger, Y & T, and many others—as well as Armored Saint, Lynch Mob and Metal Church—who they would tour all with in upcoming months; a return stop back to the Snoqualmie Casino on March 19 to give local fans a taste of the new album. This is

where they added Eddie's song, "Eye 9," into the show for the first time; On April 30, they were brought back to the M3 festival in Maryland again and played with: Faster Pussycat, Tom Kiefer (Cinderella), Night Ranger, Steven Pearcy (Ratt), Quiet Riot, Slaughter, Tesla, Y & T and others. A five-day residence with the Scorpions in May at the Hard Rock Hotel in Las Vegas; The Summer Breeze festival in Germany on Friday, August 19, 2016 with Slayer, Coheed and Cambria, Arch Enemy, Carcass, Mastodon and many others; The Full Metal Cruise IV on September 5-6 with: Blaze Bayley, Gamma Ray, The Quireboys, Uli Jon Roth and others.

Queensrÿche also toured with Armored Saint as direct support for around 20 shows, including a stop in Seattle on November 15, to play the Showbox, and the Loud Park festival in Japan (along with Blind Guardian, Dokken, Exodus, Scorpions, Shinedown and many others) on October 8. "That was a great tour [with Armored Saint], La Torre says. "They're really great people. In fact, Jeff Duncan their guitar player and I text back and forth, and he was like, 'It would be cool if we could do some more shows together.'"

Queensrÿche finally wrapped it up for the year with a show in Nevada on December 16, 2016. After that, they took the holidays off and then it would be back out on the road in the new year.

CHAPTER 23:
THE VERDICT

A fter a handful of weeks off for the holidays, Queensrÿche was back out on the road in support of *Condition Hüman*. They kicked it off on January 20, 2017, at the Turning Stone Resort Casino Showroom in Verona, New York, followed by a return gig at Snoqualmie Casino in Washington, on January 27. Following that, they played two concerts on the Monsters of Rock cruise (with Black N' Blue, Danger Danger, Girlschool, Kix, Lynch Mob, Vince Neil, Stryper, Winger, Y & T and others) in February. After this, there was some unfortunate news from their drummer that he was stepping down for a while. On March 28, 2017, Scott Rockenfield took a leave of absence to raise his newborn son, Rockson. He and his wife Misty had recently separated and had filed for divorce, which was announced a couple days later in the *Everett Herald*. It appeared he was going to stay home and raise his son as a single parent. Kamelot drummer Casey Grillo stepped in to complete the scheduled tour dates for the rest of 2017, which picked back up again on April 1 for about nine or ten more dates in the U.S. Those went on through May, and then they headed overseas. "When Scott first took a leave of absence, I'm good buddies with Casey Grillo and just called him and asked, 'Hey, can you fill in for a couple of shows?'" Todd La Torre explains. "Then when Scott wasn't letting us know when he would come back, it was like, 'Hey, can you play this show next week too?'"

On May 1, 2017, there was the first news about Queensrÿche's next record. La Torre revealed plans for their next album during an interview for the *Metal Voice* show on YouTube.com. He said he had spent a little over a week in Seattle just prior (to the interview), and a handful of songs were written at that point. He also stated that some had a faster tempo than those on the previous album. That he felt they needed a couple faster ones on this record. Queensrÿche had hoped to enter the studio by September of 2017 to start laying down tracks, eyeing early 2018 for a tentative release.

Queensrÿche continued to tour throughout 2017 with a trip through Europe for summer festival and concert dates. Some highlights were the Hellfest in France (with Animals As Leaders, Deep Purple, Devin Townsend Project, Evergrey, In Flames, Ministry, Sabaton, Tyr, Rob Zombie and others), the Rockfels festival in Germany (with Axel Rudi Pell, Blind Guardian, Helmet, King's X, Krokus, Sanctuary, Tarja and others), the Graspop Metal Meeting festival in Belgium (with Airborne, Deep Purple, Evanescence, Hardline, Hatebreed, Helmet, Mastodon, Ministry, Opeth, Primus, Sanctuary, Scorpions, Steel Panther, Suicidal Tendencies, Rob Zombie and others). An especially significant concert appearance was at the Rock Fest BCM in Barcelona, Spain, on June 30, 2017, along with Alice Cooper, Blue Oyster Cult, Carcass, Krokus, Metal Church, Paradise Lost, Pretty Maids, Running Wild, Saxon, and many others. Tobias Sammet's Avantasia also appeared on the bill, featuring Geoff Tate as one of the guest singers. Tate had a chance finally to see his old bandmates perform and chat a bit with them afterwards, as well as introduce himself to La Torre. They had a pleasant exchange and complimented each other. Following that, Queensrÿche played 15 more concerts over the next four months in the U.S, with just over 40 dates total for the year. They wrapped it up at the end of the year at home, returning to their favorite local casino, Snoqualmie, on December 29, 2017.

Geoff Tate also continued his solo touring with performing another 61 dates in North America, South America, and Europe, between January 3 and October 13, 2017 (billed as his "Whole Story Acoustic Tour"). The tour took place in very small clubs and was an intimate affair. Tate was on stage for close to two hours each night, with the setlist featuring mostly rearranged Queensrÿche songs, including several rarities. Some of the highlights included "Blood" (from *Tribe*), "Hundred Mile Stare" (from *American Soldier*), "Chasing Blue Sky" (a b-side from *Hear in the Now Frontier*), "Out of Mind" (from *Promised Land*) and "Until There Was You" (a b-side from *Q2k*). Fans in attendance remarked that Tate seemed "happy and relaxed" and enjoying the calmer acoustic atmosphere. Tate also told stories between songs, describing how some were written and recorded.

On December 1, 2017, Tate's third Operation: Mindcrime album, *The New Reality,* was released. The album was again produced and engineered by Kelly Gray and featured Gray, Scott Moughton, John Moyer, Simon Wright, and Brian Tichy. Drummer Mike Ferguson (from Kelly's old bands Lyonhouse and Dog Daze) also played on the record. Tate would launch out  on tour in 2018 with the last handful of acoustic solo tour dates in January (which included a diverse song selection of Queensrÿche songs spanning from *Rage for Order* through *Dedicated to Chaos,* but only included one song from the Operation: Mindcrime band, "The Fight"). Following that, he played a little over 100 dates throughout the rest of the year, performing Queensrÿche's *Operation: Mindcrime* for its 30th anniversary, and four *Empire* hits as the encore. 'Til Death Do Us Part, a band fronted by Geoff's youngest daughter, Emily, served as opener for the tour.

Queensrÿche took some time off in January 2018 and then made return appearances at the Turning Stone Resort Casino in Verona, N.Y., and the Monsters of Rock Cruise, both in February. They played a "pre-cruise" concert at the Magic City Casino on February 10, followed by a gig on the boat on the 12th (along with Dangerous Toys, Doro Faster Pussycat, Lita Ford, Raven, Rough Cutt, Tesla, Winger, Y & T and others).

On March 2, 2018, Queensrÿche announced a pre-order for the new album offered through PledgeMusic.com once again. It was stated they had been "locked in the studio for the last few months and still hard at work on crafting the new album." The record was offered as well as various other "exclusives" as had been done with *Condition Hüman.* Nothing was said if Scott Rockenfield was involved in the writing and recording of the new disc, or how long his leave of absence was to be.

On May 5, 2018, Todd La Torre said in an interview at the M3 Rock Festival (where they played with Ace Frehley, Great White, Lynch Mob, Night Ranger, Sebastian Bach, Slaughter, Warrant and others), that the new Queensrÿche album was about two-thirds of the way done and he was starting to lay down the vocals in his home studio again.

Interviews with La Torre and Michael Wilton in late June revealed that the album was about 99 percent done by then, and that Zeuss was working on the final mixing and then on to the mastering. They described the record as having more progressive elements, and different time signatures, and that it was unique, fast-paced and heavier. When asked pointedly who played drums on the record, La Torre joked it was "Animal" from the *Muppet Show* and laughed.

Like on the previous album, what was to be called *The Verdict* was recorded mainly at Uberbeatz in Lynwood, and Wilton's home-based Watershed Studio in Seattle. The mixing and mastering were done by Zeuss at his Planet Z studio in Wilbraham, Massachusetts. There was some additional editing done by Aaron Smith at Envisage Audio. Orchestration and keyboards were done by Craig Blackwell and Mark Lair, and Zeuss also played some keyboards and did programming. The marching snare drums (on "Blood of the Levant") were played by Jesse Smith, and the spoken Arabic was provided by Alia Rabah. The spoken word dialogue in "Light-years" was done by Eddie Jackson's sister, Olga Jackson, and is an excerpt from the film, *Stir of Echoes*. Much like the last two albums, it was again a band collaboration on songwriting and no outside writers were used. Michael Wilton co-wrote five songs, Eddie Jackson co-wrote four songs and was the sole writer on two additional ones, Parker Lundgren wrote one completely himself and co-wrote two other tracks, and Todd La Torre co-wrote lyrics and also some music for seven songs. Scott Rockenfield did not play on the album at all, nor write any material.

Todd eventually stepped in and offered to play drums on the record, as time went on and it was evident that Scott was not planning to come back for the album. The band had started to panic, as they had scheduled the record, and they had deadlines from the record company to meet. Having to search for a new drummer to play on the album would delay them another year or so at that point. So, La Torre grabbed the sticks himself and the band were able to get the album done and stay mostly on schedule.

As summer 2018 continued, Queensrÿche wrapped up the work on *The Verdict* and approved mixes and so on. They played a few more shows around the U.S. in July and August, with the likes of popular `80s hard rock/heavy metal contemporaries: Autograph, Great White, Lynch Mob, Kix, Skid Row, Slaughter, Warrant and others. These concerts were held often outside at several casinos and amphitheaters and were part of the ever more popular "package"- type bills happening in recent years. Queensrÿche additionally filled in for Whitesnake for one show in July at the Ironstone Ampthitheater in Murphy, California, as support for Foreigner (with Jason Bonham's Led Zeppelin Experience opening).

Sometime around mid-2018, Chris DeGarmo sold off a significant portion of his Queensrÿche songwriting/publishing rights to Sony/ATV Music Publishing (under the name "Screen-Gems/EMI Music, Inc.") for a sizeable amount. He sold 20 of his 70 published songs, including: "Silent Lucidity", "Eyes of a Stranger", "Jet City Woman", "Last Time in Paris", "Real World" and others (this includes all of his songs on both *Operation: Mindcrime* and *Empire*). It is unknown his reason for doing this, but it's not uncommon that publishing rights to popular songs that still generate income are sold by a songwriter. For example, K.K. Downing (ex-Judas Priest) sold off his publishing rights for 136 Judas Priest songs to a company called Round Hill around this time as well). Some people have speculated that DeGarmo got out at a good time, when there was still value to the catalog (especially their most popular and best-selling albums including their bigger hits), although he only sold less than one-third of his publishing royalties (he retained the rest of the credits from the releases of the EP through *Rage for Order* and the ones after *Empire*). Both Queensrÿche and Tate continue to perform music from past albums and those continue to sell in various forms and so on. But the reality is that will continue to decline as everybody gets older and eventually stop touring, promoting the material and so on. There's likely still enough money being generated now, though, that it was worth Sony making the offer to DeGarmo. It also doesn't stop

him from rejoining Queensrÿche at any point, for a reunion tour or otherwise. Sony likely saw the additional income potential and likely made an "offer too good to refuse" that helped expand DeGarmo's retirement portfolio. Still, the timing seemed interesting as it was around the time it looked like Rockenfield was gone for good, the 30th anniversary of *Operation: Mindcrime* was that year, and a couple years later it would be the 30th anniversary of *Empire* as well.

Although the publishing rights sale was not made public, Chris DeGarmo did make a much more "public" appearance on Alice in Chains' *Rainier Fog*, released on August 24, 2018. Chris was just down hanging out with the guys at Studio X, but a tricky acoustic guitar part Cantrell struggled with led him to ask his old friend to lend a hand (DeGarmo played on "Drone"). DeGarmo also performed acoustic guitar with the late Chris Cornell's daughter, Lily Cornell Silver, on a rendition of the Alice in Chains song "Black Gives Way to Blue" on December 1, 2020, at Museum of Pop Culture (MoPOP) 2020 Founders Award event honoring Alice in Chains.

Getting back to Queensrÿche, at the end of August 2018, the band went out with the Scorpions as direct support for them at a number of arenas, coliseums and larger casino amphitheaters. During that time, Parker Lundgren had to take a short leave of absence, and an old member filled in for him for the dates. "We did about six or seven shows with the Scorpions and Mike Stone filled in for Parker," La Torre says. "He did us a huge favor stepping in and covering those shows. He's an awesome guy. Love that guy! He's really humble and we really clicked on the tour." (Stone would also fill in for Lundgren on May 22, 2021, at the Shoshone-Bannock Hotel & Event Center, in Fort Hall, Idaho, Queensrÿche's first gig since the COVID-19 pandemic shut down touring in 2020). In between the dates with the Scorpions, they stepped out to play a couple more festivals—including the Grand Rock Timber Festival in Hinkley, Minnesota on September 8, 2018 (with Autograph, Dokken, Kix, Great White, Skid Row, Stryper, Winger and others).

On October 29, 2018, Queensrÿche officially announced the title of the new album as *The Verdict* and confirmed that Todd La Torre played all the drums on it. They also stated that it was moved up to a February 2019 release date as bonus tracks were being added to the deluxe edition. The first single, "Man the Machine," was released on November 16, followed by the second single, "Dark Reverie", on January 11, 2019.

As 2018 turned into 2019, Queensrÿche's pre-order campaign through Pledgemusic took a nosedive. In January 2019, reports surfaced that the company was behind on paying the artists or did not pay them at all. After much back-and-forth, Pledgemusic ultimately filed for bankruptcy. This was horrible timing for Queensrÿche. Just prior to Queensrÿche's drop of their new album in March, they ended up having to make an official statement in response to what was going on with Pledgemusic. On February 14, 2019, the band announced that Pledgemusic had "bamboozled them and everybody else." Simply put, Pledgemusic had money troubles and had mismanaged and misappropriated funds meant to go to bands and other artists. The band apologized for the inconvenience for fans to have to demand refunds through their credit card companies, etc. That followed with another statement by Queensrÿche on February 22, that they would still fund, at their own cost, the $70,000 worth of perks items that were promised to fans, such as signed lyric sheets, puzzle pieces, signed test pressings, art proofs, etc.

That same day (February 22), Queensrÿche kicked off their touring for the year with a return show at the Turning Stone Resort Casino in Verona, N.Y. They debuted songs from *The Verdict* such as: "Launder the Conscience", "Blood of the Levant", "Man the Machine", and "Light-years." Following that, it was another slot at the Monsters Of Rock cruise from February 24-28 (along with Black N' Blue, Bulletboys, Danger Danger, Extreme, Faster Pussycat, Jetboy, Kix, King's X, Tesla, Pat Travers Band, Vixen and others). They changed up the sets for both shows by digging out: "Condition Hüman", "Guardian", "Selfish Lives", "Toxic Remedy" and "Open Road," from the first two records with La Torre - along with playing the aforementioned tracks from *The Verdict*, and fan favorites from the band's back catalog.

The Verdict was finally released on March 1, 2019, on Century Media. It hit #16 on the Billboard charts. It also landed at #6 on the German charts, #9 on the Swiss charts, and additionally charted in the top-20 to the top-100 around the rest of the world. A music video was also made for "Blood of the Levant" and released just prior to the album's drop. Reviews and the overall response from fans on the album were positive. La Torre received praise for doing double-duty on the drums. But with Rockenfield missing in action, there were many questions about his status in Queensrÿche. "Now it's been, like, a couple of years," La Torre said at the time. "I haven't talked to Scott, and I don't know what's up. After a year of, like, him disappearing on us... I don't what he's up to. So many people have embraced Casey as the touring drummer, and a lot of people have liked my drums on the album. I'm appreciative of that. *The Verdict* has done well and made a splash."

A special deluxe edition boxset of the new album was also released in Europe and featured a second CD of bonus material (new acoustic studio versions of "I Dream in Infrared" and "Open Road" featuring Casey on drums, the three bonus tracks from the *Condition Hüman* deluxe edition, the three live bonus tracks from the self-titled 2013 album's deluxe edition, and a live version of "Silent Lucidity" from the same Snoqualmie Casino show in 2012), a patch, fridge magnet and a bottle opener.

Queensrÿche kicked off their main tour in support of *The Verdict* on March 2, 2019, in Orlando, Florida, with Fates Warning as direct support

(with The Cringe opening). They toured throughout the U.S., playing 22 dates with them on through April 3 (ending in Seattle with a sold-out show at the Neptune Theatre). Fates Warning singer Ray Alder joined the band on stage for "Take Hold of the Flame." Queensrÿche continued through the U.S. and Canada for 12 more shows with Great White, Vince Neil, Skid Row and others as direct support. Then they headed overseas in mid-July to play various festivals and concerts in Europe, and the United Kingdom, on through the end of August. First up was The Headbanger's Open Air Festival in Germany on July 25, 2019, where Seattle ruled the fest with Queensrÿche headlining Thursday night, Sanctuary performing Friday night, and Heir Apparent taking the stage on Saturday night. The following night, Queensyche played the Rock of Ages festival with Saxon, Rose Tattoo, FM, Jean Beauvior and others. Wacken Open Air was on August 2, and they joined Anthrax, Demons & Wizards, Opeth, Prong, Henry Rollins, Slayer, and many others, to the delight of 75,000 attendees. Bloodstock Open Air was in England on August 11 and they appeared with Anthrax, Cradle of Filth, Death Angel, Metal Church, Ross The Boss, Sabaton, Scorpions, Dee Snider, etc. They also played the Rock Planet in Italy in August with Firewind and Mirrorplain opening (who they played with for a few other concerts in France, Belgium, Switzerland, etc.), made appearances at the Into The Grave festival in the Netherlands, and the Summer Breeze, Turok Open Air and Free & Easy festivals in Germany. Promotion also continued for *The Verdict* with a lyric video released for the song, "Bent," on July 30, 2019, and "Propaganda Fashion" also added to their setlist around that time (that would be also be released as their third "single" from the album on October 7).

Following that tour leg, they returned to America on September 1 for a show with Dokken at the Thunder Mountain Amphitheatre in Loveland, Colorado. They played ten more concerts on through October 20, 2019, including a return appearance at the Grand Rocktember Festival in Minnesota (with Autograph, Black N' Blue, Vince Neil, Quiet Riot, Dee Snider, Vixen and others), two nights on the Megacruise (with Anthrax, Armored Saint, Phil Campbell and the Bastard Sons, Death Angel, Doro, David Ellefson, Lamb Of God, Metal Church, Overkill, Suicidal Tendencies and others.), and a spot (with Guns N' Roses, Havok, Quiet Riot, etc.) at the Fronterizo Fest in Tijuana, Mexico. Then it was back over to Europe, and the UK, for 20 more dates on through November and early December. They wrapped up their concerts for the year with four more shows at casinos in Washington and California. The last one was in Winterhaven, California, at the Quechan Casino Resort on December 21, 2019. After that, it was a couple of weeks off for the holidays for the band, having clocked another 94 concerts for the year.

Queensrÿche started 2020 with continued touring for *The Verdict*. This time, John 5 (Rob Zombie, Marilyn Manson, David Lee Roth Band) joined them, along with newer band Eve to Adam as openers, for 26 shows throughout the U.S. (with John 5 for just 20 of those dates due to other commitments). Their first show was in Ft. Lauderdale, Florida on January

17. They completed the tour on February 27, with a show at the Plaza Theatre in Orlando, Florida. This included a return to the Neptune Theatre in Seattle on February 5, to local fans' delight.

Just prior to that first leg of the tour, they dropped their fifth single from the album, "Inner Unrest", on January 10. The album continued to sell well over the last year since its release and garner more favorable reviews and press for the band.

Like many other bands, Queensrÿche had numerous other concerts scheduled and announced for 2020, but the dates were canceled or postponed due to the COVID-19 pandemic. This included ten dates with the Scorpions for another "residence" in Las Vegas, Nevada, at Zappo's Theater in Planet Hollywood (that were initially rescheduled for May 2021, but again pushed back to March-April 2022). Tate played sporadic dates in 2020 and early 2021 where they were permitted with social distancing in place. He also did a livestream event and has a full touring schedule booked for the rest of 2021. As for Queensrÿche, the band hasn't been quiet during the downtime. During 2020 and 2021, both Michael Wilton and Todd La Torre have commented that they've been writing songs for Queensrÿche's next album, with an eye on a late 2021/early 2022 release.

CHAPTER 24:
A LOOK AHEAD

S o what does the future hold for Queensrÿche 40 years into the band's life? As mentioned earlier, plans for a new album are in the works and could well be out a bit sooner than the band intially expected due to the quarantine and social distancing from the COVID-19 pandemic of 2020. In an interview the previous November in Greece, Wilton said that they had already been thinking about a new record, and that he wanted to avoid having a lengthy period of time in between albums, like the four year span between *Condition Hüman* and *The Verdict*. He also said he would like new drummer Casey Grillo to play on the next record if possible.

Michael and Todd also said in a 2017 interview that they were thinking about doing a live album with the current La Torre-fronted lineup. They weren't sure whether it would be taken from multiple shows or just one, but the idea is there regardless. It's been quite a while since Queensrÿche's last live album, and it would certainly be a nice way to capture the strength of the band's concert performances in recent years.

Capitol Records finally released the long-awaited 30th anniversary box set of Queensryche's *Empire* on June 25, 2021. The label also re-released *Operation: Mindcrime* in a similar format on the same day, giving the band's fans a double dose of classic material to consider rebuying. *Empire* is featured as a 3CD/1DVD box set, while *Operation: Mindcrime* was issued as a 4 CD/1 DVD box set. The audio from both new versions of the respective original albums is newly remastered at Abbey Road Studios in London and will also be available on vinyl. Simple two-CD versions of the records are also being released.

The *Empire* box set features the newly remastered original album on the first CD. Disc two contains three bonus studio tracks "Last Time in Paris," "Scarborough Fair" and "Dirty Lil' Secret", all of which were already available as b-sides on previous reissues and compilations, not to mention the original CD singles from the 1990s. The disc also contains edited versions of "Silent Lucidity" and "Empire," an acoustic version of "I Dream in Infrared," "Prophecy" from *Live in Tokyo* (which was available on the EP remaster in 2003), and radio edits of "Best I Can" and "Anybody Listening?" Disc three is a live performance from the Hammersmith Odeon, in London, 1990, that features 10 live tracks previously available on the 20th Anniversary box set of *Empire*. The final disc in this new box set is simply *Building Empires*, the DVD compilation that originally came out on VHS in 1992 and was issued on DVD in 2001. It's all housed in a 10x10 box with new liner notes by Alex Milas, who interviewed singer Geoff Tate for the project. The CD artwork is new as well.

The *Operation: Mindcrime* box set contents mirror the repackaging treatment given to *Empire*. Disc one is the original album remastered. Disc two has edited versions found elsewhere. The third and fourth discs contain live content. Disc three has the *Mindcrime* portion of the Hammersmith Odeon show in 1990, while the fourth live disc which is labeled *Operation: Mindcrime* Live in Wisconsin 1991. It appears to just be Queensrÿche's previously released *Operation: LIVEcrime* CD. The DVD is the *Video: Mindcrime* compilation, first released in 1989 on VHS, and then repackaged into the deluxe edition of *Operation: Mindcrime* that was issued as a box set in 2006. CD two also contains two interview tracks, "Interview with Queensrÿche: Speak the Word" and "Overseeing the Operation." Both are promotional radio interviews with the band that were previously only available on vinyl. Apparently, they've been officially digitized and are now available with this set.

For the hardcore fans, these box sets are likely disapointing. The 30th anniversary of *Empire* was the perfect opportunity for Capitol Records to do the album (and fans) justice by including a disc of album demos, and the full version of the Queensryche's much-ballyhooed *MTV Unplugged* session which has been begged for by fans for years. The same applies with the *Operation: Mindcrime* set. There are likely unreleased demos that could have been included, and/or other live shows or material from that tour. Instead, the label did the bare minimum.

Geoff Tate has continued to keep the Queensrÿche catalog alive in his concert sets as well, performing the complete *Empire* and *Rage for Order* albums in recent tours (with a new, younger lineup backing him up). He's also contributed to side projects much more in the progressive metal vein of classic Queensrÿche in recent years—with a return to guest on the most recent Avantasia album, *Moonglow,* released in February 2019 (this time singing solo on two songs, and  a group duet with: Ronnie Atkins, Bob Catley, Jorn Lande and Eric Martin)—and an album project headed by his label, Frontiers, called *Sweet Oblivion* (the first album was released in June 2019 and featured Tate on all lead vocals. A follow-up, *Relentless,* was

released on January 26, 2021.). Many people have commented that Geoff has sounded the best he has in years on these albums. And he was recently honored by being inducted into the Heavy Metal Hall Of Fame on January 15, 2020, further cementing his place in history. Eddie Trunk hosted the gala in Anaheim, California, and he was joined by Graham Bonnet, Don Dokken, Stephen Pearcy of Ratt, Joe Satriani and fellow Seattle-ites Metal Church. Tate joined the all-star band for a rendition of Black Sabbath's classic, "Paranoid", that included Chris Poland (Megadeth, Damn the Machine, Mumbo Brain), Satriani and Steve Vai.

So everybody in the Queensrÿche circle has continued to keep busy and turned things around as far as their respective legacies. But on the still most asked question of: will there be a reunion of all five original members? It's hard to say.

Geoff Tate has said in interviews in recent years that is open to the idea, and that they have had some very good offers if that were to happen. But how do Wilton and Jackson feel about that after the firing and ugly lawsuit fallout? Would they be willing to bury the hatchet with Tate for a reunion tour at the least? They were all civil backstage during the Barcelona festival in 2017, but of course that was very public. Behind closed doors there could still be a lot of bad blood. And what of their other two former bandmates?

Chris DeGarmo has followed the progress of his former bandmates and is still friends with them. Wilton has said he golfs with Chris from time to time and they attend various family birthday parties, etc. Todd La Torre said that he had lunch with DeGarmo in mid-2017 and that Chris said he respects and likes what Todd has done in Queensrÿche. Wilton has also commented that he is open to Chris working with them again and that if it did happen, they'd probably not announce it like they did with *Tribe*. Despite him selling off some of his publishing ownership in 2018, it does not in any way prevent DeGarmo for joining them onstage in the future. Yet, as of this writing, DeGarmo has elected not to perform with Queensrÿche, nor enter the studio with them. That speaks volumes, without saying a word. It is also possible DeGarmo wants to keep a more private life, despite his love of music. When he performed with Lily Cornell Silver to honor Alice in Chains, DeGarmo shunned the spotlight. So much so, that according to a social media post from Alice in Chains bassist Mike Inez, DeGarmo initially didn't want a light on him at all. He acquiesced to a small spotlight on him during the performance.

Rumors swirling around Scott Rockenfield in 2020 were that he may not be able to play drums anymore due to a debilitating muscle disease, or at least would not be able to endure a lengthy tour. Geoff Tate said in an interview that, "Scott may never play again" and, "has a lot of medical problems now." Michael Wilton hasn't commented on it recently, but stated not long after *The Verdict* was dropped in March 2019, that the door was open for Rockenfield to come back if he wanted to. Wilton also said that drumming was a tax on the body and after 35 years people change. He also said Scott was a brother, and a friend, and it was just a matter of when he comes knocking at the door again. But that Queensrÿche was a "machine that has to keep going." As of this writing in May 2021, however, Scott has resurfaced claiming he never "quit" the band, and hinted on social media that there is much more to the story than is publicly known. Rockenfield also launched a new website, https://www.queensryche2021.com, that includes a demo, "Days `O Death", an early version of "Toxic Remedy" from 2014 (which appears in its final form on *Condition Hüman*. At one point, there was other music featuring a female singer, and images of a couple of his Queensrÿche bandmates and himself, which have since been taken down. It is unknown at this time what Scott's reasoning is for creating this website, and what his plans are for it. So, rather than speculating on it we'll just have to see where it goes.

Regardless of possible reunions, Queensrÿche has certainly made a big impact on the world and the music scene in general. They have sold over 20 million records worldwide and continue to sell more. *Operation: Mindcrime* is still considered one of the greatest heavy metal and concept albums of all-time, and ranks high in many publications' and fans' top-10 lists. The storyline and the characters are part of popular culture now. "To this day, *Operation: Mindcrime* and Sister Mary are alive as ever," Pamela Moore says. "I don't see signs of it stopping any time soon. It's incredible!" Todd La Torre has rejuvinated the current lineup and they have done three albums in a more familiar hard rock/metal vein to help regain their credibility with fans and critics. They have weathered lineup changes and continue to be popular around the world. Their influence on other bands and musicians over the years has been significant, with bands (or members of) citing them specifically, such as: Angra, Blind Guardian, Conception, Crimson Glory, Dream Theater, Edge of Sanity, Gargoyle, Hammerfall, Helloween, In Flames, Kamelot, Labyrinth, Lethal, Psycho Drama, Rhapsody, Royal Hunt, Shadow Gallery, Silent Force, Stratovarious, Symphony X, Tad Morose, Therion, Unleash the Archers and others. "The two most important bands, or artists for me are Ah-Ha and Geoff Tate from Queensrÿche," said Roy Khan (Conception, ex-Kamelot). "The first one made me see that I like those kinds of high, shining vocals and melancholy lyrics and melodies. And Queensrÿche's *Rage for Order* in 1986 was great, and they were great until 1990." Despite Queensrÿche's music being mostly in the heavier vein, with progresive leanings, they have never really prescribed to fitting in any one category. Something that has likely helped them transcend those limitations. "We never thought of ourselves as a 'category', or as being part of a 'club,' Geoff Tate states. "Back when we started out, there really weren't all of these sub-genres that sprouted up by the mid-to-late `80s." Queensrÿche made original music that was their own genre.

Queensrÿche also showed local bands coming up right behind them—Fifth Angel, Forced Entry, Heir Apparent, Metal Church, Panic, Sanctuary, etc.—that there was another way to succeed. They set a blueprint for not trolling the local scene hoping to get noticed (which was the norm in 1983). Instead, you could write and record strong original material and send it out, or release it yourself, and then get signed to a major (or bigger independant) record label, get tour support to whatever degree, and break out of the Pacific Northwest. By showing you could garner a fan base, get press and publicity, and sell records around the world - without having a major record label contract to start—it made everyone take notice. Queensrÿche also helped garner attention on the Seattle music scene in general. That there were talented musicians and bands in the Pacific Northwest that were not looking to what was trending in Los Angeles or New York, but were instead creating their own original material away from that industry, and those cities you typically had to relocate to if you hoped to get signed. Queensrÿche's "breakout" was something that would help increase attention by record labels on Seattle, and eventually lead to an explosion with the "Grunge" spotlight in the early-to-mid 1990s.

Many Queensrÿche songs have been covered over the years by artists such as:

Kendall Bechtel - "I Will Remember"

Black Art - "Eyes of a Stranger"

Black Earth - "The Lady Wore Black

Black Symphony - "Deliverance"

Cyrcle IX - "I Don't Believe in Love"

Darkside - "Someone Else?"

Etheria - "Eyes of a Stranger"

Factor Five - "Nightrider"

Forte - "Prophecy"

Antonio Giorgio - "The Mission"

Ion Vein - "Take Hold of the Flame"

Karma - "I am I"

Mayadome - "Neue Regel"

Mesmerize - "The Needle Lies"

Mind's Eye - "I Will Remember"

MindMaze - "Roads to Madness"

Moon of Steel - "Anybody Listening?"

Mystic-Force - "Child of Fire"

Nightmare's End - "The Lady Wore Black"

Orange Moon - "Operation: Mindcrime"

Power of Omens - "Screaming in Digital"

Rewind - "Jet City Woman"

Shadowkeep - "Queen of the Reich"

Silent Shadows - "I Don't Believe in Love"

Swan Christy - "Someone Else?"

Talamasca - "The Whisper"

Templar - "Thin Line"

Sahaj Ticotin (of RA) - "The Mission"

Unleash the Archers - "Queen of the Reich"

So who knows what the future holds for Queensrÿche. More new albums and world tours, hopefully. Maybe more special anniversary edition box sets/editions, including one for *The Warning* (with the original track sequence and a proper remix with the guitars more prominent in the mix as the band intended with the early Triad Studios pre-production demos included perhaps?" A proper release of the great 1984 soundboard show from Harpo's in Detroit that has been floating around for many years as a bootleg? More live shows from that tour?), or one for *Rage for Order* (including the unreleased demos, various live material, etc.)? Regardless of what will transpire, Queensrÿche will likely live on as years go by as one of Seattle's biggest, not only heavy metal bands, but one of the most well-known rock bands from the Northwest in general. And one that made a huge impact on the world as a popular pioneering progressive hard rock/metal band. Their biggest hit songs continue to get regular radio and digital streaming platform rotation (Apple Music, Spotify, TikTok, etc.), and their albums and songs continue to sell. Not too bad for some musicians from the suburbs of Washington.

Queensrÿche has evolved quite a bit from the small group of friends who stayed home from parties in the Seattle suburbs to do finger exercises and work on their playing skills. Queensrÿche has had a rollercoaster of a ride, rising from the Pacific Northwest, reaching the pinnacle of stardom, overcoming the losses of its primary songwriter and record label (not to mention changing musical tastes and digital music devastating the industry) to rebuild and be in the spotlight again. Even losing one of the iconic singers in heavy metal history hasn't stopped Queensrÿche from pushing forward.

No, the band isn't what they once were—that's to be expected with new songwriters and personalities involved. But this entity called "Queensrÿche" continues to reinvent itself, album after album, bobbing and weaving its way through rock history. Whatever label you give them, "rock", "metal", or "progressive", it all fits. They find a way to survive and thrive when you least expect them to. Queensrÿche is the epitome of perseverance and one of rock's enduring success stories.

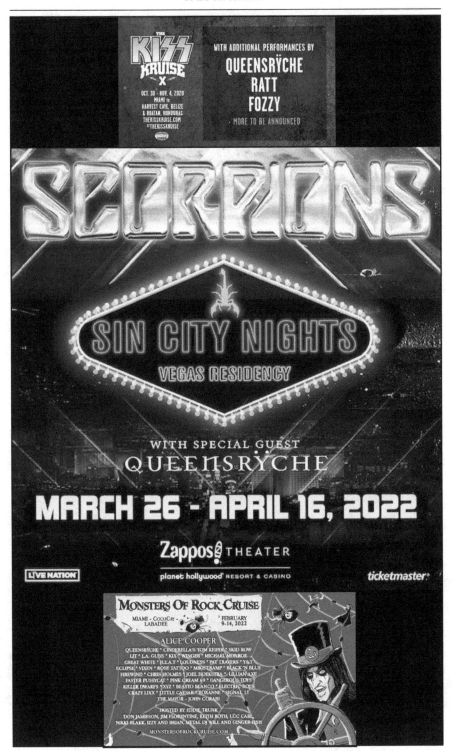

SELECTED DISCOGRAPHY

EPs & Singles (Vinyl)

Queensrÿche (1982 - 206 Records) (4 songs) (Both ASCAP and BMI editions exist. A very limited amount included a lyric sheet as well.)

Queensrÿche (1983 - EMI) (4 songs) (Major label reissue. Some came with a "hype" sticker)

The Warning (1984 - EMI) (Promo 12") (w/ "The Warning" Live)

Walk in the Shadows (1986 – EMI) (Promo 12")

The Whisper/I Dream In Infrared (1986 – EMI) (Promo 12")

Gonna Get Close To You (1986 – EMI) (Double 7" in UK and 12" in Germany. Both include "Prophecy")

Speak The Word (1988 – EMI) (Promotional 12" with Interview)

Revolution Calling (1988 – EMI) (Promo 12")

Eyes of a Stranger (1988 – EMI) (7" and 12" gatefold EP in UK, US Promo 12")

Breaking The Silence (1988 – EMI) (Promo 12")

I Don't Believe In Love (1989 – EMI) (7" and 12" Promo singles)

Overseeing The Operation (1988 – EMI) (10" Import EP – Includes "Suite Sister Mary" + Medley)

Empire (1990 – EMI) (7" Shaped Disc – Import) (Includes Non-LP "Scarborough Fair") (12" EP includes "Prophecy" as well)

Best I Can (1991 – EMI) (10" UK Import with poster and badge)

Another Rainy Night (Without You) (1991 – EMI) (US 7" w/ non-LP & 12" Import w/ 2 non-LP)

Jet City Woman (1991 – EMI) (Shaped Picture Disc)

Silent Lucidity (1991 – EMI) (12" Import EP – Includes 2 bonus live tracks)

Anybody Listening? (1992 – EMI) (7" Jukebox single)

I Am I (1994 – EMI) (12" Import – Gold Vinyl w/2 non-LP songs and prints)

Bridge (1994 – EMI) (7" Import Picture Disc – Includes "Killing Words" Live)

LPs

The Warning (1984 – EMI) (2012 Friday Music reissue with gatefold jacket and 180-gram vinyl)

Rage For Order (1986 – EMI) (both black and light grey ring cover variations exist)

Speaking In Digital: A Conversation With Queensrÿche (1986 – EMI) (Promotional LP including an interview and music)

Operation: Mindcrime (1988 – EMI) (2008 Capitol reissue "from the vaults" on 180-gram vinyl. Also 2012 Back in Black red vinyl reissue in the UK.)

Empire (1990 - EMI) (Double LP) (2011 Friday Music reissue on 180-gram black vinyl, and 2020 Friday Music limited green vinyl reissue. Also 2017 Back in Black clear vinyl reissue in the UK.)

Promised Land (1994 – EMI) (Limited U.S. pressing) (2017 Back In Black clear vinyl reissue in the UK)

Operation: Mindcrime II (2006 – Rhino) (Double LP)

Dedicated To Chaos (2011 – Roadrunner) (Double LP)

Queensrÿche (2013 – Century Media) (Released in various colors – black, gold, grey, blue, white and clear)

Condition Human (2015 – Century Media) (Released in black and clear vinyl)

The Verdict (2019 – Century Media) (Released in black, black/clear "smoke", green "petrol", clear, sky blue, red/black "smoke" and "bloodshot" (red/clear splatter) vinyl)

Cassette Singles

A Message from X (1988) (Fan club promo) (with Rosary necklace)

Eyes of a Stranger (1989 - EMI) (2 songs)

I Don't Believe in Love (1989 - EMI) (2 songs)

Another Rainy Night (Without You) (1990 - EMI) (2 songs - 1 non-LP)

Silent Lucidity (1991 - EMI) (3 songs - 2 Live)

Jet City Woman (1991 - EMI) (3 songs - 1 non-LP)

Anybody Listening? (1992 - EMI) (2 songs - 1 non-LP)

Real World (1993 - Columbia) (3 versions of song)

Bridge (1994 - EMI) (UK Import) (2 songs - 1 live)

CDs (EPs & Singles)

Queensrÿche (1983 - EMI) (4 songs) (late `80s issue with bonus song: "Prophecy")

Revolution Calling (1988 – EMI) (Promo)

Eyes of a Stranger (1989 - EMI) (4 songs) (Import) (Also US Promo single)

I Don't Believe In Love (1989 – EMI) (Promo)

Empire (1990 – EMI) (3 songs – 2 Non-LP) (Import)

Silent Lucidity (1990 – EMI) (3 songs w/ 2 Live Non-LP) (Import)

Best I Can (1991 - EMI) (4 songs w/ 2 Non-LP) (Import)

Jet City Woman (1991 - EMI) (3 songs w/ 1 Non-LP) (Import)

Another Rainy Night (Without You) (1991 – EMI) (4 songs – 3 Non-LP including "Last Time In Paris")

Anybody Listening? (1992 - EMI) (w/Non - LP song "Scarborough Fair")

Building Empires (1993 - EMI) (Promo Sampler w/ Non-LP tracks)

Real World (1993 – Columbia) (Promo w/ 3 versions)

I Am I (1994 - EMI) (4 songs w/ 3 live) (Import)

Bridge (1994 - EMI) (4 songs w/ 3 Non-LP) (Import)

Bridge (1994 - EMI) (4 songs w/ 3 live) (Import)

Disconnected (1995 – EMI) (Promo EP w/ 5 non-LP versions and tracks)

Someone Else? (1995 – EMI) (Promo w/ non-LP version)

Sign of the Times (1997 - EMI) (4 songs w/ 3 Non-LP) (Import)

Hearing Is Believing (1997 – EMI) (3 songs) (Import Promo Sampler)

The Voice Inside (1997 - Promo)

Spool (1997 – EMI) (Promo)

You (1997 – EMI) (Promo)

Breakdown (1999 – Atlantic) (Promo)

Falling Down (1999 – Atlantic) (Promo)

The Right Side of My Mind (2000 – Atlantic) (Promo)

Beside You (2000 – Atlantic) (Promo)

Open (2003 – Sanctuary) (Promo)

Losing Myself (2003 – Sanctuary) (Promo)

Rhythm of Hope (2004 – Sanctuary) (Promo)

The Hands/I'm American (2006 - Rhino) (Promo)

Justified (2007 - Capitol) (Promo)

Welcome to the Machine (2007 - Rhino) (Promo)

If I Were King (2009 - Rhino) (Promo)

Man Down (2009 - Rhino) (Promo)

Get Started (2011 - Roadrunner) (Promo)

Fallout (2013 - Century Media) (Promo)

CDs (Full-Length)

Queensrÿche (1983 - EMI) (4 songs) (2003 Remastered Edition w/ Live in Tokyo '84 concert)

The Warning (1984 - EMI) (2003 Remastered Edition w/ Bonus tracks)

Rage For Order (1986 - EMI) (2003 Remastered Edition w/ Bonus tracks)

Operation: Mindcrime (1988 - EMI) (2003 Remastered Edition w/ Bonus tracks)

Empire (1990 - EMI) (Double LP) (2003 Remastered Edition w/ Bonus tracks)

Evolution Calling (1990 – EMI) (Promotional compilation/sampler)

Operation: Livecrime (1991 - EMI) (Live CD and VHS Video Boxset)

Promised Land (1994 – EMI) (2003 Remastered Edition w/ Bonus tracks)

Road To The Promised Land (1994 – EMI) (Promotional Sampler – 10 songs)

Here in the Now Frontier (1997 – EMI) (2003 Remastered Edition w/ Bonus tracks)

Q2K (1999 – Atlantic) (2006 Rhino/Atlantic reissue with bonus tracks)

Greatest Hits (2000 - Capitol/EMI)

Live Evolution (2001 - Metal Is/Sanctuary)

Tribe (2003 - Sanctuary)

Operation: Mindcrime II (2006 - Rhino)

Take Cover (2007 - Rhino)

Mindcrime at the Moore (2007 - Rhino) (CD & DVD)

Sign of the Times: Best of Queensryche (2007 - Capitol/EMI) (Also Special Edition w/ bonus disc w/ Myth tracks, Queensryche demos, live, etc.)

American Soldier (2009 - Atco/Rhino)

Dedicated to Chaos (2011 - Loud & Proud/Roadrunner)

Queensrÿche (2013 - Century Media)

Condition Human (2016 - Century Media)

The Verdict (2019 – Century Media)

(Multi-Media)

Queensrÿche's Promised Land CD-ROM (1996 – EMI) (2-Disc Set - Interactive Game, 23 mini-documentaries and 3 music videos. A bonus fourth video is played of the unreleased song, "Two Miles High," if you beat the game.)

(Bootlegs/Unauthorized)

Triad Studios 1983 (Warning Pre-Production Demos) (CD) (Also as: **Days Before the Empire** w/ 2 Myth demos)

King Biscuit Flower Hour (1983 LP) (Split LP w/ Ronnie James Dio. 4 songs from Queensrÿche from 1983 San Jose Civic concert with Dio)

Storming Detroit (Live 1984 Radio Broadcast) (CD) (LP version called En Force)

Toronto, Canada September, 1986 (1987 LP – Live Rage For Order Tour)

The Nobility of Toxic Pharmecuticals (LP - Live in March, 1989 at Nassau Coliseum)

Operation Perfectcrime (1990 CD) (5/17/89 Japan live show)

Electric Requiem (1991 CD) (Live Amsterdam in 1990 – Radio Broadcast)

Ryche & Roll (1991 CD) (12/6/90 Milan, Italy show)

Empire Demos (1993 CD) (Unreleased demos)

MTV Unplugged (1994 CD) (Acoustic show in 1993)

In The Promised Land (1995 CD – Trademark of Quality) (San Jose show – Radio Broadcast)

Philosophy of Life (1995 CD) (Japan show – 3/17/95)

Welcome To the Promised Land (1995 CD) (1994 Germany show)

Live In The Now Frontier (1997 CD) (Import) (New Mexico show – 8 songs and interview)

(Related)

Slave to the System - Slave to the System (2002/2006 - Spitfire) (Scott Rockenfield & Kelly Gray)

Soulbender - Soulbender (2004 - Licking Lava/Rat Pak Records) (Mike Wilton w/ Nick Pollack)

Geoff Tate (2002 - Sanctuary)

Geoff Tate - Kings & Thieves (2012 - Inside Out)

Frequency Unknown (2013 - Deadline) (Geoff Tate's Queensrÿche with other musicians. Later called Operation: Mindcrime) (released on CD and LP)

Operation: Mindcrime – The Key (2015 – Frontiers) (Import) (CD and LP)

Operation: Mindcrime – Resurrection (2016 – Frontiers) (Import) (CD and LP)

Operation: Mindcrime – The New Reality (2017 – Frontiers) (Import) (CD and LP)

Sweet Oblivion Featuring Geoff Tate (2019 - Frontiers) (Import)

Sweet Oblivion (Featuring Geoff Tate) – Relentless (2021 – Frontiers) (Import) (CD and green vinyl LP)

(Related Demos)

Babylon - Rehearsal Demos 11-20-80 (w/Geoff Tate) (CD)

Myth - Live & Demos (w/ Geoff Tate, Kelly Gray and Randy Gane) (CD)

HOME VIDEOS

Live in Tokyo (1985 - Sony/Video LP) (VHS)

Video: Mindcrime (1989 – EMI) (VHS) (also Laserdisc in Japan on PMI)

Operation: LIVEcrime (1991 - EMI) (Box set with CD & VHS Tape)

Building Empires (1992 - EMI) (VHS)

Mindcrime at the Moore (2007 - Rhino) (CD & DVD set)

*Collectors note: EMI-America sent out a special promotional film-can test pressing of the EP to approximately 229 radio stations across the U.S, and Canada. An ultra rare 7" test pressing of "The Lady Wore Black" was also pressed. Only 10-15 copies of this test pressing are known to exist.

WORKS CITED

(*All interview quotes in this book were taken from ones conducted by the authors, except where noted in the book and here. All quotes used by permission.)

"Before The Storm" - By Brett Miller (Anybodylistening.net/The Breakdown Room – 2006

"Chris DeGarmo on Empire" - By Martin Popoff (The Top 500 Heavy Metal Albums Of All Time – ECW Press, 2004)

"Geoff Tate on Operation: Mindcrime" - By Martin Popoff (The Top 500 Heavy Metal Albums Of All Time – ECW Press, 2004)

"Interview With Geoff Tate" - By Bob Nalbandian (Shockwaves/Hard Radio – Episode #83 – June 12, 2018)

"Interview With Matt Bazemore" - By Dimitris Kazantzis (Rockpages. Gr - _____)

"Interview With Mike Stone" - By Bob Nalbandian (Shockwaves/ Hard Radio – Episode #15 – 200_)

"Interview: Michael Wilton of Queensrÿche" - By Dan Birchall (*Screaming In Digital* – 1995)

"Interview With Todd La Torre" - By Bob Nalbandian (Shockwaves/ Hard Radio – Episode #87 – July 8, 2019)

"John Razor Interview" - By Brett Miller (Anybodylistening.net/The Breakdown Room – 2006)

"Lyrical Lucidity: Chris DeGarmo" - By Charrie Foglio (*RIP* – October, 1991)

"Mike Portnoy on Queensrÿche" - By Jeff Wagner (*Mean Deviation: Four Decades Of Progressive Metal* – Bazillion Points Books, 2010)

"Promised Land: Serious In Seattle" - By Dave Reynolds (*Kerrang!* #516 – 1994)

"Queensrÿche Sees 'Mindcrime' As A Sign Of The Times – Again" - By Gene Stout (Seattle Post-Intelliger – September 30, 2004)

"Revolution Calling" - By Jason Arnopp (*Kerrang!* #___ - 1997; *From The Front Lines Of Rock* – Retribution Books, 2017)

"Roy Khan on Queensrÿche" - By Jeff Wagner (*Mean Deviation: Four Decades Of Progressive Metal* – Bazillion Points Books, 2010)

"The Ryche Stuff" - By H.P. Newquist (*Guitar For The Practicing Musician* – May, 1997)

"The `Ryche Way" - By Dave Reynolds (Kerrang! #433 – 199_)

"Vintage Sound Queensrÿche Turned Back The Clock for 'Hear In The Now Frontier'" - By Gene Stout (Seattle Post-Intelliger – April 20, 1997)

(*Some additional quotes by Queensrÿche band members were used from the public court records posted during the lawsuit in 2012.)

*<u>Bonus Interview Disc Credits (Hardcover pre-order exclusive)</u>:

"Queensyrche Interview" - By Beth Rivers (KZEL 96.1 Radio – Eugene, OR. – Late Spring, 1983)

"Queensrÿche Interview" - By Steve Slaton (*The Metal Shop* – KISW Radio – Seattle, WA. – August 7, 1984)

"Queensryche Interview" - By Scott Vanderpool (KISW Radio – Seattle, WA. - 1997)

INTERVIEWS BY THE AUTHORS

"An Evening With Adam "Bomb" Brenner" - By James R. Beach (*Rusted Metal: A Guide To Heavy Metal And Hard Rock Music In The Pacific Northwest: 1970 – 1995*. NW Metalworx Books, 2020.)

"The Art of Evolution: Scott Rockenfield Talks Touring" - By Brian J. Heaton (Anybodylistening.net/The Breakdown Room - October, 2002)

"Behind The Scenes With Kelly Gray At S2k1" - By Brian J. Heaton (Anybodylistening.net/The Breakdown Room – June, 2001)

"Behind The Chains With Scott Rockenfield" - By Brian J. Heaton (Anybodylistening.net/The Breakdown Room – September, 2001)

"A Chat With Craig Cooke" - By James R. Beach and James Tolin (*Rusted Metal: A Guide To Heavy Metal And Hard Rock Music In The Pacific Northwest: 1970 – 1995*. NW Metalworx Books, 2020.)

"A Chat With Tom Hall" - By James R. Beach and Brian L. Naron (*Rusted Metal: A Guide To Heavy Metal And Hard Rock Music In The Pacific Northwest: 1970 – 1995*. NW Metalworx Books, 2020.)

"A Chat With Brett Miller" - By James R. Beach (*Rusted Metal: A Guide To Heavy Metal And Hard Rock Music In The Pacific Northwest: 1970 – 1995*. NW Metalworx Books, 2020.)

"A Conversation With John DeVol" - By James R. Beach and James D. Sutton (*Rusted Metal: A Guide To Heavy Metal And Hard Rock Music In The Pacific Northwest: 1970 – 1995*. NW Metalworx Books, 2020.)

"A Conversation With Terry Gorle" - By James R. Beach (*Rusted*

Metal: A Guide To Heavy Metal And Hard Rock Music In The Pacific Northwest: 1970 – 1995. NW Metalworx Books, 2020.)

"A Conversation With Rick Knotts" - By James R. Beach (*Rusted Metal: A Guide To Heavy Metal And Hard Rock Music In The Pacific Northwest: 1970 – 1995*. NW Metalworx Books, 2020.)

"A Conversation With Paul Passerelli" - By James R. Beach and James Tolin (*Rusted Metal: A Guide To Heavy Metal And Hard Rock Music In The Pacific Northwest: 1970 – 1995*. NW Metalworx Books, 2020.)

"A Conversation With Tom Wilcox" - By James R. Beach (*Rusted Metal: A Guide To Heavy Metal And Hard Rock Music In The Pacific Northwest: 1970 – 1995*. NW Metalworx Books, 2020.)

"Eyes Of A Stranger: Michael Wilton Discusses The Future Of Queensrÿche" - By Brian J. Heaton (Anybodylistening.net/The Breakdown Room – October, 2002)

"Howard Dee (H.D.) Gray Interview" - By James R. Beach and Brian L. Naron (*Rusted Metal: A Guide To Heavy Metal And Hard Rock Music In The Pacific Northwest: 1970 – 1995*. NW Metalworx Books, 2020.)

"In The Studio With Jason Slater: Mindcrime II Producer Connects With Queensrÿche" - By Brian J. Heaton (Anybodylistening.net/The Breakdown Room - Spring/Summer, 2005)

"An Interview With Jeff Gilbert" - By James R. Beach" (*Rusted Metal: A Guide To Heavy Metal And Hard Rock Music In The Pacific Northwest: 1970 – 1995*. NW Metalworx Books, 2020.)

"James Byrd Interview" - By James R. Beach (*Rusted Metal: A Guide To Heavy Metal And Hard Rock Music In The Pacific Northwest: 1970 – 1995*. NW Metalworx Books, 2020.)

"Kim Harris Interview" - By James R. Beach and Brian L. Naron (*Rusted Metal: A Guide To Heavy Metal And Hard Rock Music In The Pacific Northwest: 1970 – 1995*. NW Metalworx Books, 2020.)

"A Look Back At Operation: Mindcrime II With Jason Slater" - By Brian J. Heaton (Anybodylistening.net/The Breakdown Room – Winter/Spring, 2007)

"One On One With Neil Kernon: The 20th Anniversary Of Rage For Order" - By Brian J. Heaton (Anybodylistening.net/The Breakdown Room – 2006)

"Randy Gane Interview" - By James R. Beach (*Rusted Metal: A Guide To Heavy Metal And Hard Rock Music In The Pacific Northwest: 1970 – 1995*. NW Metalworx Books, 2020.)

"Sister Mary Speaks: Vocalist's Role With Queensrÿche Continues To Expand" - By Brian J. Heaton (Anybodylistening.net/The Breakdown Room – Summer, 2005)

"10 Years Of American Soldier" - By Brian J. Heaton (Focus On Metal – Episode #432 – September 18, 2019)

(*Additional interviews with Sullivan Bigg, Dan Birchall, Mark DeGarmo, Craig Locicero, David Morris, Corey Rivers and Charles Russell are new to this book.)

CPSIA information can be obtained
at www.ICGtesting.com
Printed in the USA
BVHW070118211221
624506BV00018B/2014

9 781087 979700